Fearless Speech in Indonesian Women's Writing

Fearless Speech in Indonesian Women's Writing

Working-Class Feminism from the Global South

Jafar Suryomenggolo

LEXINGTON BOOKS
Lanham • Boulder • New York • London

Published by Lexington Books
An imprint of The Rowman & Littlefield Publishing Group, Inc.
4501 Forbes Boulevard, Suite 200, Lanham, Maryland 20706
www.rowman.com

86-90 Paul Street, London EC2A 4NE

Chapter 1 "Factory employment, female workers' activism, and authoritarianism in Indonesia: reading Ida Irianti's pembelaan," originally published in Critical Asian Studies vol. 44, no. 4 (2012), pp. 597–626

Chapter 4 "Surat Pendek untuk Nazik Almalaika" in Buruh Menuliskan Perlawanannya, edited by Abu Mufakhir et al., pp. 189–250, published by LIPS (2015)

Chapter 5 "Aku bukan Budak" by Astina Triutami, published by PT BPK Gunung Mulia (2011)

Chapter 6 "Geliat Sang Kung Yan" by Maria Bo Niok, published by Gama Media (2007)

British Library Cataloguing in Publication Information Available

Library of Congress Cataloging-in-Publication Data Available

ISBN 978-1-7936-5053-5 (cloth)
ISBN 978-1-7936-5055-9 (pbk.)
ISBN 978-1-7936-5054-2 (electronic)

For Māma, In Memoriam

Contents

List of Tables

Acknowledgments

This book is inspired by the remarkable lives and activism of female labor leaders whom I met in Jakarta, Tangerang, Bandung, and Surabaya during 2000–2018. I thank Emelia Yanti Siahaan, Jumisih, Kasminah, Ngadinah, Parti Darmono, Rostinah, and Yanti Kusumawati Irawan for sharing their stories with me. Over the years, I have benefited from discussions with Abu Mufakhir, Anwar Sastro, Bernadeth Lucky Rossintha, Danial Indrakusuma, Dela Feby Situmorang, Dian Septi Trisnanti, Fahmi Panimbang, Hemasari Dharmabhumi, Hendro Agung Wibowo, Indah Saptorini, Je Seong Jeon, Machmud Permana, Nurus Mufidah, Rina Herawati, Rita Olivia Tambunan, Sarinah Toeng, Syarif Arifin, Surya Tjandra, Timboel Siregar, and Yasmine Soraya.

My deepest thanks to Caroline Hau, Indrasari Tjandraningsih, and Elizabeth Chandra who read the first draft of this book in its entirety and offered detailed comments. I thank Jackie Imamura for her sensitive reading and excellent proofreading. I thank Mizuno Kosuke for his support throughout this research project. I thank friends and colleagues during my stays in Kyoto and Tokyo during 2010–2019: Akedo Masako, Nathan Badenoch, Lisandro Claudio, Ernoiz Antriyandarti, William Bradley Horton, Imaoka Yoshiaki, Ito Rinako, Kawano Motoko, Khoo Boo Teik, Kiguchi Yuka, Kiso Keiko, Kitamura Yumi, Bliss Cua Lim, Mario Ivan Lopez, Morishita Akiko, Okamoto Masaaki, Patarapong Intarakumnerd, Piyawan Asawarachan, Rosita Dewi, Shitara Narumi, Syafwina Sanusi, Takagi Yusuke, Tan Pek Leng, Veerayooth Kanchoochat, Claudia Wessel, Yamamoto Mayumi, Yoshimura Chie, and Yoshino Keiichi. My heartfelt thanks also go to A.A.S. Marliany Yunika, Irene Sujanto Lau, Ondi Nababan, Ni Putu Dewi Kharisma Michellia, Kevin Omar Sidharta, Suh Jiwon, Henny Thio, and Julia Zimpel. I thank Hélène Blanchard, Vanina Bouté, Elsa Lafaye de Micheaux, Claudine

Salmon, Catherine Scheer, and Paul Sorrentino for their support and camaraderie at the Centre Asie du Sud-Est (CASE), Paris.

I thank Judith Lakamper and Mikayla Mislak for their utter professionalism throughout the publication process and for having guided this book on its path to print. I thank the anonymous reviewers for their suggestions and comments on the manuscript. I thank Ata for the permission to reproduce one of his paintings as the cover of this book.

Support for this research has been provided by the Southeast Asian Studies for Sustainable Humanosphere research program of the Center for Southeast Asian Studies, Kyoto University (2014–2016), and the Emerging State Project of the National Graduate Institute for Policy Studies (GRIPS) under the JSPS Grant-in-Aid research project No. 25101004 (2016–2018) with Shiraishi Takashi as its principal investigator. I thank the staff of both programs for their generous support.

My family has been a constant source of support. I thank my siblings, Simon Agus, Theresia Sriwati, Cecilia Idawati, and Antonius Junanto, and I dedicate this book to the memory of our mother, Anna Liem Gwé Nio 林月娘, who first taught us to read and love books. Last but certainly not least, I am grateful to Patrick Valageas for bringing new light into my life. Mon cœur s'ouvre à ta voix.

An earlier version of chapter 1 was previously published as "Factory employment, female workers' activism, and authoritarianism in Indonesia: reading Ida Irianti's *pembelaan*," *Critical Asian Studies* vol. 44, no. 4 (2012), pp. 597–626, reprinted with permission from its editor. Responsibility for the facts and interpretations which follow rests with me alone, as does responsibility for translations.

Alésia, Paris XIV
May 2021

Abbreviations

AJI	Aliansi Jurnalis Independen (Alliance of Independent Journalists)
CLA	Collective Labor Agreement
FBLP	Federasi Buruh Lintas Pabrik (Federation of Workers across Factories)
FBSI	Federasi Buruh Seluruh Indonesia (All-Indonesia Labor Federation)
Gerwani	Gerakan Wanita Indonesia (Indonesian Women's Movement)
HPP	Hubungan Perburuhan Pancasila (Pancasila Labor Relations); it was later renamed as Hubungan Industrial Pancasila (Pancasila Industrial Relations)
ILO	International Labor Organization
KBN	Kawasan Berikat Nusantara (Nusantara Bonded Zone)
Komnas Perempuan	Komisi Nasional Anti Kekerasan terhadap Perempuan (National Commission on Violence Against Women)
LBH	Lembaga Bantuan Hukum (Legal Aid Institute)
LBH APIK	Lembaga Bantuan Hukum Asosiasi Perempuan Indonesia untuk Keadilan (Legal Aid Bureau of the Indonesian Women's Association for Justice)
NGO	Non-Governmental Organization

P4P	Panitia Penyelesaian Perselisihan Perburuhan Pusat (Central Committee for Labor Dispute Settlement)
PKI	Partai Komunis Indonesia (Communist Party of Indonesia)
PT	Perseroan Terbatas (Limited Liability Company)
SBKA	Serikat Buruh Kereta Api (Railways Workers Union)
SBSI	Serikat Buruh Sejahtera Indonesia (All-Indonesia Prosperous Worker's Union)
SOBSI	Sentral Organisasi Buruh Seluruh Indonesia (Central All-Indonesian Workers Organization)
SPSI	Serikat Pekerja Seluruh Indonesia (All-Indonesia Workers' Union)

Introduction

Indonesia has undergone tremendous changes during the last forty years, transforming a primarily agriculture-based economy into a manufacturing hub of Southeast Asia and ending the decades-long reign of an authoritarian regime. A large—and largely untold—part of this story is the lives and actions of Indonesia's female workers. This book is about some of these remarkable women. It introduces little known writings of the country's working women, writings that compel us to reconsider what constitutes working-class consciousness, the limits of political control, and the rise of female worker activism.

The authors introduced in this book write despite (and against) their social, political, and cultural limitations. As the underprivileged, many of them have attained only primary school education; a few have finished high school. As manual laborers, they have had to trade their time for earnings, leaving them little of it to spend on expressing their thoughts, feelings, and hopes in written form. Indeed, they have almost no prior writing experience. As women, they are expected to stay silent and accept the gendered roles imposed on them by society. Writing offers them a chance to overcome these limitations, and their writings also illustrate how they reflect on these issues.

These authors describe not only the settings and conditions of their work but also the challenges they face in their personal lives. Individually, these women work in a range of urban-based manual jobs and have different personal experiences, aspirations, and dreams. Collectively, their experiences are shaped by the industrialization path Indonesia has taken, their aspirations are influenced by the cultural values of the society they come from, and their dreams are induced by the conditions of economic development and their job insecurity as precariat labor, a situation shared by many in the Global South. Their writings allow us to see beyond the "economic miracle" of Indonesia's industrial policy, implemented since the late 1970s, and the political changes since 1998 that have made it one of few democratic countries in Asia. The sociopolitical conditions of these writings and their particular literary importance are the main themes of this book.

FEMALE LABOR IN INDONESIA'S MODERN HISTORY

Historians have noted the important role of female labor in both the agricultural and industrial sectors throughout the modern history of Indonesia.[1] One of the earliest records of the working conditions of female labor in Java is an observation note by Dewi Sartika, a well-known female educator, which was compiled in a 1914 Dutch colonial survey on the position of native women. She notes that

> one must not forget our women of "lower class" who, having no vocational training, have to earn their daily plate of rice by working as coolie labor in factories and plantations. As a woman it cuts through my soul that these women, although they perform as many works as men who also do not have any training, receive less pay than the men.
>
> They receive a meager daily wage as a healthy woman working in the factories and plantations, they can easily lose this job in the event of natural illness, such as during childbirth, etc., and lastly, they are treated unfairly in contrast to the male workers, although both sexes do the same job – all these will not make them want to toil in the factories and plantations. [2]

The note clearly documents that female laborers under Dutch colonial rule faced gender wage discrimination, job insecurity, and unfair treatment in the workplace—conditions that unfortunately continue to exist today. The relatively small number of female laborers in the agricultural and industrial sectors at the time might have obscured these problems as merely "a women's issue." It is estimated that in the 1920s, female industrial labor represented around 12–15 percent of the colonial economy's total labor force.[3] Thus the colonial government paid little attention to women workers, and even if it had planned to improve labor conditions more broadly, women workers would likely not have benefited.

Following Indonesia's independence in 1945 until the end of 1949, female participation in the labor market, and thus female employment, grew. Although still relatively small in number, female laborers were employed in various sectors of the economy, including in the railways department. According to the first labor survey of the postcolonial state of Indonesia, conducted in 1956 by the Ministry of Labor, women constituted a median rate of approximately 28 percent of the labor force of various sectors of the economy, with the highest concentrations of female workers in the industrial (which included home industry) and agricultural sectors.[4]

After the political upheaval in 1965, women gradually entered the labor market in relatively higher numbers than before. With the establishment of the authoritarian regime of the New Order under General Soeharto (1966–1998), structural changes to the economy accompanied rapid industrialization. Since the late 1970s, Indonesia has followed a pattern common to the newly industrialized countries of East Asia as the labor force gradually moved from the agricultural sector into the manufacturing and services sectors, absorbing many female laborers in the process.[5]

Throughout the 1980s and into the early 1990s, women workers were pushed into light industry jobs, especially in sweatshops, as a result of the nation's economic policy of export-led development.[6] With the establishment of a number of export processing zones in the country, female participation in the labor market, especially as wage earners, rose during the 1980s.[7] Economists have noted, however, that since the mid-1990s, female labor force participation in Indonesia has been remarkably stagnant, even in the face of major economic changes (see Table 0.1).[8] Nonetheless, female laborers arguably remain an important pillar of the nation's economic development.

Since 2000, Indonesia's economy has recovered from the 1997 Asian financial crisis. Increasing the rate of female participation in the labor force is considered a key to improving Indonesia's total productivity (and hence its GDP). As an upper-middle-income country (since 2020), Indonesia has high hopes of avoiding the middle-income trap and entering the ranks of high-income countries by 2045. Doing this will require reducing the female/male labor market participation gap. Beyond this economic reason, increasing female labor force participation is important to improving female empowerment in general—which is also a point of departure for the argument of this book.

Despite the lack of reliable statistical data, we know that female laborers in Indonesia are more likely to work in the informal sector of the economy. Due to the flexible nature of Indonesia's economy and particularly its neoliberal orientation in recent years, many workers have remained trapped as casual laborers in the manufacturing and plantation sectors. As subsequent chapters

Table 0.1 Labor Force Participation Rate (age 15–64), Indonesia 1990–2019

	1990	1995	2000	2010	2019
Female	49.9	50.2	51.1	51.2	53.8
Male	82.1	83	83.6	83.2	82.2

Source: ILO Labor Statistics, various years (www.ilostat.ilo.org).

will describe, female laborers are not exempt from this situation and may in fact, because of their sex, face more pressure than their male peers in the labor market.

It is telling that during the more than one hundred years since Sartika made her observation, working conditions for women in Indonesia have not improved much and due to their gender female workers are still facing the same problems that Sartika describes. However, unlike the earlier generation of female workers, whose workplace plight deeply moved Sartika yet was not documented by workers themselves, subsequent generations have summoned the courage to voice, and write, their own story. They do not necessarily need a lending hand from educated and elite sisters like Sartika, no matter how sincere and generous she was, to defend their rights and interests. Beyond defending their rights in the workplace, they also write about their lives, hopes, and dreams. As we will see through this book, their writing reflects a particular activism of women workers that is at the heart of the enormous social and political transformations that Indonesia has been experiencing during the past forty years.

LITERARY LIBERATION

Writing is a relatively new phenomenon for the working class. Working-class communities in Indonesia, as elsewhere, are imbued with oral tradition. Working Indonesians are born into, grow up, and live their lives in this tradition. Through oral speech, they narrate life and experience, feelings and thoughts, and dreams and memories. This practice is part of a broader oral tradition within the general population of Indonesia.[9] As such, orality has been the dominant mode of expression chosen by working-class communities.

While working-class oral speech shares many elements with popular oral tradition, the daily labor that shapes the lives of the working-class generates particular oral expressions. Such expressions and their usage form a distinctive culture that, in many ways, defines the class. Amid repetitive and dehumanizing routines, workers manage their day-to-day habits in specific ways to counteract the alienating conditions of the workplace. To overcome feelings of isolation and powerlessness at work and to take control of their own lives, they develop unique expressions, including aesthetic ones. Oral speech is therefore borne out of their lives and works. Despite its unique reflection of a social group, the sociopolitical significances of working-class oral speech in Indonesia have yet to be studied. Meanwhile, its cultural significances are varied and multilayered. In some ways, working-class oral tradition forms the basis of a certain mind-set and worldview, which comes through in their written expressions.

The oral tradition of the working class in Indonesia is often considered a sign of their illiteracy. This is because until the early 1980s, only a small fraction of the working class benefited from primary schooling, which only became compulsory in the 1970s.[10] Yet it can be argued that workers live their lives securely within the oral tradition because it does not conflict with the realities of their workplace, where terms of employment and workplace instructions are often conveyed orally. They understand that literacy can be an important asset, as it facilitates opportunities of entry to certain job positions, but their manual work itself may not always require literacy. Meanwhile, oral tradition provides a sense of belonging; it is where their identities as members of the working class are rooted. Thus, despite the progress of the government's primary schooling program over the years, workers have strong reasons to maintain their oral tradition.

Nevertheless, since the late 1980s, workers have steadily moved from the oral tradition to writing, and they are reading more than their predecessors ever did.[11] The feminization of the labor market, in which more women are recruited to work (especially, in the manufacturing sector), has brought with it an inconspicuous yet irreversible change: the feminization of the reading public, especially among the working class. This is a result of the new demand in the labor market for cheap industrial laborers who can read and write enough to understand workplace instructions.

In response to changes in the labor market, small independent publishers offering various publications at affordable prices began to recognize working-class communities as a bourgeoning market.[12] Although working-class readers existed in Java as early as the 1920s, they never became a significant market targeted with reading materials specifically tailored to them. This changed in the late 1980s as working people looked for stories that related to their daily lives. It was not long before workers started sharing their own stories through writing. It is in this context, of the expansion of the reading public to include working-class readers and a rising interest in the publishing industry to target those readers, that women workers started to compose a number of writings. The social context of their decision to take up the pen and distribute their writings among themselves is the focus of this book. Beyond orality, they write about their life and working experiences, personal stories, and fantasies.

PROLETARIAN WRITING, FEMINIST READING

Studies of working-class writing from the West discuss its importance as a lens to understand working-class lives.[13] Such writing expresses the experiences, thoughts, and aspirations of the working class—a perspective that is often ignored and suppressed by those in power.

Although working-class writing has existed as early as the late eighteenth century, it flourished during the early decades of the twentieth century, at the height of international socialism. As the social and cultural developments of the Russian revolution spread throughout Europe, they inspired later generations of working-class authors beyond Communist countries. Henry Poulaille (1896–1980), considered the main promoter of *la littérature prolétarienne* (proletarian literature) in France, defined the genre as that which is written by working-class authors who are active workers (or peasants) and whose written works are oriented toward the defense and liberation of the proletariat.[14] On Japan's proletarian literary movement of 1921–1934, Shea notes the serious discussion among its authors on how to approach working-class readers and "to infiltrate the working class for its reading public."[15]

Despite its progressive content promoting revolution, this proletarian tradition did not distinguish between male and female authors. Hence, contemporary scholars question whether or not this tradition is fully capable of addressing women's oppression (and emancipation), or of fully analyzing the "women question." In her examination of US proletarian fiction of 1929–1941, Foley notes that while women authors of the time were not forbidden from voicing their concerns as women, they "considered themselves leftists and knew what this meant as well as did their male colleagues."[16] Needless to say, the prime focus of authors of proletarian literature was on a political and economic revolution, not a gender or cultural one.

Based on this critical perspective, feminist scholars have noted how the significance of working-class women's writings is often ignored or sidelined by the primacy of class analysis.[17] Despite the many different understandings within feminism, Robinson has summed up the main thread of feminist readings of working-class literature as "the discovery, republication, and reappraisal of 'lost' or undervalued writers and their work" beyond commonly accepted "aesthetic standards."[18] Important studies have been carried out based on this perspective. For example, the life and collected writings of Ellen Johnston (1835–1873), a Victorian working-class female author, have been discussed with great interest.[19] In a similar vein, Liszek has discussed Marie Gulliot's life and contributions to the development of trade unionism in France, and Perrot has discussed the 1908 article penned by Lucie Baud (1870–1913), a union secretary in a small commune of Vizille, whose life and activism were largely forgotten until her writing was "found" and republished in 1978.[20] Both Liszek's and Perrot's works can be read as part of the larger project of the "discovery, republication, and reappraisal" of working-class women's writings in the development of the French labor movement. Likewise, we see a similar effort in Russia with the publication in 1998 of the autobiography of Aleksandra Chistiakova, which details the author's life as a working-class mother in a small Siberian town and was included on the shortlist for the Russian Booker literary award in the same year.[21] As these examples indicate, by uncovering previously undervalued working-class female writers, feminist literary criticism and scholarship have contributed to the historical social construction of working-class literature as a whole.

As part of a decentering of the dominant cultural context in the decades since the end of the Cold War, the feminist perspective has proven valuable in reading working-class women's writings outside the Western world and on issues that are pertinent within local contexts. For example, Perera discusses the periodical journals of Dabindu, Sri Lanka's free trade zone worker-writers collective, to highlight the collective of women workers as an important literary intervention.[22] Meanwhile, Barraclough discusses South Korean "factory girl literature" to locate the interrelationship between sexual politics and the women's emancipation movement, especially during the nation's industrialization period of the 1970s and 1980s.[23] Sun discusses China's *dagong wenxue* ("migrant literature") written by *dagongmei* (rural migrant women who work in urban factories) as a way to understand the cultural politics of their agency and the social conditions that shape their sexual experience.[24] Such works are an attempt to ground and contextualize the feminist perspective in non-Western societies and to raise issues that have remained largely uncovered. They are an important contribution to enrich our contemporary discussion of working-class women's literature, especially from the Global South.

With the exception of small circles of the academe, discussion of Indonesian working-class women's writings based on a feminist perspective rarely takes place. As a result, the issues raised in such writings do not gain the attention or appreciation in the public discourse that they deserve. A feminist perspective enables readers to see, and better understand, issues that have been ignored in mainstream male-dominated views of life and work, such as the value of domestic work and the impacts of reproductive roles on income and status. Through a feminist reading, we can analyze women's social roles and positions, sexual politics, and the moral disciplining of women's behavior. There is indeed a strong reason to read Indonesian working-class women's writing in light of the feminist perspective: it offers an unparalleled understanding of working-class women's writings, allowing us to explore the issues they raise more deeply and extensively.

It is important to note that the writings discussed in this book do not specifically talk about "women's issues" per se. Instead, they raise working-class issues as seen from the authors' own eyes as women. They are different from male workers' perspectives because they come from different experiences (both in life and at work) that are born out of the gendered roles imposed on the authors. As authors, women workers are not afraid to question, resist, and reimagine this gender construction. Their act of writing goes against the dominant social-cultural expectations of women, particularly those from a working-class background. Working-class women (and poor women, in general) are discouraged from speaking up and they do not enjoy the same access that their upper- and middle-class sisters have to voice and express themselves freely. These gendered and socially constructed experiences of writing are signified by the cultural value of *malu* (shame, shyness, or restraint).

THE GENDERED AND CLASS POLITICS OF *MALU*

While the emotion of shame is a universal human experience, in Indonesia (in particular, Java), *malu* is a potent social value that regulates behavior and forms part of the shared assumptions of the society.[25] It has been culturally ascribed to women as a valuable personal trait; every woman should strive to acquire *malu*, act according to its standard, and hold it in esteem. Members of the society work together to protect, transmit, and apply *malu* in their daily interactions. Women are expected by the society to be *malu* (or *pemalu*) and it is imperative that they act accordingly. *Malu* is an important characteristic of the social category of the "adult female." While females learn and are expected to have a deeper sense of *malu*, males are often excused for failing to express *malu* in the public, which allows them to act beyond the constraints of "proper" behaviors. Women who possess *malu* character are respected; they are therefore more desirable as wives and daughters. Beyond the economic roles she may have, a woman needs to demonstrate or be seen as *malu* by others (especially, by males) when managing her social and public appearance(s). She will be sanctioned for any transgression against what are considered acceptable behaviors so that she and those around her learn to know shame. Thus, a woman's demonstration of *malu* is the indicator by which she is judged (and projects herself) as a "good" or "bad" woman.[26]

Malu also functions as a mechanism of class differentiation. Those with a humble background and/or a subsistence level of income are expected to demonstrate *malu* in their interactions with those who have a higher-class standing than them. This does not mean that elites are not also confined by the behavior and norms prescribed by *malu*. Due to their status and power, however, elites have more leeway to ignore *malu* and in being pardoned if they fail to comply with *malu* norms. Working-class experiences of *malu* are more regimented and more closely monitored; for them, *malu* more strictly consists of elements of discipline, consequences, and punishment.[27]

Recent anthropological studies have demonstrated the importance of *malu* as a socially constructed emotion from which status and power are defined, negotiated, and maintained in the community and in the nation as a whole.[28] As an instrument of subordination, *malu* prescribes that women workers act and behave according to the mainstream norms of patriarchal society. Those who are not *malu* are regarded as women who "don't know shame" and they often find themselves battling against the cultural norms and facing social sanctions. These studies provide ample explanation of *malu* as a cultural context for us to read and understand the writings of working-class women in Indonesia.

Female workers are especially expected to know shame and incorporate it into their daily activities, both at home and at work. Although factory jobs allow women to earn an income from their labor as a step toward relative independence, they do not necessarily free female workers from family obligations and social controls.[29] In other words, the politics of *malu* follows them as they enter the formal labor market.

Most female workers secure a factory job through a personal connection (such as a family friend, neighbor, or local village head) to the factory foreman (*mandor*) and/or, in some areas of Indonesia, to Islamic community leaders who moonlight as recruiters for factories.[30] They therefore owe a "debt of gratitude" and are expected to "repay" that debt by not causing or bringing shame to the foremen or those in the community who helped them secure the job.[31] Absenteeism, refusal to work overtime, and joining a protest or strike in the factory are examples of actions considered to bring shame to the foremen and the workers' community in general.[32] The foremen monitor female workers to ensure that they practice *malu* in the workplace and do not bring shame to the community.

In the workplace, female workers often socialize and form ties among those who come from the same community (or who are recruited by the same foremen), and they identify themselves as within this group. Hometown associations are also commonly found among female migrant workers in major industrial cities in Java and foreign domestic workers abroad. These associations help them to manage life as a migrant while maintaining ties with families back home. Whether based on the same community, foremen links, or hometown association, these social ties also play a role in reinforcing workers' personal sense of *malu* and, often, dictate how workers behave. Within the group, member activities are monitored and conduct is observed; in certain situations, this functions as a form of peer pressure that reminds them to protect their *malu*.[33] As a whole, female workers need to show that they know shame and restrain themselves to "proper behaviors" to avoid bringing shame to the group.[34] Such self-restraint reflects how shame also functions as an important instrument of discipline and subordination, thus ensuring that female workers obey the expectations and commands (or, at least appear willing to do so) of their bosses in the factory and those who are part of the apparatus of social control.

Malu is hegemonic. Female members of the working-class community are expected to adopt it as part of their personal character. They learn that women who know—and demonstrate—shame are more likely to be hired for factory jobs (as foremen assume that they will not cause "trouble" in the factory) and that if they obey commands, they will be considered "good" women. Conversely, failure to demonstrate *malu* will hinder their job prospects and ruin their good name. Working-class women therefore need to emulate "desirable" women who know shame, at work and in their daily lives. Male supervisors/*mandor* use the politics of *malu* to their advantage to create an exploitable labor force. Women workers are told that in order to practice *malu*, they have to contribute their income to the family, obey their *mandor*, withhold their discontent against the factory regime, repress their anger, refrain from protest, and endure the hardship of working life—no matter how bad their working conditions are. Under pressure to demonstrate *malu*, working-class women become a docile workforce for the factory regime.

FEMALE WORKERS AND UNIONS

The politics of *malu* undoubtedly hampers union efforts to organize women workers. Historically, women workers have been reluctant to transgress "acceptable behaviors" to join unions, making it difficult for unions to attract female members. Despite union efforts to cater to women's needs and the benefits that female workers have gained as a result of union struggles to put forward their demands, for many women workers, joining a union is not as high a priority as being *malu*.

During the 1950–1965 post-independence period, labor unions clearly understood the importance of organizing female workers.[35] Although the percentage of women in the workforce was still relatively low, female workers were represented in fair numbers across all industries. The Central All-Indonesian Workers Organization (Sentral Organisasi Buruh Seluruh Indonesia, SOBSI), the largest labor federation of that time, extended its membership by recruiting women workers in major factories. It allowed women workers to join all of its activities, including rallies and demonstrations. Although allowing women to join rallies was quite uncommon at the time, SOBSI considered it an important part of the conscientization process for all of its members—including female workers.

Importantly, SOBSI did not view female workers as less capable than male workers in organizing. It documented the various *"aksi"* (actions) that women workers organized to demand better working conditions:

> Until now there are various *aksi* conducted by female workers in many differ-
> ent ways: groping, flapping, breaking-in, pinching, bringing crying children in,
> small-group picketing, rallying, marching, marching with family members, and

others . . . After joining such *aksi*, some female workers were sacked from their jobs, investigated by the police, detained, and imprisoned but in the end, it only gives birth to new cadres.[36]

A number of women's organizations supported union efforts to get more women to participate in union activities. A section of the left-wing Indonesian Women's Movement (Gerakan Wanita Indonesia, Gerwani), for instance, catered to female workers, especially those working in the agriculture sector.[37] In 1956, it successfully convinced the Indonesian Women Congress to adopt the "Piagam Hak-hak Wanita" (The Charter of Indonesian Women's Rights), which includes women workers' rights. It also campaigned for the full implementation of reproductive rights for women workers and actively advocated for the ratification of ILO Convention No. 100 (1951) on Equal Remuneration to ensure that female workers not be discriminated against based on their sex.[38] The Indonesian government finally ratified the convention in 1957. Three years after ratification, however, Suharti, the deputy leader of Gerwani, noted that the gender wage gap remained widespread in many factories throughout Indonesia.[39] This demonstrated Gerwani's recognition of the wage gap as an important issue for women workers and its commitment to work together with workers to end it.

As early as 1947, Siti Besari, a female unionist of the Railways Workers Union (Serikat Buruh Kereta Api, SBKA) noted the underrepresentation of women workers in the union structure.[40] It was not until 1956, however, that SOBSI and its affiliate unions began to increase women's share of the work of the organizations.[41] Despite SOBSI's efforts, only a few women entered the central leadership.[42] The composition of SOBSI reflected the low participation of women workers in the labor movement in general as well as the specific challenge of female underrepresentation in labor organizations.

The change of political regime in Indonesia in late 1965 and the subsequent events that crushed all leftist organizations, including SOSBI and Gerwani, had devastating effects on women's activism. During the military's 1965–1966 campaign to demonize Gerwani, many of its members were murdered, sexually assaulted, and detained without due process.[43] Many of Gerwani's political and social achievements as a progressive women's organization, including those to secure women workers' rights, were erased.[44] During the subsequent thirty years, until the collapse of the New Order regime (in 1998), the name Gerwani carried a negative political stigma, and the women's movement in general was subjugated under the regime's gendered ideology.[45] Likewise, the union movement was tamed and directed to support the regime's political agenda, which prioritized economic development.[46]

It was during the New Order period that the politics of *malu* became more pronounced as a means to control women workers. Female workers were so discouraged to join unions that there were hardly any female cadres in the All-Indonesia Workers' Union (Serikat Pekerja Seluruh Indonesia, SPSI), the only union organization allowed (and sponsored) by the regime.[47] Female union activists were considered the antithesis of the regime's idealized image of womanhood: they were therefore denounced as women who did not know *malu* (because they demanded workplace rights), who had rejected their gendered roles (as they played a public role in the union), and, worse, maybe suspected as a Gerwani cadre and thus, in the official "polite" language of the regime, should be *diamankan* (detained without due process).[48] This image has continued to have dire consequences for female union activism in the post-New Order era (1998–today).

The wave of democratization that swept the country with the *Reformasi* of 1998 has brought about tremendous political and social changes, including labor relations. Workers' rights are now legally guaranteed. As has happened in other countries of the Global South, however, forces of neoliberalism are gaining influence in Indonesia in dictating the state's economic and development priorities. It is within this tension between democratization and neoliberal challenges that a number of female workers are actively negotiating their livelihood, freedom, sexuality, and sense of self.[49] Meanwhile, male unionists continue to dominate the labor movement. Issues that are important for female workers, such as sexual harassment and maternity protection, are often sidelined or considered "women's issues" only.

FEARLESS SPEECH

Although the politics of *malu* makes female workers hesitant (and afraid) to join unions and to express their thoughts and feelings, it is wrong to assume that all female workers are obedient and submissive as is expected of them. Female workers have stood up against foremen and refused to follow orders. These women are not afraid to break the factory discipline in order to defend their rights and interests as working women. They are willing to take the risk of social sanction, even when they knew their actions might bring shame to their community. Hence, they are recognized by some as "*berani*" (fearless).

For women workers, being *berani* requires having a strong will and determination. It also includes being confident. Being *berani*, however, does not necessarily mean one is breaking the law for nothing. A *berani* worker is not a rebel without a cause: a compelling reason (usually to defend one's rights and/or a sense of justice) triggers one to act *berani*. It is important to note that although *berani* is not the opposite of *malu*,[50] *berani* can enable a person to put aside "appropriate" behavior in order to defend her rights and interests. As such, when a female worker stands up for her rights, her act might be considered a breach of *malu*, but if it is for the right reasons, she is becoming *berani* and thus will be respected.[51] Interestingly, *berani* is often identified as the most important quality of a leader. Given this meaning, it is not surprising that there is relatively strong resistance to a *berani* female worker within the union itself, as she could become a threat to the existing leadership, which is still, sadly, dominated by male workers.[52]

To be *berani* is the result of self-confidence, which is facilitated by education.[53] During the New Order period, primary education was expanded and the literacy rate among young women increased; indeed, female literacy rose faster than that of men (see table 0.2). Schooling prepared women to enter the labor market as urban laborers and enabled the extensive participation of women in the formal labor market. As with men, literacy for women is an asset when competing in the labor market, and illiterate women face higher barriers to securing good jobs.[54] Although they are often considered low-skilled or semi-skilled labor (and thus, receive low wages), Indonesian women workers, like their sisters in other East Asian countries,[55] formed the backbone of the nation's workforce in order to meet the needs of industry.

For workers to stand up for their rights, a critical conscientization process is often transmitted through conversations, dialogue, and storytelling, which facilitate exchanges of ideas, knowledge, and experiences.[56] It was (and still is) common for workers to learn about their rights in group meetings organized by legal aid or NGO activists. It is also in these meetings that workers learned to express themselves. Many learn and adopt the language of rights and come to see the social movement as part of their life and worldview.[57] Beyond primary schooling, women workers read books available in the print market and that target them as new readers. Beyond workplace instructions, women workers read leaflets, pamphlets, and other print materials produced by NGOs and other civil society organizations. Once literate, *what* they read and *how* they read it are beyond any one entity's full control.

Still, working-class women have had to find ways to raise their own voices. The New Order regime was notorious for muting any expression from the civil society,[58] and workers found it difficult—although not impossible—to express themselves. While they did carry out spontaneous wildcat strikes, the regime considered such strikes illegal and refused to acknowledge worker grievances.[59] In this context, songs,[60] poems,[61] and theater performances[62]

Table 0.2 Adult Literacy Rate in Indonesia, 1980–2016

	1980	1990	2000	2004	2011	2016
Female	57.69	75.27	82.1	86.8	90.07	93.59
Male	77.47	88.02	91.9	94.04	95.59	97.17

Source: UNESCO Data for Sustainable Development Goals (2018) (www.uis.unesco.org/en/country/ID)

created spaces that were relatively freer from the regime's surveillance and censors and in which workers could share their stories. These creative works are important because they illustrate how workers, even under the authoritarian regime, endured and were able to produce genuine expressions that meaningfully articulated their life and work.

In their writings, workers demand dignity, equality, and justice, but they neither consider nor advocate a revolution. This absence of the notion of (or identification with) a class struggle or revolution is partly due to the anti-Communist purge of 1965–1966 in Indonesia and the commonly held ideological belief, especially during the New Order regime (1966–1998), that Communist ideas are not only un-religious, but also a threat to national security.[63] Under the political surveillance of the New Order regime,[64] members of the working class (both male and female) found it difficult to produce and distribute (and also, preserve) their writings because those writings were treated as politically motivated—a legacy that sadly remains relatively intact within the society in general even after democratization in 1998. In this context, working-class women's writings challenge political norms and are therefore "dangerous" regardless of the content. How these writings are accessed, produced, and appreciated therefore reflects a class-based inequality not only in the literary landscape, but also in society in general, revealing the "silence" of the subaltern as a social process in which certain cultural and political institutions play a decisive role over working-class women's writings and lives.

Against the New Order's anti-labor policy, women workers wrote to articulate their political and economic dissatisfactions and to avoid the state's censorship. Part 1 explores how women workers navigated this articulation, in particular during the 1980s and 1990s. Chapter 1 discusses the text of a *pembelaan* (a document used for legal defense purposes in criminal courts) written in 1987 by Ida Irianti, a union leader of a Jakarta-based beverage company. Chapter 2 presents a personal note written in 1993 by Meppy Doryati Emping, a manual worker in a Taiwanese footwear factory in Surabaya, East Java. Taken together, chapters 1 and 2 represent testimonials written by female factory workers to express their discontent not only with working conditions, but also with the repressive experience of living under the military's treatment and the state's surveillance. Such testimonials represent a strategy that female workers, despite their limited power, used in the fight to defend their rights and interests as workers.

Following the collapse of the New Order regime in 1998, as discussed in part 2, women workers expressed their concerns for equal rights and social justice amid the challenges posed by neoliberalism. Chapter 3 discusses a number of short essays written by women unionists on working conditions, particularly sexual harassment, in export-oriented factories. Chapter 4 discusses an essay written by the single mother Salsabila (a pseudonym) about her struggle against difficult working conditions and to claim maternity protection, and her efforts as a union steward to defend the rights and interests of female workers more broadly. These writings illustrate the collective struggle that women workers formed to ensure a safe workplace and overcome the social limits imposed upon them.

Indonesia's large workforce, combined with the scarcity of jobs in the country, has led many young women to seek jobs abroad as domestic workers, especially in Gulf countries and the new industrializing countries of the East Asia region (Singapore, Malaysia, Taiwan, and Hong Kong). Many of these workers write in various literary forms and on many different subjects. Chapter 5 analyzes published accounts written by Rini Widyawati and Astina Triutami about their lives as overseas domestic workers. Chapter 6 discusses short stories and novels written by Indonesian overseas domestic workers in Hong Kong, focusing on two pioneering anthologies of stories: Tarini Sorrita's *Penari Naga Kecil* (Little Dragon Dancer) and Maria Bo Niok's *Geliat Sang Kung Yan* (Writhes of the Kung Yan). These personal accounts and stories, written far from home, illustrate how overseas domestic workers are creating a space of their own to demand their rights (and, the implementation of these rights) and to experience freedom outside of their manual work.

Throughout the last forty years of industrialization and twenty years of political changes in Indonesia that this book covers (from the late 1980s to the 2010s), women workers have written in many different forms. They write defense speeches (chapter 1); personal notes (chapter 2); short articles (chapter 3); protest essays (chapter 4); personal accounts (chapter 5); and works of fiction, mainly, short stories, (chapter 6). Unlike upper- and middle-class authors, they write in various forms not because of literary pretentions but because of the urgency of the issues they raise and the limited time they have to write. The forms that these writings take were shaped by the particular situation that each author faced—situations that limited their writing capacities and at the same time also allowed (or force) them to express themselves. As authors, they are constrained by the limited time they have in between their physical labor, activism, familial obligations, and writing. In terms of form, they write to explore the limits of their expression. Content wise, they write to confront matters important to them as women workers. They must be versatile and creative in narrating their stories so that fellow workers (who also have limited time) will read and enjoy their writings.

Due to the social and political limitations these women had to face in producing (and distributing) their texts, it is not easy to determine how well these texts are consumed, circulated, and reflected among their intended readership and beyond. Nonetheless, by writing their own stories, these working-class women document and preserve a "collective sensibility."[65] Not all working-class women have the courage to break the politics of *malu* and go beyond the cultural and social conventions that surround them. Not many can afford to spend their time or have the capacities to write—an activity that is considered a luxury—because they must prioritize their physical survival first. Not all working-class women are ready to have their writings read in the public sphere. Therefore, these authors, although writing as individuals, also write for their fellow working-class sisters, and in so doing convey an experience shared among a wide range of working women.

This does not necessarily mean, however, that these authors represent working-class women as a whole. In fact, none of the writers discussed in this book ever claim to represent the working class.[66] They write, first and foremost, from their own personal experiences. These experiences, however, are shared (and inherited) among working-class women. As writers, they knowingly write for their fellow working-class sisters. They describe the world they are part of—both the world of economic and political transformations that Indonesia and common Indonesians are experiencing and the larger world of the (unfair) global production system and the (restricted) regional mobility of labor in Southeast Asia. Beyond any claim of representation, their writings as a collective work provide a window into the struggle of working-class women, in their own words.

Do their writings form the basis of a working-class feminist idea in Indonesia? To answer that, we need to note that these women workers do not write with a feminist agenda in mind. Although some have had contacts with local and international feminist groups, many do not identify themselves as feminists or align their activism to feminism. They may not even write to consciously question or challenge the patriarchal values of society. Nonetheless, by writing, these authors actually do challenge women's gendered roles and advance a feminist agenda, although they may not set out to do so. The politics of *malu* (still) works as an important indicator to judge any woman, but working-class women, through their reading and writings, have taken a part in shattering it. They write based on their gendered experiences in a labor market that exploits female labor and diminishes their contributions to the economy. Indonesia's forty years of industrialization and twenty years of political change, particularly the problems generated by the capitalist mode of production, have deeply impacted their lives. Their writings therefore question economic inequalities and demand fair treatment. Furthermore, compared to upper- and middle-class writings, their writings constitute a distinct sociopolitical consciousness that is shaped by their working experiences as manual laborers. This consciousness is the main feature and also the main contribution of these writings to women's literary production. Thus, their words and actions may be classified as part of a feminist activism that stems from working-class experiences typical of the Global South. Women's literacy and engagement with written literature comes in various forms and are based on diverse experiences. Their writings may not be seriously considered by the literary establishment, but they inspire fellow workers to take on their own struggles in the workplace and beyond. Therefore, their writings can be considered a progressive force, one that illuminates the often-suppressed voices of the nation's working population and that has become a pillar supporting women's political and economic empowerment in modern Indonesia.

NOTES

1. See Locher-Scholten (2000); Chandra (2002).

2. Welvaartscommissie (1914: 23). Among the nine elite native women who were interviewed in the 1914 colonial survey, only Dewi Sartika mentioned at length her concerns about the conditions of working-class women.

3. Chandra (2002: 113–115).

4. Vreede-de Stuers (1959: 121).

5. See Heyzer (1986); Deyo (1987); Hadiz (1997).

6. Adoption of such a policy saw the manufacturing sector's share of the country's GDP rise from 8.4 percent in 1980 to 14.3 percent in 1990; real growth rates of the sector exceeded 10 percent during the 1980s. Indonesia's economy did grow and it was considered a newly industrializing economy—until the 1997 Asian financial crisis.

7. The rapid development of the textile, garment, and footwear industries began in Indonesia in the mid-1980s after the relocation of these industries from East Asia in search of cheaper labor in Southeast Asia. Since then, exports from these industries became, and have remained, the bulk of Indonesia's non-oil and gas exports, even after 1998. See Benjamin (1996).

8. See Schaner and Das (2016); Cameron et al. (2019).

9. See Smith-Hefner (1989); Hoskins (1998); and Teeuw (1994). For studies on oral tradition in Southeast Asia and Polynesia, see Kemp (2004).

10. While six-year-primary education became compulsory based on Presidential Instruction No. 10 Year 1973, the government did not fully implement the Instruction nationwide until 1984.

11. White (1993) notes that the Indonesian workforce of the early 1990s period is more literate than cohorts in earlier periods.

12. Pulp novels were commonly circulated among working-class readers in the 1980s as cheaper paper became more available and small-scale printing presses popped up across in many industrial cities in Java. Rini (1995: 88) observes that female workers read some pulp novels/dime novels, such as those authored by Freddy S., Abdullah Harahap, and Maria Monica (all author's names are aliases).

13. See, for example, Aron (2006) on Belgian proletarian literature; Vincent (1981), Goodridge, and Keegan (2017) on the British working class; Lauter (2005) on American workers; Pierse (2018) on Irish workers; and Traugott (1993) on French workers from the early industrial era.

14. Poulaille (1986) considers *la littérature prolétarienne* the modern expression of literature created precisely out of industrialization and the progress of capitalism. See also Ragon (2012 [1974]); Geneste (1992).

15. Shea (1964: 87). For a survey of Japanese proletarian authors, see Kobayashi (1988). For a translation of Japanese proletarian literature in English, see the anthology edited by Bowen-Struyk and Field (2016).

16. Foley (1993: 242).

17. On how working-class women identify themselves with dominant middle- and upper-class aspirations and values, see Steedman (1986).

18. Robinson (2006: 249).

19. See Boos (2003); Hart (2015).

20. See Liszek (1994); Perrot (2012). Based on Perrot's book, a TV drama of the same title by Gérard Mordillat was produced in 2017 and was broadcast on August 24, 2018.

21. The autobiography, titled *Ne mnogo li dlia odnoi? (Enough for one?)*, was edited by a journalist, Vladimir Shiriaev. On the importance of Chistiakova's published autobiography, see Rotkirch (2004).

22. See Perera (2008, 2014).

23. See Barraclough (2009, 2012).

24. See Sun (2014).

25. Shame as social sanction is common in maritime Southeast Asian societies. For comparison, see Frank (1984) on *hiya* (in Tagalog) and Mageo (1991) on *ha'amã* (in Tahiti).

26. Based on his fieldwork observation, Peletz (1996: 228) notes that "females have a stronger and more developed sense of 'shame' than males," but also that, "if they did not, they would be 'like wild animals' and the world would be in chaos."

27. For the working class, *malu* functions as a reminder of one's "debt of gratitude." Based on his fieldwork in a working-class/urban-poor area of Manila (the squatter settlement of Tatalon), Pinches (1991: 174) notes that

> shame is frequently used or invoked as a principal sanction in reciprocal relations, most notably in those involving a debt of gratitude (*utang na loob*). The pairing of shame and debt of gratitude arises generally in interpersonal relations, but it is of particular importance in relations of patronage, including political patronage.

28. While acknowledging the analysis first proposed by Geertz based on his fieldwork in Bali (1973), recent studies have highlighted how the socially constructed emotion of *malu* is central to the various cultural fabrics of life in societies. See, for example, Lindquist (2009) on migrant workers in Batam and Spiller (2010) on the ideals of masculinity in West Java.

29. In a survey of three industrial zones in North Sumatra, Hutabarat (2006: 93) finds that female workers, even when they are single, are expected to financially support their family, in contrast to male workers. In one case, a female worker of a furniture company had to put aside approximately 20 percent of her monthly income to support her younger sibling's education. Many factory women feel *malu* if they fail to send a portion of their income home.

30. See Mather (1983).

31. Widiawati (1995: 37) notes that female workers often borrow money from their respective *mandors* to cover basic living expenses. In a study of family consumption patterns of daily workers in a palm-oil plantation in North Sumatera, Situmorang et al. (2008: 110) note that the wife of the *mandor* who operates a grocery stall (*tukang warung*) that caters to the plantation workers often monitors the workers' shopping lists, and how they handle their income. This financial dependency of the workers on their *mandor* often complicates their "debt of gratitude" and determines the depth of the politics of *malu* in their lives.

32. Based on in-depth interviews during her fieldwork in an industrial town in Java, Silvey (2003: 144) notes that "women who worked in factories . . . saw the avoidance of strike activity as appropriate behavior for women."

33. Based on his fieldwork in the Northern Region Industrial Estate in Thailand, Hirai (2008: 143) notes that "For many women, relatives in the factory are generally considered a symbol of village constraint and oppression. As a result of the need to maintain family honor, relatives keep each other under constant surveillance, even in the factory."

34. Based on his fieldwork observation among the migrant female workers in Batam, Lindquist (2009: 59) notes that

shame, or *malu*, is more important than the fear of sin. Certainly, religious practice can lead to the formation of new forms of subjectivity and religious enlightenment, but it is the negotiation of *malu* that is critical for female migrants.

35. Praptini (1951) notes the importance of joining unions in defending the rights of women workers (such as reproductive rights). Interestingly, she also notes that "it is important to have a women's organization that specifically tackles the needs of working women."

36. SOBSI (1961: 45).

37. Vreede-de Stuers (1959: 95) notes that at Gerwani's second congress in Jakarta (March 25–31, 1954), Umi Sardjono, the organization's chairwoman, mentioned five main agendas of the organization that included the extension of social protection for female workers. In 1961, Sri Ambar, the head of the Women's Bureau of SOBSI, emphasized the need for special social protection for female workers due to their "dual roles in the society, as a worker and a mother" (see SOBSI 1961: 36).

38. See Pandjaitan (1963).

39. See PKI (1960). Throughout 1959–1960, gender wage gap cases were commonly reported to the Central Committee for Labor Dispute Settlement (Panitia Penjelesaian Perselisihan Perburuhan Pusat, P4P).

40. See Besari (1947).

41. SOBSI (1957); Hindley (1964: 208–209).

42. Sri Ambar notes that in 1961, the SOBSI had sixty-six female union activists in its central and local structures (see SOBSI 1961: 46).

43. Only a handful of Gerwani's members were ever brought to trial. In 1975, four women leaders were brought to trial: Suharti Harsono, Sri Ambar, Sudjinah, and

20 Introduction

Sulami. See Sulami (1999) and Sudjinah (2003) on their detention, trial, and later imprisonment under the New Order regime.

44. See Wieringa (2002).

45. The New Order regime promoted "state-ibusim" that reinforced women's subordination (see Suryakusuma 1996). It is interesting to note the many similarities between the New Order's state-ibuism and the Japanese state's construction of womanhood as "ryosai-kenbo" (良妻賢母/ good wife, wise mother) (see Kondo 1990; Uno 1993), as both ideologies domesticated women workers' gendered roles.

46. See part 1 for more details of the labor policy of the New Order regime.

47. The SPSI established Institute for Women, Teenagers, and Children (Lembaga Wanita, Remaja dan Anak, LWRA) in 1986 as its "women's section." This was a response to foreign donors' appetite for "gender programs" for laborers in developing countries. The LWRA managed to receive financial assistance from a number of international organizations (including foreign and international trade union confederations) to organize educational programs for women workers. Hadiz (1997: 144) notes that it "could not conceivably encourage the use of strike action as a weapon by workers."

48. This was a common method of containing striking workers and union activists during the New Order period.

49. For a comparative note, see Werbner (2014) on the agency of women unionists in Botswana's labor movement, and Britwum et al. (2012) on the strategies of women workers in the Philippines to push for gender equality programs in their workplace.

50. Spiller (2010: 30) notes that "(s)ometimes overcoming *malu* and being *berani*—the Indonesian word for daring or brave—has rewards, in the form of increased status. I am unaware of instances in which *malu* and *berani* are used as direct opposites."

51. In Tagalog-speaking societies, Lindio-McGovern (1997: 128) notes that a woman who is courageous (*hindi takot, matapang*) "is respected by members because she also respects them."

52. Based on an interview with a female union activist, Ford (2008: 24) notes that "women activists who take these steps are not always appreciated by their male counterparts, because once they become 'brave,' they are considered a threat." Ockey (2004) notes that in Thailand, women unionists find it difficult to get elected as leaders because many do not believe women can lead.

53. From their analysis on the effects of education on women's empowerment in Indonesia, Samarakoon and Parinduri (2015) find that education increases women's stock of knowledge, in line with similar studies in Asia.

54. See Gallaway and Bernasek (2004).

55. Barraclough (2012: 58) notes that "Working women were the poorest paid and usually the youngest and least educated of South Korea's modern waged workers in the 1960s and 1970s."

56. Similar to conditions in Indonesia, in the Philippines, as Lindio-McGovern (1997: 130) notes, "(lower class) women were actually teaching each other, and perhaps changing each other's views about a woman's place in society."

57. See Tjandraningsih (2003).

58. "Muted expression," or political oppression under the authoritarian regime, was an important theme for many critical artists of the time. McGlynn (2000) discusses the "muted expression" of Indonesian literature, but does not pay much attention to women workers.

59. Ironically, in its typical usage of euphemisms, the regime named such worker strikes *unjuk rasa* (or "show of expressions"). For a detailed discussion of this issue, see Smyth and Grijns (1997).

60. For example, see "Untukmu buruh: lagu-lagu perjuangan buruh" (For all the Workers: Workers' songs of struggle), a collection of twelve songs produced by Indonesia Prosperous Worker's Union (Serikat Buruh Sejahtera Indonesia, SBSI) in 1995. Some of these songs were arranged by NGO activists, but nonetheless became part of the workers' identity. For a comparison of the context of working-class songs, see Werbner (2014) on the working-class protests in Botswana and Ramaswamy (1993) on Tamil folk songs among women farmworkers.

61. A well-known working-class poet was Wiji Thukul (born on August 26, 1963). His collections of poems were published posthumously; see Thukul (2000, 2014).

62. Bodden (1997: 40) notes that

(t)hroughout the 1980s, a number of Indonesian grassroots LSMs [NGOs] had already experimented with theater as a means for building solidarity, increasing confidence, and conscientizing peasants, students and scavengers . . . [because] role-playing techniques were more effective than lectures as a means of informal education for workers.

63. Aspinall (2005: 5) notes:

The regime's primary claim to historical legitimacy was that it had "saved" the nation from communist treachery in 1965 . . . . Anti-communism, expressed by repetitive warnings of the *bahaya laten PKI* (latent danger of the PKI) and *ekstrim kiri* (extreme left), remained central to regime discourse until the very end.

64. Indonesia's New Order was not, by any means, unique in suppressing the working class in the name of the nation's economic development, as authoritarian regimes in East and Southeast Asia, past and present, have similarly done. In describing the activies of Korean women unionists during the 1970s, Park (2005: 27) notes the general attitude under the military regime that, "People thought workers forming a labor union and doing union activities was something that only communists did, and therefore [they] deserved to be treated like animals."

65. Zandy (1990: 10).

66. For this research, I could not find any writing by Indonesian women plantation workers or miners. This appears to be common in other countries as well, and leads us to conclude that oral history remains predominant in these sectors. On working conditions in oil palm plantations, see Li (2017); Pye et al. (2012). On how women workers see their working conditions in mines, see Lahiri-Dutt (2006) and Lahiri-Dutt and Robinson (2008). Jala PRT network has organized domestic workers since 2004. See their website: www.tungkumenyala.com.

Part 1

DEFYING AUTHORITARIAN RULE

Female labor is indispensable to the global production regime. Since the latter half of the twentieth century, the growing international division of labor has triggered the creation of industrial factory zones in the Global South to accommodate light manufacturing industries that relocate operations in search of cheap labor. This has been accompanied by a worldwide feminization of labor, as women, often seeking wage labor for the first time, find that the low-paying jobs in these factories are their only option to enter the formal workforce, typically in the consumer electronics, food and beverage, and clothing and footwear sectors. Indonesia is no exception to this global phenomenon, also having witnessed a feminization of its workforce since the mid-1970s.

As Indonesia opened its doors to global production and embraced export-oriented industrialization policy, it enjoyed a period of relatively high economic growth during the 1980s and 1990s. This allowed the New Order authoritarian regime to consolidate and entrench its power under the hand and patronage of Suharto, who in 1983 claimed the title of "father of development." Invoking national security, the regime effectively neutralized social protests, silenced critical voices, and suppressed human rights (especially, freedom of assembly and freedom of speech). Control and suppression extended to labor as well. As early as 1973, the regime established the All-Indonesia Labor Federation (Federasi Buruh Seluruh Indonesia, FBSI) as the only legal labor union after securing tight control over various labor groups and eliminating the left-wing unions. It later formulated the doctrine of "Pancasila Labor Relations" (Hubungan Perburuhan Pancasila, HPP), the central premise of which is that workers and employers are "partners in production."[1] For the sake of establishing "harmony in the workplace," the right to strike was undermined, labor grievances and disputes were dismissed, the minimum wage was kept low, and the ability of workers to voice collective interests was impeded. In 1985, the regime centralized the FBSI's organizational structure under its control and changed its name to the All-Indonesia Workers' Union (Serikat Pekerja Seluruh Indonesia, SPSI). Workers' attempts to organize any independent union were thwarted, often with the help of the military. Under the repressive authoritarian rule, workers, just like everyone else in the society, could not exercise their freedom of expression: any open criticism or explicitly political writing put them directly under the state's surveillance.

The New Order regime understood that a constant pool of cheap and obedient labor was necessary to ensure the continued ascent of export-led industries. Female laborers, regardless of their skills, were considered passive, docile, and suitable for tedious manual work. They were therefore mainly employed in the light industries, which required uninterrupted production on assembly lines to meet the demands of the global market. Labor-intensive and long-working hours, it was in these export-oriented factories where workers began testing the limits of the New Order's tight authoritarian rule.

It is within this context that part 1 discusses two important writings, individually penned by Ida Irianti (chapter 1) and Meppy Doryati Emping (chapter 2). Both Ida Irianti and Meppy Doryati Emping entered the labor market in the mid-1980s, at the height of the regime's export-led industrialization policy. The feminization process prompted rural young women to search for jobs in urban areas; they found those jobs as manual workers in factories. During this time, urban life lured millions of young women with the promise of earning enough to fulfill their social obligation to support their family's income and, importantly, to gain a sense of freedom in a life of their own. As they attained formal employment as manual workers in the factories, their lived experience of work and urban life led them to union activism.

Ida Irianti came from a rural background and worked as manual laborer at a factory in urban Jakarta. Her union activism began shortly after the restructuring of the FBSI into the SPSI, in 1987–1988. Her struggle was partly shaped by this institutional change; as the union's structure became more directly controlled by the regime, she had to fight on her own. Due to her activism, she was criminalized and brought to the criminal court, a maneuver that employers often use to bust unions—even until today. She wrote her *pembelaan* (defense speech) in 1988.

In the early 1990s, a time of rising labor protests in many industrial areas of Java, Meppy Doryati Emping was working in an export-oriented footwear factory in Surabaya (East Java). The regime's control over civil society, especially the labor movement, was tightening and the military often acted to "harmoniously settle" labor disputes.[2] In this climate, her union activism was branded a security threat. In 1993 she penned a personal account of "bitter tragedy," which chronologizes her actions and the retaliation of the employer and the state that left her traumatized.

Both Ida and Meppy's writings reflect a working-class consciousness against social injustices of the time. As the regime censored, suppressed, and imprisoned its critics, these two women wrote about and against those injustices as experienced by the working class. In so doing, they created a zone of resistance in which they told the truth. Although their writings may not possess a sophisticated argument or literary complexity, they are based on actual experiences as female laborers. The writings are therefore an authentic portrayal of how their labor was commodified under the state's export-led industrialization policy, how workers had to toil to earn a living while being denied their rights, and how workers found strength in the collective power of the union. Their writings not only inform us about the reality the regime wanted to hide and suppress, but also embody the authors' courage in putting pen to paper. In that sense, the writings are a testament of a working-class struggle that refused to submit to the factory's discipline or the state's ideology of "industrial harmony."

The writings of Ida Irianti and Meppy Doryati Emping are a literary expression of what they saw and experienced, what they felt and thought. Having learned to write in school as part of their basic education, they knew writing was useful for them, even if they may not have had a polished literary skill. As workers, they were not afraid to write. Both women wrote with a specific purpose: they used writing as an instrument to articulate collective concerns that they were not allowed to voice at the workplace, to convey a call to struggle to their co-workers, and to let others understand what they were going through. As such, their writings demonstrate that although female workers during the New Order regime were politically silenced, they were not mute.

NOTES

1. The Indonesian state doctrine of Pancasila consists of five principles: belief in one, Supreme God; just and civilized humanity; national unity; democracy led by the inner wisdom of unanimity arising out of deliberations among representatives; and social justice for the whole of the Indonesian people. "Hubungan Perburuhan Pancasila" ("Pancasila Labor Relations") was later renamed as "Hubungan Industrial Pancasila" ("Pancasila Industrial Relations").

2. For dispute settlement regulations of this time, see Surat Keputusan Menaker tentang Petunjuk Penyelesaian Perselisihan Hubungan Industrial dan Pemutusan Hubungan Kerja di Tingkat Perusahaan dan Pemerantaraan no. 15A/ Men/ 1994 (Letter of Decree of the Minister of Manpower on Guidelines of settlement of industrial relations dispute and termination of employment at factory level and mediation) (dated January 4, 1993).

Chapter 1

Reinventing Defense Speech

No one today seems to know about her. Labor activists would often get puzzled looks on their faces when I asked if they knew or had ever heard of Ida Irianti.[1] Not only have many of her contemporaries forgotten her name, but sadly, they also do not realize what Irianti accomplished in her ground-breaking efforts to organize workers during the 1980s, a time of tight political control under Indonesia's New Order authoritarian regime. Although she and her work have been consigned to an obscure past, her *pembelaan* (defense speech) leaves an important footprint of the collective struggle and resistance she once led.

In May 1987 Irianti led a strike of around 300 unionized workers at the P.T. Sinar Sosro (Sinar Sosro, Ltd.) plant in Jakarta. The strike against the giant beverage manufacturing company shocked the New Order regime and sparked a heated debate in the national media about workers' basic right to strike.[2] Yet, Irianti is noteworthy for reasons other than her leading role in this strike. She was the chairperson of the local union at P.T. Sinar Sosro, and one of only a few women workers in a leadership role, entrusted with such a position by her coworkers at a time when female involvement in unions was rare.[3] Significantly, Irianti was elected by her coworkers at the local plant and not appointed by the union hierarchy. This ran counter to the norm of the All-Indonesia Labor Federation (Federasi Serikat Buruh Indonesia, FBSI), the only union federation that was allowed and sponsored by the regime. In the federation, selected individuals were appointed to union leadership roles in order to guarantee worker compliance with the dictates of the regime.

It was her union activism that brought Irianti before a criminal court, and the *pembelaan* we examine in this chapter was written for that forum. She was the first factory worker tried for a criminal offence after the New Order regime promulgated its labor law in 1969 and was the first female worker to draft her own *pembelaan*.[4] She presented her eloquently written document before the district court of East Jakarta in July 1988.[5]

This chapter introduces and discusses Irianti's *pembelaan* to highlight the importance of reading workers' writings as part of scholarly efforts to understand how members of the Indonesian working class embody the narrative of class in their articulations for social justice. Irianti's *pembelaan* is the result of her personal experiences as a female worker and was an integral part of her union activism. As a factory worker, she received meager wages and labored without the benefits of social security or job protection. Still, she was expected to work long hours, voice no complaint and avoid union activities. These were the working conditions that she and her coworkers set out to change.

Irianti makes no claim to speak for the entire working class, but her document illuminates the general conditions of Indonesian workers in the 1980s. Its value is as a legitimate articulation by a member of the working class about the world she experienced and at the same time aspired to change. Her *pembelaan* also reveals her position in the larger political and economic constellation of global capitalist production and Indonesia's authoritarian state, as well as her and her coworkers' efforts to stand with dignity within that constellation. Thus, it transcends the boundary between the individual and collective and helps us see beyond standard explanations of the authoritarian state's domination of the working class.[6]

More than just a historical artifact of the 1980s, when labor's freedom of association was suppressed by the state,[7] Irianti's *pembelaan* has contemporary relevance as well. It documents changes in the workplace that initiated the informalization of work by means of outsourcing labor—an issue that has continued to haunt the labor movement in Indonesia despite workers having enjoyed relative freedom of association since 1998.[8] As a text, Irianti's *pembelaan* compels readers to reconsider the image of illiterate, passive, and defenseless female workers. It questions these stereotypes in a manner similar to recent studies that critically interrogate the one-dimensional portrayal of Third World labor in East Asian industrialization. It presents a more complex understanding of the issues of precariat labor toiling under globalization. Regardless of the sociopolitical constraints imposed on them, workers describe their own world and reflect on how to change and improve their situation. Thus, Irianti's *pembelaan* is an important manifestation of the experiences of a "conscious worker" and, as such, it casts a new light on the issues of her time.[9]

This chapter first sets the stage of Irianti's time within Indonesia's arc of industrialization and political transformation, focusing on the feminization of labor and its social implications. It then turns to the significance of the *pembelaan* in the historical context of Indonesian political thinking. Far from merely being a written speech presented before the court as a legal document to defend oneself against a criminal charge, Indonesian political actors have long used the *pembelaan* to command the attention of the audience in the court and to educate the wider public by delineating the political contours of the case. Soekarno's "Indonesia Accuses" (in Dutch, "*Indonesië klaagt aan*"), delivered before the Bandung district court in 1930, is the finest example of the political-pedagogical use of a *pembelaan*.[10] Other examples include Sudisman's "Analysis of Responsibility" ("*Uraian Tanggungdjawab*"), which he read before the New Order's Special Military Tribunal in 1967,[11] and Heri Akhmadi's 1979 trial defense against charges of insulting the head of state.[12]

The original purpose of the *pembelaan* as the defendant's legal document loses its meaning once the defendant sees (or believes) that the court he/she is standing before is nothing but a kangaroo court (and the trial, a show). This is precisely how Irianti saw her trial, and she therefore wrote her *pembelaan* not merely in hopes of a legal acquittal, but, above all, to narrate her personal story to illuminate the economic injustice, social alienation, and political repression of the working class as a whole—the class she belonged to and identified with. She hoped that her audience would understand and sympathize with the workers' desperation and their attempts to change their situation through industrial action. The *pembelaan* gave Irianti a social forum at a time when Indonesia's working class had no access to other written forms of literary engagement and very few fora to speak out. Thus the *pembelaan*, as a vehicle for timely and suitable intervention, was Irianti's chance to tell the public about her, and her coworkers', struggle.

This chapter reads Irianti's *pembelaan* as a narrative of "tactical essentialism"[13] to examine two important issues: (1) the involvement of female workers in union activities in authoritarian Indonesia in the 1980s and (2) how changes in the workplace weakened the union. Irianti's *pembelaan* offers a clear account of how workers saw, experienced, and understood these two issues, and assessed the implications to their lives. Lastly, the chapter analyzes the 1987 strike as a climax in the union's struggle and situates its results in the political context of the day. Throughout, Irianti's reinvention of defense speech deepens our understanding of the twin issues of factory employment and female worker activism during Indonesia's authoritarian regime of the 1980s.

IDA IRIANTI AND HER TIME

Irianti took up factory work in early 1983, during the so-called second wave of the feminization of Indonesian labor (1979–1986), when factories began to hire women in greater numbers to help Indonesia compete in the global production process.[14] This pursuance of a competitive edge and the reality of the New Order regime also made it a time of worker subordination. Irianti went to work for P.T. Sinar Sosro, a domestic beverage manufacturing company. Although beverage companies followed the general trend of hiring women workers, the percentage of women in production was not as high as it was in the textile, garment, and footwear (TGF) companies.[15] I would suggest that differences in industry sectors, global linkages, and market shares within companies in the 1980s do not necessarily account for the conditions that led to the involvement of female workers in unions, but they may help to explain the company's responses to perceived worker militancy, as shall be discussed below.[16]

As with other women workers of the time, Irianti was confined within and bound by patriarchal social institutions and factory discipline. Far from being submissive and "loyal" to the factory's regime of discipline, however, she chose to voice her grievances and act to address them.[17] Irianti organized her coworkers and protested against both the economic injustices in the workplace and the sociopolitical barriers that limited her organizational capacity. By raising her "voice," Irianti broke the silence of the Indonesian working class, especially women workers, under the authoritarian regime. She showed enormous courage in taking a leading role in her union and then putting pen to paper to document her, and the working class, struggle. Her activism with fellow female workers shatters the myth of the docile and passive East Asian female workers. Indeed, the May 1987 strike that she led stirred a national debate on workers' right to strike (as shall be described below).

Irianti's *pembelaan* illustrates the social conditions of female workers under the export-oriented policy that Indonesia took at that time. Indonesia was not the only (authoritarian) country in East Asia to implement a policy of exclusionary corporatism in the 1980s. A decade earlier, South Korea and Taiwan had embraced a similar policy, becoming models for other aspiring countries in the region, including Indonesia. Examining the literary forms that other Asian female workers used helps in contextualizing Irianti's *pembelaan*. The writings of South Korean female workers, for instance, provide a fruitful comparison.[18] Under the rule of Chun Doo Hwan (1980–1988), with its iron fist policy toward South Korea's democracy movement, "slum romances" written by working-class women began to flourish as part of the *minjung yesul* (people's art movement) and become "a source of revitalization."[19] Romance was a literary form that was easily accessible to the working class of the time, and Korean female workers used it to tell their own stories of hardship and struggle as factory workers during the rapid industrialization pursued under Chun's authoritarian regime.[20]

The difference in form between Irianti's *pembelaan* and the "slum romances" written by her Korean sisters reveals a divergence in the social circumstances that Indonesian and Korean women experienced in their work environments. The authoritarian sociopolitical environment of Indonesia in the 1980s was not conducive to the development of a genuine people's movement, such as the one that women workers were able to form with the support of grassroots organizations in South Korea beginning in the 1970s.[21] While the percentage of unionized women workers in South Korea was quite low—only 18.6 percent in 1989[22]—it was high compared to the percentage in Indonesia.[23] Moreover, Korean women workers in small- and medium-sized industries in the late 1980s were organized into independent unions,[24] while union organizers paid no attention to women workers in similar-sized industries in Indonesia. In Indonesia, members of the middle class dominated the production of short stories and novels in the 1980s and their literary writings were consumed for personal leisure by the same class. The most striking difference of women workers' labor activism in Indonesia was the high rate of illiteracy among poor rural women, for it was these uneducated women who were most often recruited for factory work.[25]

Irianti therefore faced numerous obstacles as a (female) labor activist trying to maneuver Indonesia's specific sociopolitical circumstances. As readership among (female) workers was low, union organizing became her priority. She took up the pen only when she decided to write a *pembelaan*. Knowing that this might be her only opportunity, Irianti determined to use her *pembelaan* not simply to defend herself before the court, but also as a political act. She wanted her life story to illuminate the poor working conditions and the sociopolitical oppression of the Indonesian working class, many of whom did not have the same literary opportunity (or necessity) she had at that time.

THE *PEMBELAAN* AS A POLITICAL DOCUMENT

Although its origins can be traced back to an earlier time, the *pembelaan* as political rhetoric appeared in its most refined form in Soekarno's defense speech (*pleidooi*).[26] As a key leader of the nationalist movement during the late Dutch colonial period, Soekarno decided against asking for a pardon or a lighter sentence, as a defendant would normally do in court. Instead, he ingeniously seized the machinery of the legal process to lay bare his understanding of the charges made against him[27] and, more importantly, to describe the political and economic context of his case, namely, the dire condition of colonialism in Asia, particularly in the archipelago. Soekarno did so eloquently, with scholarly citations from his readings on the subject clearly illustrating the depth of his knowledge.

Contemporary readers of his *pleidooi* may think of Soekarno as a native writing back to his colonial master by employing the tools invented by the colonial world.[28] This may have been his intention, but Soekarno did not write his *pleidooi* for the colonial master alone. A split in the text makes this clear: he addressed the colonizer in a formal sense, but explained the details of his case to the court's general audience, the colonized natives. To the colonizer, he articulated the natives' discontent; to the natives, he spoke as if he was giving a lecture (in the courtroom!) on the subject of the colonial world. Soekarno ridiculed the legitimacy of the (Bandung) court, but, more importantly, he successfully turned the court that was supposed to try him into a stage upon which he accused the colonial government of its decades-long history of humanitarian crimes against the natives. Thus, he titled his *pleidooi* "Indonesia Accuses." The political sleight-of-hand he performed in the court evidently caught the colonial government so off guard that for his second "crime against the state" in 1933, he was exiled to the town of Ende (on Flores island) without trial. This prevented him from utilizing the public forum of the court to air similar (or, even more telling) accusations against the colonial government. Soekarno indeed opened a new arena in political rhetoric to convey his message. While the content of his *pleidooi* was undeniably a compelling message on its own, the way Soekarno used the court to reach a wider audience for his political cause is equally important.

Seen from this perspective, Soekarno's *pleidooi* marked the beginning of the use of the pembelaan as a standard document for legal defense in court into a means of conveying a political message to a wider audience.[29] Soekarno certainly understood the nature of the colonial court he was facing: far from conducting a fair trial, the judges had already decided upon a verdict before the first session opened. In this situation, he had no reason to pursue a legal defense and instead seized the chance to challenge the colonial government by using his case as an instructive example of colonial repression of native aspirations. By using the *pembelaan* the way he did, he refused to participate in the sham proceedings, thus exposing the court's illegitimacy.

Soekarno's *pleidooi* is a model against which to read subsequent *pembelaan* delivered by political dissidents to the ruling powers to highlight the *political* nature of their case. For example, in his "Analysis of Responsibility" ("*Uraian tanggungdjawab*"), read in July 1967 before the Special Military Tribunal of the New Order regime, Sudisman describes the political nature of his trial: "sessions of the *Mahmillub* [Special Military Tribunal] are open, yet closed, and are 'public' . . . but not *public* at all, or what in the language of ordinary people, would be called *dictated*, in other words, undemocratic."[30] As in Soekarno's case, Sudisman did not write in hopes of a political pardon.[31] Instead, Sudisman produced a personal reflection on the political conditions that led to the downfall of the Communist Party of Indonesia (PKI).

That is my regret and thus, I would like to use this occasion to apologize to all my friends. (p. 1)

When Irianti drafted her *pembelaan*, she was undoubtedly thinking mostly about her coworkers rather than giving her own fears room to take charge of her mind. However, her *pembelaan* was written free of the jargon of the union movement—expressions so often associated with socialism, communism, or international solidarity. She evidently suspected that political terms such as these would have no resonance and even be counterproductive in the courtroom.[35] Her *pembelaan* also does not pretend to be sophisticated in the manner of Akhmadi's document, which is full of political catchphrases. Her *pembelaan* shows clearly that she is close to, and knows intimately, her audience. They are the common workers, the manual laborers who do not have much time to play with fancy words, thus the language she uses is clear and easily accessible. Far from taking the position of a leading demagogue who preaches to workers with the ideological virtue of a political agitator, whose noble mission is to disturb the "false consciousness" of the working class, Irianti comes close to her audience as one of them, as an equal to them.

Precisely in this quality the difference between Irianti and Soekarno and Heri Akhmadi is evident. As political dissidents, Soekarno and Akhmadi were intellectuals and members of the fortunate elite, so their *pleidooi/ pembelaan* speaks to "the people" from a higher ground. Irianti, by contrast, is a member of the working class, herself an oppressed subaltern. As intellectuals, Soekarno and Akhmadi had more than one opportunity to take up their pens to write down their thoughts and concerns about the nation; their *pleidooi/pembelaan* were just one part of this larger effort. Irianti, however, did not share this luxury; drafting her *pembelaan* was her one and only opportunity to express her opinions and concerns to a general audience.

Significantly, Irianti was the first woman to write a *pembelaan* in such a political fashion; even today, most such *pembelaan* are written by men. Women in Indonesia have produced writings in many other forms, including "political" novels, such as Soewarsih Djojopoespito's *Buiten het Gareel* (*Out of Harness*), but autobiographies and novels as a literary form are dominated by educated and middle-class women.[36] As a member of the working class under an authoritarian regime, Irianti understood that any aspirations she might have to join literary circles that the middle class then dominated had little chance of being realized. In this respect, her *pembelaan* is comparable to the *testimonios* (testimonial narratives) used by members of marginalized groups in Latin America as a literary genre that suits their needs.[37] Her *pembelaan* may not be as narratively compelling as the *testimonio* of, for example, Guatemala's Rigoberta Menchú, but reading Irianti's document (and speech) against this background reveals evidence of a similar collective consciousness and a desire to articulate the voices of Indonesia's working class. Like the *testimonios*, then, the political *pembelaan* became a literary instrument of the working class in 1980s Indonesia.[38]

As a literary instrument, Irianti's *pembelaan* describes the world of the Indonesian working people as seen, experienced, and understood by one of its members. The literary value of her *pembelaan* rests on its original form and its content aims to strategically accommodate the primary expressions of the working class in times of economic and political oppression under the authoritarian regime. She felt an urgency to spotlight the miserable conditions in a time when the regime was embarking on the demanding project of economic development through export-oriented production to the detriment of its working people. In this spirit, she had two important stories to share: one about the union activities of female workers, and the other about the ongoing changes in the workplace that were weakening the union.

THE MAKING OF A FEMALE LABOR LEADER

The social context that shaped Irianti's *pembelaan* was characterized by a low level of female workers' involvement in union activities in the 1980s. The politics of *malu*, as described in the introduction, had confined female workers to certain social roles that limit their public lives, including union activities. Irianti's *pembelaan* details this condition as she personally experienced it. More interestingly, it also paints a picture of her personal transformation from a *(pe)malu* to a *(pem)berani* young woman.

Irianti informs us that when she started working in the factory, the dreams she had were rather limited and centered on herself and her family. The *pembelaan* starts with the feeling she had during her first days in the factory:

> It started in 1983. At that time, I started working at P.T. Sinar Sosro, and was stationed as a typist. There was a hope to be promoted as an assistant accountant. I worked with a big hope. I could contribute to the family's income, could save up for my children's future education, and could enjoy life a little bit better. I hoped my children could have a better life than I had, so they wouldn't need to work so hard just to meet basic needs. I hoped they could enjoy a higher education to secure a position better than their mother's. (p. 2)

The "big hope" she had was for a better financial situation; nothing was more important to her than securing her children's prospects for higher education. Education would be a means to improve her children's living situation and gain control over life's uncertainties. Irianti is not ashamed to admit that her early dreams might be judged as unwarranted or superficial because she wanted to give an honest description. In so doing, her *pembelaan* informs us that these dreams are not hers alone, but also are shared by working-class women in general.[39] Although often considered supplemental, the income of women workers is essential to meet household expenses, including education expenses for children, to help them secure their own dreams.

It was not long before Irianti began to realize that these dreams were beyond her reach, however. What started as a simple dream began to shatter just months after she began working:

> It was such a joy for me to get work. Although my [monthly] wage at that time was 50,000 rupiahs, there was a hope [for me] to depend on. But this joy lasted no more than three months. I had signed a contract that stated that after three months [probation] work, I would get a letter of appointment as a permanent worker and a wage increase of as much as 10,000 rupiahs. I had waited for the three months [and then for another] four months . . . and what was promised never came to be realized. It was not the 10,000 rupiah-wage increase that really mattered, or the letter of appointment. Under such a working situation, how could I have a hope for the future and my family? The promise could not be relied on; I did not have the power. Not that I didn't try. I raised this issue several times. The answer stayed the same: "[Some] workers here do not have a letter of appointment. If Ida Irianti is given that letter of appointment, others would also ask the same." Evidently, I was not the only one who experienced this, but also many others. (p. 2)

Three months working in the factory opened Irianti's eyes to the reality: there was and never would be any job certainty. On the one hand, Irianti's expression that she "was not the only one who experienced this" signals the end of her hope for a stable income. On the other hand, it opened up her mind to the common plight of her fellow workers, other urban proletariats in Java. Many manual workers indeed had no employment security during the time of export-oriented industrialization under the authoritarian regime; this had been the case since the early 1970s.[40]

Irianti's self-identification with the working class can be read as part of her personal transformation—a transformation that took place only after she started working in the factory and began to see herself as a worker. Thus, her *pembelaan* contains the important element of "collective consciousness," something also seen in *testimonios*.[41] Comparing her situation with that of her coworkers in the factory, Irianti discovered a common similarity and few differences: the basic absence of employment security affected *all* workers in the factory. The significance of this self-identification for her *pembelaan* is to argue that her problem was not an isolated case; her experience was tied to, and was the result of, the regime's economic repression of the working class.

Without her identification with the working class, her *pembelaan* would be no more than a document for legal defense in the court of law that notes her individual situation. By acknowledging the commonality of her experience among other workers, her *pembelaan* became an overarching affirmation of the marginalization of the working class.

Her personal transformation was also shaped by one particular industrial action that took place in the factory. As she related in her *pembelaan*, the most influential event that confirmed her personal transformation was the worker strike in 1984, which took place a few months after she started working:

> One day I witnessed fellow workers who were gathering in the factory yard for a strike. I went out and asked what they were demanding. Apparently, the union chairperson was suspended due to a wage negotiation; they demanded their chairperson be reinstated and the negotiation be continued. I was amazed and moved at once. Amazed, because a union chairperson was put under suspension simply after conducting a negotiation and whose demand was in fact a reasonable demand. And that [such an event] was taking place where I worked, in my country that upholds the ways of the *musyawarah* [deliberations]. I was moved seeing fellow friends whose lives were meager yet they had a sense of justice, still had a sense of solidarity, and still had immense courage to defend their leader. I was then just a keen onlooker, wanting to see what would happen, while a feeling of sympathy for fellow friends was blooming inside [my] heart. I soon left [my] stance as an onlooker after I witnessed how the regional board of the Food and Beverages Workers Union and the officials of the local office of the Ministry of Manpower started to get involved and [instead] ordered my friends to go back to work without even trying to settle the issue of their demand. (p. 4)

The three-day strike that Irianti witnessed (her first) in 1984 called for the reemployment of the union's leader, who had been suspended from work while negotiating a wage increase. The workers brought their claim to the Panitia Penyelesaian Perselisihan Perburuhan Pusat (National Committee for Labor Dispute Settlement), which soon ruled in favor of the company and allowed it to impose performance-based wages in the factory.[42] Thus, the union's efforts to improve the welfare of the workers were stymied. In practice, the new wage system stalled the possibility of any wage increase for all the manual workers and it eliminated a seniority system.

Although the strike was short in duration and yielded no direct results for the workers, it changed Irianti forever. Initially she was just a spectator, a still-*malu* factory worker. After having witnessed the action, she was curious enough to approach the workers who had been on strike. In her *pembelaan*, Irianti mentions how surprised she was by the strike, but also that she was so curious that she approached the striking workers and asked what their demands were. A conversation between her as a young *malu* female worker and a group of *berani* workers might have taken place. This conversation was important for her transformation; she dared to take a step and crossed the boundary, marking her transition from being *malu* to becoming *berani*.

Talking with the workers, she learned about their "reasonable demand"—a demand that reflected hers, too. Instead of withdrawing from the crowd or becoming a "free-rider" worker, she began questioning the startling contrast between the harsh realities of the social injustices she was experiencing as a worker and the ideals of "industrial harmony" the regime pushed with its "Pancasila Industrial Relations" policy.

In her *pembelaan*, Irianti wrote that the strike made her "amazed and moved at once" (*heran dan terharu sekaligus*). The change in her feelings is significant: from being indifferent to being a concerned worker.[43] Her reference to the feeling of sympathy as the original spark that eventually changed her life so dramatically contrasts with other motivating factors in building labor activism, including political indoctrination and advocacy training, the aim of which is to shake workers' "false consciousness" and lead them to the "right path" of union activism.[44] This raises the subject of class consciousness. The language, and analysis, of class was of course prohibited in public discourse of the time, so not surprisingly, Irianti's *pembelaan* contains no reference to Marxism or socialist ideas. Furthermore, nongovernmental organizations (NGOs) at that time had not yet employed class analysis in their activities among workers. Irianti's motivations, however, did not make her any less of a union activist than more class-conscious workers of subsequent generations.

In her own way, Irianti describes her real feelings as a worker and the varied experiences she encountered on her own journey of self-development. Her *pembelaan* paints a picture of one worker's personal transformation, the social background that shaped her involvement in union activities, and her process of self-becoming. Her *pembelaan*, therefore, issues a persuasive call to reconsider the nature of women workers' activism under the authoritarian regime's policy of exclusionary corporatism.

The three-day strike in 1984 hastened Irianti's personal transformation and solidified her self-identification with the working class. She was no longer a *(pe)malu* female worker concerned only with her family dreams and afraid to confront her employer. Instead, she became one of the *berani* female workers who outspokenly challenged the social authority and no longer ignorantly or humbly accepted her oppressive working conditions. Her saga began with workplace changes in the factory where she was working.

WORKPLACE CHANGES AND
THE UNION'S STRUGGLE

During the 1980s, especially in the years 1982–1987, wage growth in Indonesia's industrial sector was below the real rate of inflation and thus the real value of workers' income diminished and their purchasing power weakened.[45] Meanwhile, under the regime's export-oriented industrialization policy, companies were encouraged to expand production and, especially with the decline in oil prices after 1981, to export non-oil products such as timber and rubber. To further this effort several bold deregulation packages were put in place and companies enjoyed a more relaxed economic climate.[46] In this environment, companies developed managerial strategies to compete for a greater market share. That these strategies brought about workplace changes at the factory level is a subject rarely discussed in microeconomic analysis and in anthropological reports on labor. We have therefore yet to see a comprehensive picture of how these changes were decided and implemented and, more important for our discussion, how they impacted workers' lives.

Read against this background, Irianti's *pembelaan* provides a bottom-up perspective based on the real experiences of manual workers who had to face company strategies to rationalize some aspects of their operations. P.T. Sinar Sosro was a domestic company whose production, for the most part, targeted the domestic market. Its domestic competitors, however, took advantage of the regime's liberalization policy, putting new competitive pressure on the company. Irianti's *pembelaan* details, in her own words, the sequence of events after the 1984 strike and how subsequent workplace changes progressed in steps.[47]

The restructuring of the wage system was the first of such steps:

[T]he employer wanted to implement a new wage system. According to this new rule, the wage is based on two components: a basic minimum wage (GPM) that is 30 percent of the whole wage, and a basic professional wage (GPP) that forms the remaining 70 percent. Together they are called the basic standard wage (GPS). If a worker is absent from work due to sickness or is on leave, what shall be paid is only the basic minimum wage (that is, 30 percent). . . . The employer would then impose a standardization of wages based on each worker's position in the company. Those who had worked long [for years] would have their basic wage reduced in accordance with the standard. Some workers who previously had a basic wage of as much as 150,000 rupiahs would get [their wages] reduced to as little as 70,000 rupiahs, and so forth. . . . In implementing this new wage system, neither workers nor their union were consulted; we just had to obey the decision taken alone by the employer, although it impaired workers as a whole. We are merely an object, regardless of how its [the company's] decision impacted our life and future. The employer decided and implemented what it had decided arbitrarily.I could see the impact on myself and other workers of the policy's implementation. If we got ill, we would only receive 30 percent of our already-meager wage. The company does provide a polyclinic inside the factory [but] with very minimum facilities. The doctor visits [the factory] four times a week and only for one hour to serve all the four hundred workers. It is very difficult to get treatment in the polyclinic and the medicine is very limited. If we go for treatment outside [polyclinic], we have to pay for it ourselves. (p. 3)

Restructuring the factory wage system to a performance-based one was meant to stall general wage increases. Irianti explains that this policy was implemented without any prior consultation with the workers or their union. The issue, however, was not only about the decision-making process, for, as the *pembelaan* makes clear, the basic premise of the unions' negative response was the enormous financial loss workers would have to bear under the new wage system, since the basic wage (30 percent of the minimum wage) could not cover their basic life necessities.

The second workplace change was the "rationalization" of the employment system through the outsourcing of employment. This meant that workers were no longer employed by the factory; they now signed employment contracts with an external company. Irianti describes this process:

The accounting department, the most important department of the company, was about to be dissolved and all of its activities in bookkeeping were to be handed over to a service company named Infosos, to support P.T. Sinar Sosro. Workers in the accounting department were to be transferred as workers of Infosos. At first, I didn't really understand this step taken by the company; why a department that is so important and keeps all the company's secrets should be handed over to an outside service company. But gradually I came to an understanding. . . .

These workers, who were transferred to work at Infosos, were then offered a wage increase as long as they would sign a fixed-term contract. They, again, became confused. On the one hand, they needed the increase, as wages had stagnated. On the other hand, they didn't want to work as a fixed-term worker because they had been permanent workers and their job was by nature, not a temporary job. (pp. 5–6)

The factory thus outsourced its accounting work by transferring workers— without their prior consent—and offered a wage increase once they agreed to sign a fixed-term working contract with an external company. In that way, the factory no longer needed to employ workers for bookkeeping work; this job was outsourced to Infosos.

Irianti explains that this outsourcing strategy did not stop at the accounting department, but was also later applied to all new hires. In describing this practice, she names Prapto Raharjo, the factory's human resources manager, as the mastermind behind this workplace change—a change that advantaged Raharjo's own outsourcing business:

> In the past, to recruit workers, P.T. Sinar Sosro acted as a party in the employment relationship with the workers; now [however], a new policy currently under implementation [means] that workers won't have [any] employment relationship with P.T. Sinar Sosro, but shall form an employment relationship with a labor agency managed by Mr. Prapto Rahardjo, S.H., and this labor agency shall hire workers to work at P.T. Sinar Sosro. Therefore, in the upcoming days, inside P.T. Sinar Sosro there will be workers whose employment relationship is with Infosos, workers whose employment relationship is with the labor agency managed by Mr. Prapto Raharjo, and also, probably, other ventures that support P.T. Sinar Sosro and place their workers at P.T. Sinar Sosro. In this kind of condition, establishing a labor union proves difficult and in reality, impossible. (p. 16)

The outsourcing of workers to different entities created a situation in which new recruits no longer had an employment relationship with the P.T. Sinar Sosro; thus the company had no legal liability for workers' economic welfare. Irianti astutely foresees the consequence of this new practice in terms of union activism: the labor union will lose its power to organize workers in the factory, as its organizational struggle is now confined only to defending existing members without being able to recruit new ones. Even if workers could re-form the union and recruit new members, they would have to deal with the labor agency than with P.T. Sinar Sosro.[48] Thus, it will find it difficult to establish itself as a legitimate party that represents all workers in the factory.

Irianti's *pembelaan* makes clear that outsourcing had been in practice in Indonesia since the early 1980s.[49] Her *pembelaan* demonstrates that workers were not ignorant of the implications of outsourcing and could clearly express their thoughts about its consequences to their material conditions.

The third workplace change Irianti discusses involves control of the workforce. Under the New Order regime's policy of exclusionary corporatism, Minister of Manpower Sudomo[50] reorganized the All-Indonesia Labor Federation (FBSI) into the centralized All-Indonesia Workers' Union (SPSI) in 1985. Having to operate under the state's surveillance system gave local unions less freedom to assemble and plan labor actions. Irianti's *pembelaan* explains from her factory-floor level perspective how this policy of labor control was imposed hand-in-hand with other workplace changes. Prior to 1985, the local union at P.T. Sinar Sosro had a relative degree of autonomy from FBSI as a central organization. The union's first strike, in 1984, is evidence of how free the union was to plan and organize itself with no direct interference from FBSI. After 1985, however, all local unions came under the SPSI's direct control. This change seriously impacted the power of labor to organize at the factory level. Irianti describes what happened to the P.T. Sinar Sosro union:

> As has been known, the second congress of FBSI was organized at the end of 1985. At the congress, it was decided that FBSI would change its name to SPSI. The federation form would be changed into a centralized one (*unitaris*), and its organizational structure would change. There is no more Branch Officials, Regional Officials, or National Officials of the Industrial Sector Union (SBLP). What we have now is a Branch Board, a Regional Board, and a National Board. The local union's name was changed to a Work Unit (UK) and its organizers as Work Unit Officials, simply abbreviated as PUK.
>
> Therefore, we requested a letter of statement [to confirm the local election] from the SPSI Branch Board (DPC SPSI) of Jakarta Timur (East Jakarta), and not from the Regional Board of Jakarta, Food and Beverage Workers Union (RBJ/ PD SBMM FSBI Jakarta). It was not letter of statement that came [to our office], but representatives of the National Board of SPSI of Tourism, Food and Beverage Workers Union (PARMAMIN), who questioned the validity of the local election and ordered a reelection. The Branch Board also stated the same opinion and reasoned that it did not witness the election process. For us, this is so strange. If some of our members requested a reelection, automatically we would do it. But the fact is that our members predominantly supported us, yet these officials insisted it was not valid. For me, it was not about my position [as chairperson]. That was not important. The most important thing was how far the voices of our friends are appreciated and counted, how far we can foster our rights for self-determination. (p. 7)

Irianti's *pembelaan* provides a detailed account of the organizational change (from FBSI to SPSI) at the local level and how it affected the work of a local union. Her union, for all of its autonomy to elect its own leadership, was not recognized by the national board of SPSI. It is important to note that leadership of the SPSI was based on appointment (by the regime), not by election. Thus, the leadership of the local unions, such as Irianti's, that were elected by the rank-and-file challenged the new normal of the SPSI structure. The invalidation of the union's election illustrates the degree of control exercised by the authoritarian regime over labor, and how this control cut off the relationship between workers and unions. Thus, the SPSI, rather than representing workers, served as the regime's surveillance agent.

Irianti also explains that the tightening control of the workforce, which began right after the 1984 strike ended, involved Indonesia's military:

> [W]e had to face a screening team, whose chairpersons were the owners of the company, Mr. Sutjipto Sosrodjojo and Suryanto Sosrodjojo, and its members were Mr. Sudadian, a TNI-AD (army) major and his son Lies Faturachman as assistant. The task of this team was to interrogate all workers, both the experienced and the newly recruited ones, about who were the *dalang* [organizers] of the strike, what the demands were, and so on. This team also gave us a lecture about Pancasila. The working method of this team initially required us to answer a list of prepared questions and then we were interrogated one by one. We were confused as to how Pancasila could be interpreted by and for the interests of the employer; we did not have any suspicions about what could be imposed on us at that time. (p. 5)

The involvement of the military in workers' strikes was not new; since the late 1970s, Minister Sudomo had spoken of labor disputes as a national security threat. This concern led the regime to use the military to contain worker discontent and deter workers from going on strike, as in the case of P.T. Sinar Sosro in 1984.[51] As Irianti explains, these military personnel individually interrogated workers and lectured them on Pancasila. For some workers, the interrogations led to their dismissal; those who "passed" the interrogations were ordered to attend lectures on Pancasila as a way to dissuade them from organizing any future strikes.

Irianti's *pembelaan* forthrightly questions the legitimacy of the regime's interpretation of Pancasila according to "the interests of the employer." While the regime used various means of control to neutralize the labor movement as a political threat, employers saw an opportunity to weaken the union's bargaining power by refusing to acknowledge the union as a bargaining agent, instead forming its own company "union":

> A few months after I was suspended [from work], the company started to introduce an organization of workers, named as "The Extended Family of Sosro" (Keluarga Besar Sosro, KBS). Newly recruited workers were expected to apply to be a member of KBS instead of becoming a member of [our union] the SPSI local union of P.T. [Sinar] Sosro. (p. 16)

By forming its own replacement organization for the local union and forcing new recruits to become its members, the company dealt a final blow to the workers' independent union. As Irianti notes, this move crippled workers' capacity to resist.

Although Irianti's *pembelaan* may not be the best or most accurate account of the workplace changes of her time (at least in the eyes of economists), it does document how workers saw, faced, and dealt with the changes that management and the regime imposed on them. Irianti convincingly conveys that these changes made it more and more difficult for workers to exercise their right to organize, defend their rights, and collectively claim benefits for their economic welfare.

THE 1987 STRIKE AND ITS AFTERMATH

In her *pembelaan*, Irianti describes how changes in the factory "delivered me to slowly become active in the labor union" (p. 5). She had been involved in union organizing for two years prior to being elected as the union chairperson in 1987. Under her leadership, the union began actively taking measures to respond to the wage issue, which led to a strike. She explains how the strike began:

> We drafted a letter to the employer to request a negotiation on a wage raise and THR [holiday bonus]. A few months passed without any reply at all. We informed our members about this situation and asked for their patience. Soon we ensued with a second letter; no reply also.
>
> It isn't difficult, for fellow workers, to imagine the feeling when one's wage hasn't been raised for years. Each time [it becomes] a headache to figure out ways to trim down expenditures, what expenses could be lessened, get confused if children are ill, become embarrassed in front of the [owner of the] food stall as [our] debt increases, and so forth. Not to mention questions at home about the wage raise that could lead to a quarrel. Friends could also imagine how furious we could be [since] the letter that means so much to maintaining our members' lives, had received no response at all. It hurts to know that our existence is considered as nothing more than [our physical] as a pile of bones and brawn with some strength left. That's how we felt Your Highness, Madam Prosecutor, and respected Counselor. (p. 10)

The union contacted its affiliate, the Regional Board of Jakarta (RBJ) and asked for its organizational support. Unfortunately, its request was rejected (for reasons never made public); ironically, the RBJ even called the legitimacy of the union's leadership into question.[52]

The Board's action robbed the union of time and energy—and the union soon abandoned this route. It then changed tack and invited management to have "periodic consultative meetings" (*secara teratur berkonsultasi*) about work-related matters. Factory managers showed up for the first meeting, but then refused to meet with union representatives again.

Finding no alternative, workers launched a strike on May 13, 1987, crippling factory production. To convey the desperation of workers to defend their interests, Irianti ingeniously notes that "the fear of screening and superfluous accusations," as had happened after their 1984 strike, "was easily outweighed by the urgency of fulfilling basic needs" (p. 10). Workers perfectly understood the risks, Irianti confirms. The strike continued for three days without any reaction from the employer. On the fourth day, two representatives from the Regional Board of SPSI came to the factory, but "they couldn't understand what our burdens were, [and] their words sounded like the words of the employers" (p. 10). The union soon refused their assistance.

On the sixth day of the strike, two representatives from the Ministry of Manpower came to the factory. After a talk with the union, the representatives called for the employer to participate in a negotiation. The employer refused to cooperate and declared that the dispute would be only settled under the guidance of the Minister of Manpower. Legally speaking, this decision was surely an extrajudicial move for the law required a voluntary negotiation between the two opposing parties. However, Minister Sudomo appeared to want to isolate this dispute and settle it as quickly as possible behind closed doors. In a comment to the press, Sudomo insisted that "workers do not need to strike as the case is very sensitive [*peka*] and besides, their endeavor more often than not is being exploited [*ditunggangi*] by a third party."[53] By using words such as "peka," Sudomo made his contention clear: the workers' strike was an issue of political security and not one of working-class welfare. When he mentioned "the third party" who might exploit the strike, he raised the specter of "latent danger of communism"—a political scare tactic the regime employed to curb criticism from the social movement.

With this move, Minister Sudomo forced the employer to enter negotiations with the union, and the strike came to an end, at least for a few days. The employer agreed to draft a collective labor agreement as required by the law, but refused to reinstate ninety-eight workers whom they considered to be the instigators of the strike. The employer maintained "it is necessary because Sosro [company] as a beverage producer is prone to sabotage."[54] Faced with the employer's obstinacy, the workers once again asked the Ministry of Manpower to intervene. Minister Sudomo agreed to meet with the workers and he reportedly summoned the employer to come to the Ministry so that all parties could discuss the issue. As a result of this meeting, the employer began reinstating all the workers to their former positions in the factory.

Sudomo used the strike at P.T. Sosro to illustrate his security concerns over worker strikes in general. "In principle," he said, "a strike isn't allowed, although it isn't against the law. Striking isn't in accordance with Pancasila Industrial Relations and could invite *kerawanan sosial* [social hazard]."[55] In other words, no matter how miserable working conditions might be, security concerns outweighed them. Social protest—including that based on workers' grievances—was thereby stifled.

Critics of Sudomo's position came from a surprising corner: Imam Sudarwo, chairperson of the SPSI whom Sudomo had supported during the reorganization of FBSI/SPSI in 1985, insisted that "striking isn't illegal." He clarified, however, that strikes had to be "the last resort, only after the union has taken all procedures as prescribed in the Pancasila Industrial Relations."[56] In response, Sudomo warned that Sudarwo's statement should not be taken literally or in a way that might "hamper *stabilitas*" [stability]).[57] The press portrayed these conflicting views as polar opposites: on one side, Sudomo bans strikes because they are not in line with the Pancasila Industrial Relations; on the other side, Sudarwo reasons that the law, in fact, guarantees workers' rights to strike. For months in 1987 a debate raged in the media. "Experts" entered the fray, but none of them analyzed worker strikes in the context of the authoritarian regime.[58]

Despite this media attention, Irianti and her fellow union members continued to face difficult times in their negotiations with their employer. On August 29, 1987, management and employees finally agreed to sign a collective labor agreement, but issues of interpretation arose regarding its implementation. The employer searched for loopholes in the agreement in order to discharge workers (especially, union organizers) whenever it wished. On one occasion when some sixty-seven factory workers were taking a work break, the employer accused them of refusing to work. The workers were suspended and the dispute was brought to the Ministry of Manpower. Minister Sudomo reportedly condemned the union and urged it "not to take arbitrary actions," believing that this incident was the workers' fault. Speaking in his usual tone, Sudomo warned that the workers' arbitrary action "could disturb the stability of the economy and security."[59]

While negotiations to reinstate the sixty-seven workers continued, Irianti, as the chairperson of the union, had to face a most upsetting challenge. Having become the employer's target, she was suspended from work. At this time, a long-repressed conflict between Irianti and Prapto Rahardjo,[60] resurfaced and brought the labor dispute to a climax. In her *pembelaan*, Irianti describes the situation:

The event that led me to stand before your honor took place on December 23. I saw [Prapto Rahardjo] coming [to the office] and it soon came to my mind to talk [with him] to explain the matter and state my reasons for refuting the warning he gave. My request for a talk and to discuss [the matter] was rejected harshly and emotionally [by him]. I raised my arm to call him, and for reasons unknown to me, he raised his hand high and said in high tone: "What do you want?" I was caught so caught off guard that I raised my arm to ward him off, and at that moment his collar was pulled off. [Because of that] it seems that office matters have become personal matters. (pp. 15–16)

The police investigated this incident and charged Irianti with "defamation, unpleasant behavior and conducting an insult," simply on the grounds that she "pulled off" Raharjo's collar. She was brought before the criminal district court of East Jakarta in July 1988, where she produced her *pembelaan*. She was found guilty of the charges, as she predicted in her *pembelaan* that she would be. She served her time in prison,[61] but more importantly, her effort to write down her story in the form of her *pembelaan* surpassed the limitations that reality imposed on her as a worker and awarded her the freedom to define her world.

Reinventing the *pembelaan* was indeed a tactical move by Irianti (and the working class) to express themselves. While the *pembelaan* was an instrument appropriate to the political context of the time, it also carried a lasting message about workers' experiences during the authoritarian regime as seen from their own perspective. Irianti's *pembelaan* was a voice from below that strategically confronted the FBSI/SPSI leadership and also challenged the state's authority to repress labor. Her *pembelaan* is more than just a dose of "alternative narrative." By putting forth her perspective as a worker, the *pembelaan* weaves together the seemingly contradictory premises of the oppressive nature of factory work and the liberating consequences of female activism in a time of authoritarianism and rapid industrialization in Indonesia in the 1980s.

Far more than merely a document of legal defense, Irianti's *pembelaan* is distinctly political. It describes her personal transformation and experiences as a female worker who had developed a critical consciousness and had no fear to confront an oppressive regime at the factory level. The *pembelaan* reveals Irianti as the finest example of a female labor activist, one who was exceptionally *berani* in her own time. However, the workplace restrictions she describes in her *pembelaan* portray how workers were cornered to the point of being unable to organize independently. These restrictions, as we will see in chapter 2, had dire effects on labor organizing capacities in the 1990s.

NOTES

1. Personal details about Ida Irianti have been impossible to find. I was unable to find anyone who knew about her background or keeps in touch with her now. She evidently retreated from union activism and her whereabouts today are a mystery.

2. One reason why the strike was quickly reported in the national media was the factory's proximity to Jakarta.

3. See Smyth and Grijns (1997).

4. See Law No. 14 Year 1969 on Manpower (promulgated on September 19, 1969). Article 13 of the Law states, "The use of strike, demonstration and lock-out shall be regulated further in government regulation(s)."

5. This case was registered as criminal case no. 608/Pid/S/88/PN.Jkt.Tim. All related documents are from the archives of the Jakarta Legal Aid Institute, which provided legal services for her. This is where I encountered the document for the first time. No document was able to be retrieved from the East Jakarta court. Irianti's *pembelaan* was produced on a manual typewriter. Page numbers are given for all extracts of the text. The text is in Indonesian, and is 5,669 words long.

6. See Robison (1986); Wolf (1992).

7. The suppression of labor's freedom of association in the 1980s is well documented in INDOC (1981, 1983).

8. For a discussion on outsourcing and employment agencies, see Mather (2004); Breman (2010); Juliawan (2010).

9. Wright (1997: 246) notes that

class content of consciousness can refer to those aspects of consciousness which are implicated in intentions, choices, and practices which have "class pertinent effects" in the world, effects on how individuals operate within a given structure of relations and effects on those relations themselves.

10. Soekarno (1951, 1975). Soekarno may not have been the first prominent nationalist figure to exploit the *pembelaan/pleidooi* to voice his political views, but his rhetoric was the finest. For historical consideration, see Semaoen (1919); Marco Kartodikromo (1922).

11. Sudisman (1967, 1975).

12. Akhmadi (1979).

13. In the Latin American context, the *testimonio* (testimonial narrative) genre of literature provides a space for the subaltern, or members of disadvantaged/marginalized communities, to narrate their life stories in a first-person account of the human right abuses and social oppression they have experienced (or witnessed). *Testimonios* may take the form of an autobiography or memoir, but they represent the experience of the narrator's community (or the group or class that she/he belongs to) as a whole. As such, *testimonios* serve as a basis for public articulation of the subaltern as a collective—without essentializing their experiences. The *pembelaan*, like the *testimonio*, functions as a "tactical essentialism" in the sense of political practice. See Beverly (1992).

14. In certain sectors of industry, the demand for female workers surpassed the demand for male workers.

15. Caraway (2007: 85) presents the data on the changes to the women's share of industrial employment for 1971–1996. The beverage sector had a 13-percent increase, while rises in the export-intensive sectors were higher: textiles, 20 percent; wood processing, 38 percent; garments, 23 percent; footwear, 71 percent; and wood products, 26 percent.

16. Hadiz (1997: 106) notes that "domestic investment firms were the site of an overwhelming number of strikes" in the early 1980s, notably in the textiles, assembling, pharmaceuticals, metals, and ceramics sectors.

17. Mather (1983) describes women workers in Tangerang choose to leave the factory (to "exit") than to voice their grievances. The decision to "exit" that these workers took depended on the conditions of the labor market at the time. When demand for labor was high, workers could easily find other factory work. Thus, choosing to leave does not imply an unwillingness to stay and try to change unsatisfying working conditions (i.e., passivity).

18. Although a number of short stories in Taiwan have workers as protagonists, workers and their activism are not the dominant theme (see, for example, Hsiao 1996). This literary activity is the domain of professional writers, not of members of the working class.

19. See Barraclough (2009).

20. I thank Jeon Je-Seong for sharing his insight on this matter.

21. Kim (1997: 104) notes: "Throughout the entire period of Park Chung Hee's presidency [1962–1979], while male workers were somewhat distracted by a formal structure of the unions designed to coopt them, women workers became increasingly important within the informal labor movement." In that process, the role of the Catholic Church and community groups is noted for supporting the struggle of women workers in their local unions, as exemplified by the case of Tongil and the Seoul-based Y.H. Company.

22. See Moon and Broadbent (2008: 137). This is the percentage of the total female workforce that was unionized.

23. Exact numbers are difficult to come by. One International Labour Organization report (1997) put the unionization rate (of male *and* female workers) in Indonesia in 1995 at 3.4 percent. No percentage was given for unionized women workers.

24. See Koo (2001); Chun 2003).

25. Inspired by Freirean literacy methods, labor activists approached workers for community education. This proved to be instrumental in organizing workers, especially in Java's urban cities.

26. Soekarno and three other leaders of The Indonesian National Party (PNI) were arrested on the accusation of "opposing imperialism and colonialism," based on articles 169 and 171 of the Criminal Code (*Wetboek van strafrecht*). An additional charge was based on articles 161 bis. and 153 bis. Both articles—known as "hate-sowing articles" (*de haatzaai artikelen*)—were by definition loose and open to various interpretations. Thus, the colonial government invoked these articles as a legal means to neutralize political dissidents, especially native insurgents.

27. There is no standard template for a *pembelaan* (*pleidooi*), in contrast to most other legal documents. The legal counsel may give suggestions to the defendant in drafting it, but the defendant (who may not understand legal terms) is left to speak his/her mind openly before the court in his/her own language(s) and according to his/her own understanding.

28. Comparing Soekarno's *pleidooi* with Dangir's minutes of interrogation (*process verbalen*) illustrates the different contours of their language and worldviews.

In 1928, two years before Soekarno's arrest, Dangir, a Samin from Genengmulyo village, was arrested and immediately interrogated by a native vice regent (*patih*). As Dangir's *process verbalen* was written for colonial administrators to read, it was framed within the logic of colonial anxiety about the Saman movement. Reading Dangir's *process verbalen*, Shiraishi (1990: 120) concludes that Dangir had not, in fact "liberated himself from the words. . . . [H]e was brought back to the administrative language of the *patih*, the language of administrative rules and classification under which he had lived in the past." Soekarno's *pleidooi*, on the other hand, shows that he did not confine himself to the colonial legal framework. Instead, he constructed his own frame, one that placed the colonial world under the political and economic lens of his microscopic historical argument.

29. A Jakarta-based publisher, in an introduction to the reprinted edition of "Indonesia Accuses" in 1951, noted "the defense speech has become a political document." See Soekarno (1951).

30. Sudisman (1975: 2).

31. Sudisman was perfectly clear about this. In his own words: "Saya sengadja tidak menamakan uraian saya ini suatu pembelaan. . . ." (I intentionally did not title my analysis as a defense.) In fact, he admitted that it occurred to him to title his *pembelaan* "*PKI Menggugat*" ("PKI Accuses") as a reminder of Soekarno's *pleidooi*.

32. Sudisman (1975: 2).

33. Anderson (1990) juxtaposes Sudisman's "*Uraian Tanggungdjawab*" with Soetomo's autobiography, which is "somber and centers on death rather than birth," in order to note the differences of language expressions between the two authors, who both had a Javanese background, but came from different generations.

34. Under a complete modification of criminal procedural law in 1981—which incorporated due process (presumption of innocence and the burden of proof)—a defendant is explicitly guaranteed his/her right to a fair trial. See Law No. 8 Year 1981 on Criminal Procedural Law, promulgated on December 31, 1981. History demonstrates, however, that this "guarantee" was not always ensured. There were strong indications that the judiciary was not free under the New Order regime.

35. I thank Caroline Hau for sharing her insights on this matter.

36. See Watson (2009).

37. *Testimonios* allow members of a marginalized group (e.g., a minority ethnic community) that is excluded from its own literary representation (or has no access to such) to tell their life stories with the intention of communicating the sociopolitical problems of being the subaltern in the society. The issue of authorship is crucial to stress in the production of the *testimonio*, as the narrator is supposed to be orally relating her/his life to an interlocutor, who writes everything down on the narrator's behalf. See Beverley (1999: 97). In the case of Irianti's *pembelaan*, however, I could not find any evidence to suggest that there was an interlocutor assisting her.

38. For a similar case in the mid-1990s, see Pakpahan (2002).

39. Steedman (1986) notes how working-class women, despite the rhetoric of class, may aspire to achieve typical middle-class status in society.

40. See Mather (1983): 4. Women who had been working for more than three months were commonly still considered to be on probation. Many were employed

as casual/daily workers (*buruh harian lepas*) or put under long probationary periods (*percobaan*).

41. Beverly (1992: 103) notes:

> *Testimonio* represents an affirmation of the individual subject, even of individual growth and transformation, but in connection with a group or class situation marked by marginalization, oppression, and struggle. If it loses this connection, it ceases to be *testimonio* and becomes autobiography, that is an account of, and also a means of access to, middle- or upper-class status, a sort of documentary *Bildungsroman*.

42. *Tempo*, May 30, 1987.

43. There is no doubt that in Irianti's case, emotions played a powerful role in consciousness raising. Witnessing the strike became an affective element of mass solidarity that helped form her activism as a female worker. The intricate connection between "emotion" and "political consciousness" is a subject often left ignored in labor studies in the Asian context. Referring to the situation of Polish workers during the authoritarian regime, Scott (1990) describes how emotions as "subjective experience" may become a "shared hidden transcript" that lays the foundation for social change.

44. As we will see in chapter 2, the labor movement in Indonesia also adopted the human rights discourse to foster labor rights.

45. See Mather (1983); Manning (1998).

46. See Hill (2000).

47. These workplace changes paralleled what was happening in the West and was known as the shift to post-Fordism. Harvey (1989: 150) describes the shift as part of a "flexible accumulation" whereby

> employers have taken advantage of weakened union power and the pools of surplus (unemployed or underemployed) labourers to push for much more flexible work regimes and labour contracts. . . . [T]he apparent move away from regular employment towards increasing reliance upon part-time, temporary or sub-contracted work arrangements.

48. I thank Jackie Imamura for sharing her insight.

49. With no government regulations on this practice, factory owners were free to outsource at various levels of manual work in the factory. It was only in 1989 that outsourcing as part of a sub-contract business became regulated for the first time. See Keputusan Menteri Perdagangan No. 264/Kp/89 tentang Pekerjaan Sub-Kontrak Perusahaan Pengolahan di Kawasan Berikat (Decree of Minister of Trade No. 264/Kp/ 89 on Sub-Contracting in Manufacturing Industries in the Export Processing Zones).

50. Sudomo was the Minister of Manpower during 1983–1988. He had been the head of Command for the Restoration of Order and Security (Komando Pemulihan Keamanan dan Ketertiban, Kopkamtib)

51. The security approach laid down by Sudomo claimed that it was the duty of the military to step in in the case of labor disputes. The presence of military personnel (especially from the army) in the factory was indispensable in curbing labor protests. For the company, employing military personnel (either active or retired members)

is part and parcel of their labor relations strategy; these personnel were expected to handle any labor protest in the factory as a security issue.

52. As noted above, the RBJ was surprised to find that the local union had organized a factory level-election for union representatives with Irianti elected as its chairperson. This election, organized by the local union, showed that the union was capable of being autonomous, while union officials at that time (including RBJ's) were appointed by the central federation under the control of the New Order regime. Thus, the RBJ questioned the "legitimacy" of the union leadership under Irianti.

53. *Merdeka*, May 19, 1987.

54. *Tempo*, May 30, 1987.

55. *Suara Merdeka*, May 25, 1987.

56. *Kompas*, June 2, 1987.

57. *Kompas*, June 3, 1987.

58. See *Pelita*, June 12, 1987; *Kompas*, August 6, 1987; *Jakarta Jakarta* no. 58 (July 24–August 6, 1987). The media sensation lasted for months. Sudomo finally acknowledged the legality of workers' right to strike, while also referring to Law No. 7/PRP/1963 on Prevention of Strikes and Lock-outs at Vital Enterprises. P.T. Sinar Sosro was considered to be a "vital enterprise."

59. See *Pelita*, September 30, 1987, and *Suara Pembaruan*, September 30, 1987.

60. This was not a personal conflict. Rahardjo was a member of the management committee for the negotiation of a new Collective Labor Agreement (CLA) at the factory and, at the same time, the manager of the outsourcing company that supplied a workforce to P.T. Sinar Sosro. Rahardjo was also the one who signed Irianti's suspension letter. Thus, the tension between Irianti as chairperson of the union and Rahardjo as part of the factory's management was long-standing.

61. No record exists of the time she actually spent in prison.

Chapter 2

Soliloquy of Disobedience

As noted in chapter 1, the industrialization policy of the New Order regime in the 1980s boosted the country's economic profile. Although the regime still relied on exporting oil and gas, by the 1990s it started to see the results of a growing manufacturing sector, especially in export-oriented industries. With firm growth in manufacturing contributing to the country's overall economic performance and employing more workers, the agriculture sector, although still the largest contributor to total employment, was slowly declining. Industrial areas were established and growing throughout the country, with a major concentration of factories in the Jabotabek (Jakarta, Bogor, Tangerang, Bekasi), Surabaya-Sidoarjo (East Java), and Medan (North Sumatra) areas.

The rise in the number of industrial workers, however, was not accompanied by sufficient social protection and welfare for them. Freedom of association was still taboo, and the only labor union recognized by the regime, the All-Indonesia Workers' Union (SPSI), was notoriously corrupt; it rarely defended workers' interests and rights. As noted earlier, emphasizing "harmonious relationship," the regime's ideology of Pancasila Industrial Relations (Hubungan Industrial Pancasila, HIP) did not allow any organization outside the FSPSI, and denied workers their basic rights, including to strike.

During 1990–1995, however, labor unrest mounted. Workers voiced their economic, social, and institutional frustrations through various forms: *unjuk rasa* (protest), *demo* (rally), and *mogok* (strike). This period was also a witness to events that became important landmarks in the development of the country's labor movement. In 1991, 14,000 workers staged a massive strike against P.T. Gadjah Tunggal, a multi-factory tire company, in Tangerang (West Java), near Jakarta. Military personnel, as expected, were dispatched to pacify the workers, and cracked down violently. In 1992, Muchtar Pakpahan, a Medan-based lawyer, established the All-Indonesia Prosperous Workers'

55

Union (Serikat Buruh Sejahtera Indonesia, SBSI) as an independent labor union outside the FSPSI. In 1993, Marsinah, a twenty-four-year-old female worker at P.T. Catur Putra Surya in Sidoarjo (East Java), was kidnapped and murdered (presumably, by the military) following the strike she led against the company during May 3–4. Her murder was later called the "Marsinah case." In 1994, a string of strikes in the Medan industrial area started in early March. By April 13, they had grown into a general strike of approximately 20,000 workers from at least twenty-three factories, many of whom were affiliated with the SBSI. On April 14 and 15, the strike turned into an anti-Chinese riot that took the life of a businessman. Pakpahan was detained on the next day and a number of SBSI union activists were physically tortured during interrogation; some were jailed without trial. All these events marked 1990–1995 as a peak period of urban unrest and military violence in Indonesian modern history.

At the local level, East Java provides an illustrative example of the rise in worker strikes. As we can see from table 2.1, beginning in 1991 there was an "explosion" in the number of worker's strikes in East Java, doubling from 1991 to 1992, and steadily increasing until 1994. This trend corresponds to the increasing number of strikes reported at the national level during the same period.[1] The most common demand from workers in the strikes during 1991–1994 was proper payment of the minimum wage, and it was only after the government raised the minimum wage in 1994 that the number of strikes gradually decreased and workers' wage demands became less of a priority. The strikes took place across all labor-intensive industries, but were mainly in the manufacturing and service industries. As the sociopolitical impacts of these strikes were high, the authoritarian regime saw them as a security threat.

Of the 155 strikes in East Java in 1992, at least 27 (17 percent) occurred in establishments with 500 workers or more.[2] This means that there were at least two major strikes per month in the Surabaya-Sidoarjo industrial area that involved a total of more than 1,000 workers. Military personnel were present

Table 2.1 Number of Strikes in East Java, 1991–1998

Year	Number of strikes	Number of strikes that demanded the proper payment of minimum wage (in percentage)
1991	60	43 (71.6%)
1992	155	120 (77.4%)
1993	185	161 (87%)
1994	314	177 (56.3%)
1995	135	72 (53.3%)
1996	132	72 (54.4%)
1997	142	65 (45.7%)
1998	202	98 (48.5%)

Source: LBH Surabaya 1998 (based on newspaper reports)

at walkouts; it was considered legitimate and normal. Workers were always defenseless, however, when their strikes ended in violence. What happened in East Java is illustrative of the "explosion" of labor unrest in early 1990s Indonesia.

A number of studies have proposed explanations for the rise in labor actions during 1991–1995. Scholars mostly agree that a set of social-political conditions and the military's violent approach to the unrest influenced its rise. Manning points to the "the abundant supply of labor still locked into relatively low productivity agriculture and non-farm activities,"[3] which made industrial workers, who were relatively better off than agricultural workers in terms of bargaining power in the labor market and awareness of rights, more primed to demand better working conditions. Hadiz also points to workers' relatively young age and education background as "important with regard to an understanding of the inner dynamics of the wave of industrial unrest that has occurred in the industrial centers of Indonesia in the 1990s."[4] As noted earlier, the New Order's industrial development policy required supplying the labor market with an increasingly educated workforce, and the government therefore instituted a basic education program. By the 1990s, many industrial workers had spent six to nine years in school and were young (in their twenties) when they entered factory work for the first time. These characteristics formed a common basis from which this generation of workers was able to aspire to a better standard of living, and increased wages specifically. In the process of organizing themselves, they were made aware of their legal rights as workers through advocacy and training programs facilitated by middle-class NGO activists.[5] The strike became their answer to the political barriers that had impeded the fulfillment of their economic rights and aspirations.

It is also important to note that industrial areas in the 1990s, compared to the previous decade, had more large-scale, multi-factory operations that employed 500 workers or more (such as P.T. Gadjah Tunggal). This reflected the changing spatial landscape of capitalist production under globalization, a common feature in the Global South.[6] The urbanization and concentration of workers in industrial areas created a pool of urban *massa* ("the masses")[7] that was dissatisfied with poor working and living conditions. Many of the industrial workers were (internal) migrants who were forced to look for jobs in the industrial areas after being uprooted from agricultural work.[8] The nature of the new labor regime—large numbers of people working for a single factory or single company—also made it easier for workers to collectively organize toward a common goal.[9] Thus, the regime's industrialization policy not only brought changes to economic production; it also transformed the urban landscape with labor-intensive industries operating in large-scale factories, and the increasing number of labor strikes during 1991–1995 was the unintended outcome of this.

The new workers had a loose connection to the traditional order of their hometowns, and as *massa* in the urban landscape, were seen by the military as a threat. They could easily be mobilized to participate in industrial actions— with or without instructions from the SPSI, the official state-sanctioned labor union.[10] This meant that they were "out of control." As such, the military had a rationale to "secure" them from being used by any *aktor intelektual* ("political provocateurs"), and made it a military duty to identify and arrest any *dalang* ("puppet master") behind a strike.[11] Yet despite the risk of the presence of the military, industrial workers did demand better conditions through strike actions.[12]

Against the backdrop of these social changes, economic conditions remained the main underlying reason for urban workers to strike: they wanted higher wages and better welfare. The cost of living and inflation had been increasing since 1990, pushing workers to their limits.[13] Conditions were so pressing, particularly in East Java, that even after the government decided to increase the minimum wage in 1994, nearly 50 percent of East Java workers were receiving low pay.[14] East Java workers, who were paid much less than those in other regions, had particular incentives to organize to demand better wages.[15] It was precisely in this context that Meppy Doryati Emping (here-inafter, Meppy) began working in a factory and got involved in the largest workers' strike in East Java in 1992.

Meppy was twenty-seven years old in April 1992 when she started work-ing as a manual laborer at P.T. Victory Long Age, a Taiwanese company in Surabaya (East Java) that produced sports shoes for export.[16] In late October 1992, when workers of the factory organized a general strike, she was one of their leaders. Within that six months period, she had seen and experienced various injustices under the factory regime. But it was the aftermath of the general strike, when she and two of her coworkers were kidnapped (and sub-sequently, detained) by the military in late December 1992, which made her pen her story. The trauma of the kidnapping forms the basis of her account, in which she details not only the key events of and feelings she had just after the kidnapping, but also narrates her experiences of working in the factory, organizing the strike and the aftermath of it.

This chapter discusses Meppy's account to better understand the condi-tions of the working class in the 1990s, especially under the surveillance of the military. It will unpack the social and political tensions that workers were experiencing at the factory level and the power of the military in protecting the factory regime. As we will see, Meppy was fully aware of what was going on in the factory and willing to come together with her coworkers to change conditions in the face of the military's security approach to the workers' cause. While the "Marsinah case" illustrates the excessive brutality of the military in controlling worker strikes, Meppy's account moves beyond the politics of *malu* to describe both the personal and political sides of a worker strike, based on her own perspective and feelings. This chapter offers a reading of her account in light of the traumatic experiences she had, to highlight her struggle not only personally, but also collectively with her coworkers. Her account is a testament to what workers had to face once they started organizing under the authoritarian New Order regime during the 1990s. By reading it, this chapter shows that despite the terror that the state unleashed to tame labor activism, female workers bravely took the risks to participate in the collective struggle to organize.

TRAUMA AND WRITING

In contrast to Ida Irianti's public defense (see chapter 1), Meppy's account was originally not intended for the public to read; it was written in a notebook and kept as a personal memoir.[17] The twenty-five-page account consists of five sections, each with its own title and a date (presumably, the date it was written) on the top of the page.[18] The titles of the five sections are:

1. "The bitter tragedy, detention at Korem Bhaskara Jaya 084, Waru Sidoarjo" (dated December 31, 1992)[19]
2. "Accusation against me" (dated January 29, 1993)
3. "The start of our strike on October 30, 1992" (dated March 15, 1993)
4. "The start of my paralegal training" (dated March 17, 1993)
5. "The end of my working period at PT Victory Long Age" (dated April 6, 1993).

The sections are not arranged chronologically, but rather are based on the events that Meppy remembered at the time of her writing or that she considered more important.[20] The account begins with the key event that precipitated her writing: her kidnapping and detention. The "bitter tragedy" consisted of a series of traumatic experiences; she recounts these in detail, as well as her feelings about what happened to her.

Meppy as an author struggles to communicate what happened not only to her physical body, but also to her inner self. Taken against her own will, the trauma of the kidnapping led to her breakdown.[21] Writing about it, however, allowed her to remember it and overcome its impacts. As a victim of abuse (by the state), her act of writing can be considered a catharsis.[22]

Despite the traumatic experiences she had to bear, her account is simple, direct, and without many turns of phrase. It was written in her own personal expression. This feature may reflect Meppy's working-class background, and that she was writing first and foremost to remember and understand the experiences she had, without planning to make it public. Her account details the various abuses she endured without taking refuge behind a veil of obscurity. Similar to the accounts of political prisoners during the New Order regime,[23] her account tells the truth from the victim's perspective, a perspective that was denied and silenced under the regime's official history.[24] Rather than being locked in a cave of fear, Meppy as author uses the act of writing and expressing herself as a way to regain her humanity. Her account thus not only exposes the logic of state terrorism in controlling its people,[25] but also illustrates the capacity for the traumatized to come to terms with the pain and trauma associated with ill-treatment and overcome suffering. Through writing, she emerges not only as a witness but also as a survivor that the regime failed to subdue.

It is in this light that this chapter reads Meppy's account. Her writing is a narrative strategy that allows her to recount her experiences under the authoritarian regime and at the same time deal with the scars from those unforgettable events in her life as a female worker. The following paragraphs will describe those events as written in her account, from the time she started working in the factory (April 1992) to her involvement in the strike and its aftermath (October–November 1992), as well as her kidnapping and detention (December 31, 1992–January 2, 1993), and finally, when she was forced to resign from her job (late January 1993).[26]

FACTORY WORK AND ORGANIZING

Similar to many other female workers of her time, Meppy started working in the factory after she graduated from high school and when she was still single. From the account, it seems that she must have worked elsewhere before she started to work at P.T. Victory Long Age. Born and raised in Surabaya, she was one of many local female workers at the factory and lived with her parents.

In her account, Meppy does not write about her childhood or school days (understandably, as a personal record it was not necessary for her to write this kind of information).[27] She describes her factory work experience briefly, as follows:

> I started working at P.T. Victory Long Age, Tanjung Sari Street No. 24, Surabaya, on April 28, 1992. I was assigned to the packing department; I was in that department for 2 months. . . . Since I worked there, I started to know other (P.T.) Victory workers and I was getting familiar with the security personnel. (p. 12)

Although the description was quite short, we can assume that her first two months working at P.T. Victory Long Age went smoothly and there was no significant problem that was important enough to be recounted.

As Meppy started to get to know her coworkers at the factory during her training period, she also began to know about their activities at work.[28] It was after her training period that she was first introduced to the workers' efforts to organize. She wrote about it as follows:

> After a two-month training, I became assistant supervisor and was responsible for delivering finished shoes boxes to the main storeroom and taking notes of the outflow of all kinds of boxes from the main storeroom. I was assigned to this job for 2 months. It was at that time that we started to plan a strike that was instigated by one of my colleagues, Mr. Imam. I was in my third month of work when he shared his early plan for a strike, but at that time I hesitated to join in as I did not yet know all the colleagues and was still new in the factory. But Imam kept insisting to me to join in his plan. (p. 12)

As noted above, it was only after she finished her training period and started to work on regular tasks in the factory that she was approached by Mr. Imam, who "shared his early plan for a strike." Mr. Imam (full name: Imam Basuki) was one of the worker-activists in the factory and he was later kidnapped along with her (on December 31, 1992).[29]

Meppy did not write down how she was approached and why Imam trusted her enough to share his plan, given that she was a new worker in the factory. Presumably, their interaction started because he was in charge of the storeroom. There is no information to confirm whether they were from the same hometown. Nonetheless, there is little doubt that it was their daily interaction at work that allowed them to foster mutual trust as coworkers. It could also be that Imam was trying to organize workers in the factory based on their working department, and Meppy was a useful contact person in the packing department. It was common at the time for workers to organize themselves based on their work departments and select a representative or coordinator for their department. Meppy must have been aware of this organizing practice in the factory.

As Meppy notes, it was in her third month that Imam told her about the strike plan. By sharing his plan, he expected her to organize workers in her department. But it seems she was hesitant to do so (in her own words "to join in") because she "did not yet know all the colleagues." Although she used this excuse, it did not deter Imam. It could be that Imam had tried persuading some other workers from the packing department to organize before Meppy started her work there, but failed, and Meppy, as someone relatively new in the department, offered a hope that Imam needed for the strike plan.

Imam's repeated efforts to get Meppy to join in the plan did not bear any results, but she admitted that she was "curious to know," an indication that she might have thought about some action, too. However, strangely, she was not very interested in attending the workers' meetings:

> Finally, after a while, I followed his request, as I myself was curious to know what they would do. And on one day, I received a written invitation to a meeting at the home of Ms. Supartun, and if I am not wrong, they always had meetings on Wednesdays and Fridays in different places. But I was reluctant to attend their meetings for a few times. (p. 13)

Despite being invited to attend the meeting, Meppy did not go, noting that she "was reluctant to attend" despite her curiosity in the strike plan. She reasoned that the meetings were mainly a "long-winded discussion" (*pembicaraan yang bertele-tele*) (p. 13). This, and possibly because she was kept informed of the results of the meetings, or she generally heard about them (as workers commonly exchanged news in the factory) could have kept her from going. Despite not attending, however, she continued to be regularly invited to the meetings.

In her account, Meppy does not write anything specific about being political or the evolution of her consciousness as a worker. Nonetheless, the written lines in her account reveal her complete understanding of what was going on in the factory: workers were mounting grievances. Just like any other worker at that time, she knew the risk of attending such meetings. She also understood, however, that workers did not have many options (or enough time) outside of the factory to talk among themselves as fellow workers. She must have understood the importance of these semi-clandestine meetings as a space (and the only space) for workers to share news among themselves and more importantly, to organize. She did finally attend one of the meetings, but she did not enjoy it; she notes that she was just "sitting outside the house" (p. 13).

It was at that meeting that the workers decided to visit the office of the LBH Surabaya (Surabaya Legal Aid Institute) to consult about their common grievances at the factory. Meppy joined in this visit:

> The next day after the meeting all of us together went to the office of LBH at Kidal Street No. 6, to meet Mr. Munir to discuss all the problems we encountered and it was there at the LBH office that I started to learn about labor law and related regulations. After we were confident enough about what we had, we started to plan a strategy and we always organized meetings in various places that were safe from being seen in the public—at the home of Mr. Urip, Ms. Tina, Ms. Sudarsih (Ciwit) and in the LBH office—to discuss all the things we were going to demand to the company later. Finally, we came to an agreement and started to decide the "D-day." (p. 13)

Meppy writes that she "started to learn about labor law and related regulations" at the LBH office from Mr. Munir whom the workers met there. Mr. Munir (full name: Munir Said Thalib) was a labor lawyer who had been working at LBH Surabaya since 1989. He was the same age as Meppy (both were born in 1965 and were twenty-seven years old at that time).[30] There is little doubt that Mr. Munir was already well known among the workers in the Surabaya area at that time, and the high-profile name of LBH as an institution that defends human rights must have garnered workers' trust (and hopes) to assist them on legal matters.

As Meppy notes, the meeting with Mr. Munir was a very educational one for her and her coworkers. They learned about their legal rights and were encouraged to organize to defend their rights. It was at this meeting that Meppy and her coworkers together became "confident enough" (*menguasainya*), a sign that they all had come to realize their legal rights as workers, and buried their fear against the factory regime. This development in their perception of themselves as individuals and as a group gave them the strength to move beyond "long-winded discussion" into action. After meeting at the LBH office, they held at least five follow-up meetings (in different places) to make necessary preparations, including listing their demands to the company and setting a date for the strike, or "D-day." In her account, Meppy conveys the excitement that was palpable at these meetings as the workers were now meeting not just to talk or share information, but to prepare to strike.

Meppy notes how everyone worked together in preparing all the materials and divided tasks among themselves. While some were assigned to collect strike funds,[31] Meppy was assigned to type letters "to several government institutions" about their grievances. They succeeded in collecting 600,000 rupiah (around 260 US$) as a strike fund, more than enough to support their plan. With that, they were ready. They used the LBH office for their final meeting, to prepare what they needed for the strike[32]:

> Once all the equipment was ready, on October 29, 1992 at around 9:00 at night, we went to the Legal Aid office at Kidal Street No. 6. After we arrived, we briefly had a discussion. Mr. Munir even asked: "are you guys ready with all the risk that you will need to shoulder?" All of us replied that we were ready to face all the risks that would come. With that, Mr. Munir just surrendered to what all of us wanted. Then we started to paint banners while others were listing all the demands to distribute the next day. (p. 14)

In addition to preparing materials and equipment, this final meeting also prepared the workers mentally. Mr. Munir asked if they were ready to strike, not to check if the workers were physically ready, but to confirm if they were aware of the potential consequences of their strike, especially if the military

would intervene and break it up violently. Meppy and her coworkers confirmed that they were ready. And with that, the strike they had planned for
months was about to begin.

THE STRIKE AND ITS AFTERMATH

Meppy and her coworkers (approximately thirty persons) prepared throughout the night of October 29. They grouped themselves into six teams; each
team was assigned a specific task and a particular post within the factory.[33]
Meppy was assigned to make photocopies of the strike leaflets (3,000 copies)
and distribute them. She was also, together with Mr. Imam, on the team to
represent the workers.

They all spent the night at the LBH office, and in the early morning on the
day of the strike, they went to the factory. It was much earlier than usual:

> All of us departed from the LBH office at Kidal Street No. 6, Surabaya at 4:30
> in the morning and arrived at Tanjung Sari at 6:00. And all of our colleagues
> started to disperse to their posts as we had planned it last night. (p. 15)

Meppy made the 3,000 photocopies of the strike leaflets that included a
list of the workers' demands. There were twenty-two demands in their list:

1. A fair wage according to the minimum wage of 2,250 rupiahs (0.97 US$)
   per hour
2. Health benefits
3. Transportation coverage of 500 rupiahs (0.22 US$)
4. Meals allowance of 500 rupiahs (0.22 US$)
5. Other work-related benefits
6. Work-related bonus
7. Overtime pay according to the Decision of the Minister of Manpower No.
   Kep. 72/Men/84 and Regulation of Minister of Manpower No. Per. 03/
   Men/1987
8. Menstrual leave, maternity leave, and annual leave
9. Full wages during a strike
10. Severance payment for any worker whose work is terminated
11. Payment of all fees until worker recovers from work-related accidents
12. Better workplace safety
13. Double overtime pays on Sundays
14. No work on national holidays and days-off
15. Maximum regular working hours of forty hours per week
16. No layoffs

17. A mosque or prayer room on the company's premises
18. No pay cuts
19. Simplification of permission procedures [for bereavement leave]
20. No illegal charges or pay cuts without explanation
21. Payment of unpaid overtime income
22. No more job agents or brokers

It is interesting to note that the list, compared to lists from other worker strikes in East Java in 1992, was very long. Although the list was mainly about income (minimum wage, overtime pay, severance pay, and benefits), it also demanded rights: the right to leave (menstrual, maternity, and annual leave) and the right to rest (maximum working hours, no work on national holidays, and permission not to work). It also sought to improve facilities (to establish a prayer room and provide safety equipment), and address the dominance of job agents and brokers over their work.

The long list of demands does not necessarily mean that their factory had more problems compared to others, or that they suffered the worst working conditions in East Java in 1992. Other factory workers surely faced similar issues, especially when payment of minimum wage and overtime were the most common demands in worker strikes in 1992. Rather, the length of the list indicates that Meppy and her coworkers were better able than workers from other factories to articulate their demands. The LBH Surabaya (Mr. Munir and his colleagues) must have assisted them in identifying problems in their workplace and formulating these problems in light of their legal rights as workers. Indeed, it was common practice at the time for workers to list all the problems in their workplace, contrasting the laws with what they saw and experienced in reality in the factory, as part of a learning process. The list of demands was also a medium to alert other workers of their rights, no matter how "trivial" they may have seemed.

The long list of demands could also mean that Meppy and her coworkers had been observing these problems in their factory for some time, but could not do anything to overcome them. It expressed their common frustration and they wanted to let the company know that they were fully aware of all the problems in the factory and that the company had been violating their rights as workers. Meppy and her coworkers did not necessarily expect the company to address all these issues at once, which was, of course, quite impossible. Instead, they most likely planned to ask the company to improve working conditions over time, and this would give them the time to organize workers. This would also allow workers to organize more easily while monitoring if the company made any improvements.

Meppy does not describe the walkout itself in detail, especially after she finished distributing the leaflets. It is safe to assume that the walkout went as planned. In fact, Meppy notes that it did not take long for the company to respond:

> It was not long before some of my colleagues and I were called upon to repre-
> sent all the workers; in total we were 30 persons. When we got inside [the office
> building], the security personnel informed us that only 16 of us were enough to
> enter the office room, it was around 10:30 p.m. when we were ordered to enter
> the office room to discuss the demands that we made. (p. 16)

The workers soon decided thirteen persons to negotiate with the employer as a representative team (Meppy was one of the thirteen).[34] She details the non-workers that attended the negotiation:

> When we entered the office room and sat on the chairs we saw, among others:
> Mr. Kong, Mr. Lukman Wijaya, Mr. Tai, Mr. Akiok, Mr. Mahmud, the human
> resource manager, Mr. Edi (from the SPSI union), Mr. Ichsan Rahmad (from the
> SPSI union), Mr. Chen, Mr. Hutomo, the Babinsa, the Koramil, the Korem Mr.
> Samsudin and Mr. H. Katrup (from the Department of Manpower),[35] Kapolda,
> Kapolres, and journalists. (p. 17)

Besides the employer (Mr. Khong Hsien Mou), and his assistants and legal representatives, two SPSI officers and two officers from the Department of Manpower also attended the meeting. The SPSI officers did not represent the workers; they were attending the negotiation as a formality. Whenever a strike took place, the SPSI was an official witness to the negotiation. It was commonly reported that SPSI officers would support the employer's position in negotiations, and push workers to accept the employer's argument. Although two officers from the Department of Manpower attended the meeting, they did not mediate between the employer and workers. It was common practice for such officers to merely act as witness to the negotiation and, if necessary, issue an official memo about the meeting that might favor the employer. A number of military and police personnel were also present at the meeting (the Babinsa, the Koramil, and the Korem).[36] As noted earlier, it was then a common procedure for the military and police to monitor worker strikes and attend negotiation meetings. They had a high stake in maintaining order in their territory, and worker strikes were considered a security issue. They needed to attend the meeting because Meppy and her coworkers had succeeded in organizing 4,000 workers to participate in the strike. This was the largest strike in East Java in 1992. Thus, Meppy and her team, as representatives of the workers, had to face sixteen men of power at the negotiation table.

As expected, the negotiation was tough, continuing through lunchtime and lasting until 2:30 p.m. Meppy describes:

it was when we discussed the minimum wage that the negotiation got tough and we got into a heated argument. Finally, at around 2:30 in the afternoon we came to an agreement and it was signed by all attending parties. The meeting was over by 3:00 p.m . . . in front of the factory some workers were still waiting to hear the arguments during the negotiation. After explaining what we had faced [during the negotiation], we went back home. (p. 17)

Although it took hours to negotiate, it seems Meppy and her coworkers were satisfied with the result. They might have felt that they had done their best to defend their rights during the negotiation. In fact, the written agreement showed that the employer acknowledged their list of demands and agreed to fulfil the demands accordingly. The minimum wage would be 2,250 rupiahs (0.97 US$) and the employer would pay for overtime work according to the law and related regulations, as demanded by the workers. The employer also agreed to provide menstrual, maternity, and annual leaves, health benefits, and safety facilities. There were two workers' demands, however, that the employer would not accept. First, the meal allowance would not be 500 rupiahs (0.22 US$) as demanded by the workers, but instead, 300 rupiahs (0.13 US$). Second, the employer would pay workers only 50 percent of wages during the strike, instead of full wages as demanded by the workers.

In general, the agreement was in favor of the workers. After all, most of the workers' demands were based on violations of their rights and thus, the employer just agreed to comply with the law. It was, indeed, an irony that workers had to organize a strike to force the employer to respect their rights and comply with the law, even to provide the minimum wage. Most worker strikes in the 1990s were similar, with the main objective to force the employer to comply with the labor law.

Although on paper the agreement favored the workers, its implementation was a different matter. Meppy and her coworkers understood this: they continued to monitor the employer to ensure that working conditions were improved as agreed. Agreeing to worker demands was a common tactic of employers of that time to tame workers and contain their strike so as not to lose many working days. Meppy and her coworkers must have been aware of this or observed this from other strikes. However, it seems that they were not fully aware then that their employer was waiting to strike back.

It did not take long. Within a week after the strike, their employer had devised a strategy to retaliate that included targeting those who were members of the representative team during the negotiation. As organizers of the strike, they were considered "troublemakers."

A few days after the strike, Meppy was accused of stealing the company's employment book (which kept a list of workers' names).[37] She was asked to fetch a book from the company's office. Because the book was fully wrapped, she did not know what book it was, and sincerely did what she was asked to. On the way to deliver the book, she was stopped by her supervisor who "caught" her red-handed "stealing" the company's employment book. With that, the employer had a valid reason to punish her. She was transferred from one department to another, especially to jobs that required physical strength. She explains:

> For a week I was punished—I was not allowed to enter the packing department. [At first] I had to work outside with my friend, Ilham, to arrange cardboard boxes on the pallets. . . . After that, I was dismissed from work on November 9, 1992. (p. 8)

Her dismissal was sudden, though not unexpected. Two of her coworkers, Mr. Imam Basuki and Ms. Nur Sontini, were also treated similarly: they were transferred from their usual posts as a punishment, and when they failed to perform the required tasks (or, in Meppy's case, refused to perform the job), the employer had reason to dismiss them.

With the dismissal of the three, workers now understood that their employer was targeting those who had organized the strike on October 30, 1992. They quickly reacted against this by organizing another strike to demand the reinstatement of the three. The strike started on the following day:

> On November 10–12, 1992, all of our colleagues organized a strike for 3 days to demand the company reinstate the three of us, Imam Basuki, Nur Santini, and I, back to work. On November 12, Imam Basuki and I were asked by the company to represent all workers and discuss together with the company and the military. (p. 9)

Once again, the employer was forced to negotiate with the workers. This time the workers demanded the full implementation of the previous agreement of October 30, 1992, and also, the reinstatement of three of their coworkers. The strike lasted for two days until the employer finally could not manage it and called Imam and Meppy to represent the workers on November 12, 1992.

The workers' demands were accepted, similar to the previous meetings. In the written agreement, the employer also agreed to reinstate the three workers back to their original posts and not retaliate against them anymore. The agreement was signed by the employer, all of the fourteen worker representatives,[38] and two officers from the Department of Manpower, on November 12, 1992. It seemed that everything was settled; especially, Meppy and her two coworkers could go back to work as usual from November 13. Another strike, however, was lurking.

Meppy devotes two full pages to her involvement in the strike of the supervisors (*mandor*). She was invited by one of the supervisors (Mr. Gunadi) to come to a meeting on December 14. To her surprise, the meeting was attended by all of the supervisors, many of whom she did not even know before. She notes that Mr. Munir and two young lawyers from the LBH Surabaya also attended the meeting.

It is important to note that in the factory's regime, supervisors were paid more than the minimum wage. This difference was intended to drive a wedge between the supervisors and the manual workers, and hinder the formation of any alliance between them. This management strategy works well in many situations. In this case, however, it began to collapse when Meppy and her coworkers succeeded in organizing a strike in the factory. The supervisors, witnessing the workers' strike and what they had achieved started to realize that they also needed to organize to defend their rights. Meppy discussed wages as their main problem in that first meeting, and at a second meeting on December 20, together with Mr. Imam Basuki, she shared organizing strategies. As many as 141 supervisors attended the meetings; they all agreed to organize a strike to demand better wages.[39]

On December 28, 1992, while the workers were entering the factory to work, all the supervisors declared a walkout at the factory gates. The company refused to deal with them on the first day of the strike. It was only on the second day (December 29) that Meppy and Mr. Imam Basuki were asked to meet with the striking supervisors and mediate between them and the company. Meppy explains:

(T)hey demanded an improvement in their wages, for two full days. On the second day [of the strike], as their representatives, we were asked [by the company] to go out of the factory to deal with their issue. Unfortunately, the company could not come to an agreement and thus, the matter was taken to the Department of Manpower [for mediation]. It was there that finally, after going through various arguments, Mr. Lukman Wijaya agreed with all of the demands. (pp. 10–11)

Meppy and Mr. Imam Basuki acted as representatives of the supervisors during the mediation process at the Department of Manpower office. They succeeded in getting the company to agree to the supervisors' demands for better wages and more annual holidays (seven days). With this, an alliance between the supervisors and the manual workers in the factory was coming to fruition. If the alliance was not stopped, it could bring together both the supervisors and the workers in a common struggle to demand better wages and welfare for all, a serious threat to the company. To protect itself, the company began preparing a plan to break the joint organizing efforts by targeting

Meppy and Imam Basuki, whom they must have considered key troublemakers in the factory (and key to the success of the alliance). Although it was then a common practice for companies in Indonesia, especially in East Java, to report to the military and contact them in the case of any worker strike, it was a malicious plan to intimidate the workers to stop organizing. This unchecked mechanism created the abuse of power.

RETALIATION

Although the military and the police were always present during the negotiation meetings they had with the company, the workers were not pressured to accept the company's arguments. In fact, as Meppy notes, they were allowed to argue against the company, especially when it came to workers' rights. They were well versed in defending their rights based on the labor laws. The company was losing ground, as it had, indeed, violated workers' rights. But Meppy's activism in leading a strike and acting as a representative of the workers, and later, of the supervisors as well, must have earned her the attention of the company and the military.

Two days after the strike of the supervisors ended with an agreement, Meppy and two of her coworkers, Mr. Imam Basuki and Ms. Dasmiati, were summoned by one of the company's security guards to see Mr. Masrihadi, the human resource manager, in his office. Mr. Masrihadi informed them that officers from the Department of Manpower had requested that they, as representatives of the workers, bring their wage slips as evidence of their wages to the department's office. Mr. Masrihadi offered to go together with them to the office. His offer seemed like a nice gesture by the company to accommodate the workers. Meppy and the others did not see anything strange with this sudden request, and they all agreed to go with him, as they trusted that he would have prepared their wage slips also. Meppy describes what happened next:

> Finally at around 10:30, Imam, Dasmiati, and I, together with Mr. Masrihadi, two Korem officers, Mr. Tri and Mr. Edy, rode in the dark-green company car, driven by another Korem officer, that was supposedly heading to the Department of Manpower office. Strangely, I noticed we took the road through Darmo Satelite, a different route than that to the Department of Manpower. But at that time, I didn't have the courage to ask about it and decided to stay quiet. (p. 1)

Indeed, the car was not heading toward the Department of Manpower. Instead, it went to the military office of the Korem.

Upon arrival at the Korem office, they realized that they had been tricked and kidnapped against their own will. They were detained without any charge, and abused by the military personnel:

we were surprised and shocked, why were we brought to the Korem office and treated rudely and with offensive words coming out from their mouths, such as "you thief," "you crook." They shouted such words at my friend, Imam, and shoved him into the office. He was beaten by several Korem officers until his face was left black and blue. Meanwhile Dasmiati and I were treated similarly in a different room; both of us were slapped as if we were notorious criminals. The three of us didn't know what our mistake was, but they accused us as rebels in the strike. (p. 2)

The three were beaten up all through the lunchtime until about 3:00 p.m. From around 5:00 p.m., military officers began to interrogate them, separately in different rooms:

It was where we were interrogated in detail with a lot of questions, including about our personal identity and also about our family members [it was so many questions] that [it] took 7 pages with 4 copies, and it ended at around 1:00 a.m. (p. 3)

While forced interrogation is a common method to extract information from detainees, prolonged interrogation (in this case, for almost six hours straight) is meant to make them tired and psychologically torture them so they surrender themselves completely to the military's control.

Although they had met a number of military personnel during the negotiation meetings after the strike, Meppy and her coworkers were not fully aware of the power the military had in maintaining control over the society, including with severe punishment. In fact, Meppy even thought that after the interrogation ended, she and her coworkers would be "allowed to return home" (p. 3). It was when she heard that was not the case that she fell into shock:

Then Mr. Rangai replied that according to the order of their commandant, Mr. M. Ali, we were not allowed to go back home, and upon hearing that I started crying uncontrollably. I was so sad that I could not pay obeisance (*sungkem*) to my parents on New Year's Eve like I always did every year, that I collapsed on the chair. (p. 3)

Held for the night, Meppy could not pay obeisance (*sungkem*) to her parents on that New Year's Eve, a painful denial of her ability to perform her (annual) filial obligation.[40]

The next day, January 1, 1993, she and her coworkers were again interrogated from the morning. They were asked about their activities, and the paralegal training organized by the LBH Surabaya in Malang. The interrogation continued in the afternoon and lasted through the night. They were asked "the same questions just like yesterday" (p. 4).

On the morning of January 2, Meppy witnessed two military personnel sexually harassing her coworker Dasmiati. Mr. Siswandi had interrogated Dasmiati the day before; it is possible that he had targeted her then. Both he and Mr. Cholil, another military interrogator, knew that because it was so early in the morning and other personnel had not yet arrived, Meppy would be the only witness to their actions. Meppy recounts:

> And in the morning of January 2, 1993, at around 4:00, Dasmiati woke up earlier to have a shower, and at 5:00 I was waken up to take a shower. After the shower, both Dasmiati and I went back to our cubicle to take a nap . . . that Mr. Siswandi entered our cubicle and laid his body on Dasmiati and ordered her to caress him. After him, one of his friends, Cholil, if I am not mistaken, took his turn. Cholil even fell asleep for a while and after he woke up, Dasmiati wanted to take a nap, but Siswandi followed her; he jabbed his fingers in Dasmiati's buttocks, saying that was the way to wake Dasmiati up for breakfast. Dasmiati was upset with it, and she protested to both of them, but in response, they laughed and replied that even if she protested to Mr. Ali, he would certainly tell them to do so without hesitation. Dasmiati didn't say [anything] and was upset with their treatment. I witnessed all of these from the reception room. After they harassed Dasmiati, they went for a shower. (pp. 4–5)

We are not sure how common or widespread sexual harassment was as part of the military's ill-treatment of detainees at that time. Reading Meppy's account, however, it is clear that the commandant (Mr. M. Ali) at the Korem office knew about it. Regardless of whether it was done purposely or strategically (as a method to crush the detainee's spirit of resistance), the perpetrators were free to sexually harass. Even without the express consent of their commandant, they knew that they would not be punished, even if Mr. Ali found out about it later. This blanket impunity shows the pervasive power that members of the military had over society, especially female detainees. Indeed, although Meppy herself was not harassed, the fact that she took notes about this incident shows the dark impression it made on her and demonstrates her insecurity in fearing that it could also happen to her.

Interrogation continued on that day as before. Meppy notes that they were "repeating the same questions again" (p. 5). The questioning ended during lunchtime and after that, Meppy and her coworkers were taken to the office of

Mr. M. Ali where he gave them some "advice" (*dinasehati*) about "not-to-do things." Meppy explains:

> Then the three of us were warned not to do it [the strike] anymore and Mr. Ali said that it was all right for us to demand our rights as long as it was exercised genuinely and not orchestrated by an outsider (*dalang*), and some other things . . . after that, we were ordered to write a letter of statement that stated, among others, as I remember, that I wouldn't tell anyone what I just felt, saw, and heard [in the Korem office]. That's the only statement I remember. (pp. 5–6)

The commandant's warning to Meppy and her coworkers not to organize any more strikes shows that labor actions were a security issue for the military. The goal was to be able to report zero strikes to higher commands; lower officers would not hesitate to do whatever it took to maintain security in their territory. Mr. M. Ali also warned Meppy and her coworkers about the role of outsiders or masterminds (*dalang*) who orchestrated worker strikes. It was part of his duty as commandant of the Korem office to investigate any strike and identify its organizer(s). This notion of the role of the *dalang* was based on two assumptions: (1) that workers would be better off if they just trusted the state (and the military) to protect them rather than protesting against any violations and injustice at their workplace; and (2) that workers were incapable in articulating their problems and formulating grievances on their own. Thus, under the state's patriarchal ideology of Pancasila Industrial Relations (Hubungan Industrial Pancasila, HIP), workers were expected to remain docile and passive under the state's fatherly protection, and avoid any *dalang*, or political provocateur who might take advantage of the workers to create political instability.[41] The military assumed workers were just puppets.

Meppy notes that she and her coworkers "just said yes" to Mr. M. Ali's advice (p. 6); they did not see any point in arguing. They were tired of being detained and just wanted to be released and go home as soon as possible. As the commandant, he was the only person who held the power in the room; it was therefore a strategic choice for them to look compliant and obedient.

They were finally released on that day at around 3:00 p.m., and Meppy notes that she arrived back home at around 3:40 p.m.:

> When I arrived at the front of the house, my mother and siblings were crying so that it pained my heart. But I had to stay cheerful so that my family wouldn't get stuck in sadness. (p. 6)

Although Meppy does not write in detail about the reaction of her family to the kidnapping, it is clear that they were extremely worried because they had no idea where she and her coworkers had been taken. In fact, on the morning of that day (January 2, 1993), the father of Imam Basuki reported to the Surabaya police office (Polsekta Tandes) that all three of them were missing. The police must have suspected why they were kidnapped and where they were detained, but they could not perform their civilian duties to protect citizens as they were officially under the military.

AFTERSHOCK AND SURVEILLANCE

Meppy went back to work on January 7, 1993. She notes that at first, she worked as usual, but she was uneasy because she was "always being monitored and they searched for our mistakes" (p. 21). She knew that it was part of the employer's strategy to have an excuse to fire her and her coworkers. She tried to hold out against the employer's treatment and encourage her coworkers who had "little courage" (*nyalinya kecil*) (p. 21).

The employer tried to intimidate her and her coworkers from continuing their organizing activities. When they were collecting funds from other workers (for organizing activities), the employer confiscated the money and asked them to explain what they were going to do with the funds and show the balance sheet. As days passed, the employer was "monitoring more closely" (p. 22), checking when she entered the factory gate to sign in for work, how long she went to the toilet, and her conversations with her friends. Although she tried to stay calm, she finally decided to give up:

> And on January 26, 1993, I went to work again, but I already had a plan to leave without informing them [the employer]. I brought my camera with me and took some pictures with friends. When the lunch break came, at 12:00 noon, I said goodbye to my friends, supervisors (*mandor*), and the security guards. Then I walked out and went home. (p. 22)

Meppy does not say directly why she gave up her work three weeks after she resumed it that January. Yet we can safely assume that it must have been that she could not tolerate the employer's surveillance anymore. While she understood there was nothing she could do to stop it, she knew that she could not submit herself to the factory regime. Walking out on the job was her last act of defiance.

Upon learning that Meppy had abandoned work during lunchtime on that day, the employer soon retaliated:

> (A)t exactly 2:00 p.m., my friends, one by one, were summoned by the human resource manager and asked to sign resignation letters; there were 15 workers and they were given severance payments on the spot. They were photographed when they signed the resignation letters. (p. 23)

Meppy must have heard about this incident from her coworkers. With Meppy gone, the employer took the opportunity to dismiss her coworkers, all of whom were members of the negotiation team. It was the employer's way of normalizing the factory back to the way it was and breaking the workers' organizing efforts.

Meppy writes that the human resource manager and some Korem personnel (including Mr. Agus Tomo who interrogated her) visited her home that night to get her to sign a resignation letter. She was not home at that time. They returned the next day, but she was not at home then either. They came again the following day (January 28), at noon. She was asked to write her own resignation letter and only after she did so, was she given the severance payment.[42] In the end, as she notes, "After that, they advised me that if I would work elsewhere, I should not repeat all the things I had done at PT Victory Long Age" (p. 24). Meppy nodded in response to their "advice," although she quickly replied that if she found problems in her next factory job, she would "negotiate with the employer in a peaceful and relaxed manner." It is obvious that she knew what they wanted to hear from her, and that the military personnel would monitor her activities from that day on. She also understood that it would be difficult, if not impossible, for her to find a new job in the Surabaya area.[43]

NARRATING REPRESSION, SYMBOLIC DISOBEDIENCE

As we have seen, Meppy's account expresses the types of repression that workers had to bear under the New Order regime's ideology of Pancasila Industrial Relations (*Hubungan Industrial Pancasila*). Her experiences were less intense than what the New Order's political prisoners experienced and witnessed during their detention. The events that took place in her account took place during the ten-month period of her factory work, while political prisoners like Pramoedya Ananta Toer endured fourteen years of brutal imprisonment.[44] Her twenty-five-page account stands thin compared to the volumes of *oeuvre* written by political prisoners. Nonetheless, Meppy was not exempt from experiencing similar ill-treatments: she was kidnapped, (illegally) detained, and put under surveillance by military personnel. She was intimidated at the workplace to such an extent that she had to give up her only livelihood. As a worker, she was targeted due to her activism. As a female worker, she witnessed her coworker being sexually harassed in the Korem office while the perpetrators laughed about it.

Similar to Toer, she was forbidden from sharing her feelings, thoughts, and experiences and thus, her account evokes the violation of freedom of expression prevalent during the 1990s in Indonesia. Fearful of further retaliation, she was forced to keep the repressive experiences she and her coworkers had in the Korem office to herself. Despite these difficulties, she did write down her experiences of being kidnapped and detained, and provided the background of her activism in the factory that gained her the attention of the military. Instead of feeling ashamed (*malu*) of the harassment and intimidation, she put them center stage in her account. She wrote her account to remember the experiences and to record how the military had treated her. In a similar vein with the New Order's political prisoners, her act of writing was a way to overcome the trauma initiated by the repressive experiences. While political prisoners write and publish their accounts to educate the public, Meppy wrote her account as a record to herself. She knew she needed to release the tensions psychologically associated with the trauma and to free herself through writing, without worrying about being censored (by the military). In that way, the repressive experiences she went through would not become a prolonged repressed experience. Instead, she transformed them as part of her story of the struggle against human rights violations and injustices at the workplace.

Her account illustrates the real condition of the workers in Indonesia in the 1990s: they were not allowed to establish their own organization outside the government-sponsored FSPSI and they were not allowed to express grievances about working conditions or organize a strike to defend their rights and interests. As she could not tell others freely about these experiences, she wrote to herself and for herself. Her account provides a detailed record of these human rights violations as experienced and written by a member of the working class. Her account also sheds light on the case of Marsinah, who was kidnapped, detained, and murdered (presumably, by the military), roughly one month after Meppy wrote her account.[45] Marsinah's case follows a similar pattern in how the military viewed worker strikes, how they threatened workers by kidnapping, illegally detaining, and harassing them (and in the case of Marsinah, by taking her life), in order to put an end to their activism. Both Meppy and Marsinah still stood against these threats to defend their rights. They were exemplary fearless female workers of the 1990s. As a survivor of these ill-treatments by the military, Meppy proves her strength twofold by writing these experiences. She is the only worker that leaves us with this courageous record.

Her account itself is solid evidence that she, as a worker, was capable of understanding the world she lived in, articulating the problems at her workplace, and formulating demands for change. Workers were not just following instructions from a *dalang*; Meppy's account confirms that workers had their own concerns and thoughts on matters that were important enough to them to defend. Meppy gave an honest account of her initial hesitation to join the workers' meetings, and that it was only out of curiosity she began attending it. She would later participate only after she saw action as a chance (the only chance?) to better her working conditions and living standard. Once she was part of the movement, she gave her full attention and dedication to it. The LBH Surabaya, with Mr. Munir as its head, facilitated this rising consciousness of the workers. It was her own courage, not any *dalang*, however, that moved her. It was also through her own initiative, not any instruction from a *dalang*, that made her write about her experiences. Therefore, her account is not only a soliloquy of the repression that workers experienced in the 1990s, but also their disobedience—an important account of fearless female workers defending their collective rights as workers and at the same time, their freedom of expression.

NOTES

1. On the increasing number of strikes during 1991–1993, Hess (1997: 45) notes,

(t)his trend has paralleled the growth of manufacturing, but indicates more than an increase in discontent and a greater willingness to express it. It also indicates the failure of the industrial relations system to cope with the demands workers are making.

2. According to newspaper reports, at least twenty-seven strikes took place at factories that employed more than 500 workers: at P.T. Tjung Dong Indonesia (2,000 workers) on January 7, at P.T. Sekar Laut (2,000 workers) on January 21, at P.T. Quinci Kota Mas (850 workers) on February 5, at P.T. Tulus Tri Tunggal (700 workers) on March 10, at P.T. Food Specialites Indonesia (700 workers) on March 13, at P.T. Komega (1,200 workers) on March 17, at P.T. Grating Jaya (600 workers) on March 25, at P.T. Hari Terang Industri (1,800 workers) on March 30, at P.T. Telaga Maspertiwi (1,103 workers) on March 31, at P.T. Multi Manua (600 workers) on April 1, at P.T. Ten Hang Fan (500 workers) and P.T. Alim Surya Steel (3,000 workers) on April 3, at P.T. Gincu Kota Mas (600 workers) on April 12, at P.T. Keramik Diamond Indah (600 workers) and P.T. Gesti Avis Sidoarjo (1,000 workers) on April 20, at P.T. Koyo Mulya (1,600 workers) on April 22, at P.T. Hyatt Regency (500 workers) and P.T. Ereuka Aba Mojosari (600 workers) on May 1, at P.T. Satrindo Utama Makmur (600 workers) and P.T. Drakindo Kencana Tama (530 workers) on May 14, at P.T. Asia Tile (1,612 workers) and P.T. Surya Sakti Utama (650 workers) on July 14, at P.T. Elang Perkasa Makmur (750 workers) on August 27, at P.T. Murni Makmur Sejahtera (600 workers) on September 2, at P.T. Indaco Aneka Jaya (600 workers) on September 15, at P.T. Asia Victory Surabaya (1,600 workers) on September 23, and at P.T. Victory Long Age (4,000 workers) on October 30.

3. Manning (1993: 87).

4. Hadiz (1997: 126).

5. A number of labor NGOs were established during the 1980s–1990s. In Surabaya, these included: Kelompok Kerja Humanika (Humanika Working

Group), Yayasan Arek Surabaya (Surabaya People Foundation), Lembaga Studi Kemasyarakatan dan Bantuan Hukum (Institute for the Study of Society and Legal Aid), and Pendampingan Buruh Keuskupan Surabaya (Outreach for Workers of the Surabaya Archdiocese).

6. See Herod (2001).

7. Siegel (2001: 120) notes, "The *massa*, a transformation or perhaps a remnant of the *rakyat*, are the product of the imagination of the middle class; they are the menace left once the body of the nation has divided in two and identity . . . a fear cultivated by the government in different forms during the New Order: fear of Communism, fear of criminality, and fear of the *massa*."

8. Although most workers saw factory employment as a better option than hard labor in the agricultural sector and as part of the path of social mobility, they primarily migrated because their livelihood in their hometown and access to land were already made difficult due to the impacts of the industrialization process.

9. Although subcontract and outsourcing practices were already introduced in a number of factories as early as mid-1980s (as discussed in chapter 1), conventional factory system was still the norm.

10. A number of factory-level unions, although officially affiliated with the SPSI, were quite independent. After 1991, there were efforts to establish non-affiliated unions (primarily by or with the help of concerned NGOs' activists).

11. *Dalang* is the puppet master in Javanese *wayang* performance. On depictions of *dalang* during the New Order period, see Williams (1990: 116–120).

12. It is interesting to compare this situation with Brazil during Vargas's dictatorial regime (1937–1945), as Wolfe (1993: 117) notes, where "(w)omen textile workers used factory commissions to coordinate their various survival and resistance strategies. Sao Paulo's metalworkers, who trusted neither Vargas nor their co-opted union, also organized independent comissões to press for higher wages and safer work conditions." The authoritarian regime with its military arms in turn contributed to solidifying workers' collective awareness as a repressed group.

13. Workers could not afford to fulfill basic needs. Dhanani and Islam (2004: 58) note that in 1999, "(t)he national minimum wages (of 1.4 persons) can, at best, meet only 65 percent of the basic expenditure needs of households (of four persons)."

14. See Instruksi Gubernur Kepala Daerah Tingkat I Jawa Timur No. 7/1994 tentang Peningkatan Upah Minimum Regional di Jawa Timur (Instruction of the governor of East Java No. 7 Year 1994 on minimum wage increase) (dated March 2, 1994). In its efforts to pacify worker strikes, the central government even reintroduced *tunjangan hari raya* ("bonus for religious holidays"). On this, see Peraturan Menteri Tenaga Kerja No. Per. 04/Men/1994 tentang Tunjangan Hari Raya Keagamaan bagi Pekerja di Perusahaan (Regulation of Minister of Manpower No. PER-04/MEN/1994 on Bonus for religious holidays for company's employees) (dated September 16, 1994). The bonus was common during the Sukarno years (1955–1965) to supplement workers' meager incomes. During the early years of the New Order regime (1969–1972), however, it was considered a financial disadvantage for investors and in 1972, companies were no longer obligated to provide it. Throughout the 1970s and 1980s, many workers did not receive the bonus.

Reintroducing the bonus in 1994 (as extra income) was one strategy of the government to prevent further strikes.

15. Dhanani and Islam (2004: 59) note that, "in 1994, the incidence of low pay varied from 7.5 percent in Central Kalimantan to 47.6 percent in East Java."

16. P.T. Victory Long Age was established in May 1988.

17. The notebook was part of a pile of documents on the kidnapping incidents of three P.T. Victory Long Age workers kept at the office of the Surabaya Legal Aid Institute (LBH Surabaya). I thank Jeon Je Seong who shared all the documents with me. For background analysis, see Jeon (2002).

18. There were originally no page numbers on the notebook, but for the purpose of this reading, I have assigned page numbers to the account as a reference. On one page, Meppy writes the lyrics of a pop song, Merry Andani's "Dinding Pemisah" ("Separating Wall") (dated January 9, 1993).

19. We know for certain that December 31, 1992, could not be the date of the writing of this section. Instead, it is the date of her kidnapping and detention by the military. By putting December 31, 1992, at the head of the section, it seems that Meppy wanted to point out the importance of the event that pushed her to write. It is more likely that her account was written between January 9, 1993, and April 6, 1993.

20. Chronologically speaking, the list would logically be in this order: Section 3, Section 4, Section 1, Section 2, and Section 5.

21. Psychology informs us, as McNally (2012: 1) notes,

(t)he dynamics of abduction and kidnapping are similar in that in either instance the hostage taker holds someone against his or her will, and the victim then becomes a pawn for either ransom, bargaining, or negotiation. . . . Kidnapping thus continues to impact the world with the resultant psychological traumatic affect thrust upon the victims of the hostage taker as well as their families, friends, and the involved first responders.

22. Garland (2005: 249) notes that "if the original events are brought into consciousness and put into words (the 'talking cure'), especially if they are accompanied by the original intense feeling they provoked, then the symptoms will disappear."

23. For a comparison, see Toer (1995), Sulami (1999), Sudjinah (2000, 2003), and Setiawan (2004) as examples of the traumatic experiences of political prisoners during the New Order regime. For a discussion on Sudjinah, see Watson (2006: chapter 3).

24. "Truth" here does not indicate a legal sense of being a witness in a court of law under oath to tell the truth. The victims' truth is supported with facts and evidence. Telling "truth" here means sharing their experiences for what they were.

25. Agger and Jensen (1996: 69) note that

(u)nder state terrorism, the frequency of the stressor events is characterized by an enduring, repetitive and chronic impact of stressors which take place in a context of power, where fundamental human rights are violated in a systematic and deliberative way.

26. Some details in her account are left out here to maintain the story line.

27. She did write that she liked "to make friends" (*berkawan*), and her dream (*cita-cita*) was "to be a successful person in many things." We are not sure the reason she

wrote it, but it seems that it was written as part of a self-description to emphasize her own characteristics.

28. It was then a common practice for workers to be required to work through a three-month training period as a probation to the job. During this time, they would earn 70–80 percent of the minimum wage.

29. One document from LBH Surabaya notes that Mr. Imam Basuki was born in 1970 (he was twenty-three years old then).

30. On Munir and his murder case, see Avonius (2008).

31. This fund was primarily used to buy equipment and materials, make photocopies, and pay transportation fees.

32. It was common for workers to have meetings in the LBH office, as they did not have many other options and LBH always opened their meeting rooms for workers to use.

33. These six teams included: two teams to organize workers from the east and west sides of the factory, one team to organize workers from neighboring factories, one team to secure the area by looking after the parking lot and traffic lanes, one team to make photocopies and distribute the strike leaflets, and one team to be the workers' representative.

34. The agreement has the names of the thirteen workers: Meppy, Sudarsih, Puji M, Kasiono, Rusmini, Isa, Imam, Nanik, Nur, Sri, Nuhudiyanto, Urip, and Mujito.

35. Understandably, some of the names were not spelled correctly. Officers from the Department of Manpower were Mr. Syamsuddin and Mr. H.M. Katroep UZ. Officers from the SPSI were Mr. Abu Bakar and Mr. Edi W. They were all men. The Babinsa (Bintara Pembina Desa/Village Military Advisor) and the Koramil (Komando Rayon Militer/Military Sub-district Command) are village-level military units. The Korem (Komando Resort Militer/Military Resort Command) is regional-level military unit that supervise Koramil and Babinsa.

36. In its efforts to monitor and control the population, the military established "territorial commands" that stretched from regional and provincial to district, sub-district, and village levels, and were structured in parallel to the civil service. The Korem was in charge of the province and sub-province level (in this case, East Java province). The Koramil was in charge of the sub-district level (in this case, the Surabaya-Sidoarjo area). The Babinsa was a non-commissioned military officer at the village level. Although the police had its own internal structure, it was under the military command. The Head of the Regional Police (Kapolda) was in charge of the provincial level (in this case, East Java province). The Head of the Resort Police (Kapolres) was in charge of the regency/city level (in this case, Surabaya city area).

37. Meppy does not mention the date of this incident; she only notes that, "it was Monday" (p. 7). It could be November 2, 1992.

38. They were Imam Basuki, Puji M., Sudarsih, T. Hery Christiani, Meppy, Samsuti, Dasmitai, Isa, Mujita, Kasiono, Sri Kusmiati, Rusmini, Puji, and Urip. This team had different members from the previous negotiation team of thirteen persons.

39. Meppy's account does not mention any follow-up meeting with the supervisors. She notes that during this period, she went for a paralegal training organized by the LBH Surabaya in Malang city, on December 25–26, 1992, together with four

coworkers (Mr. Imam Basuki, Ms. Damiati, Ms. Suhartini, and Ms. Titik Sulistiyo). Workers from other factories also attended the paralegal training, in which they learned about workers' rights and labor laws.

40. *Sungkem* (literally, kiss the knees) is a symbolic act of submission of a child to his or her parents by kissing their knees. It is a common practice in Javanese families, especially on New Year's Eve, the first day of Idul Fitri (Eid al-Fitr, the celebration of the end of the Islamic holy month of fasting), and as part of the wedding ceremony. During the New Order regime, it was commonly taken as part of the state's patrimonial rituals under Soeharto.

41. Similar cases happened in many parts of Indonesia. Sih Handayani (1995: 278) notes how three union activists from an industrial complex in Central Java were interrogated (and abused) by the police to identify the *dalang* of their strike. It is obvious that the state failed to grasp that the *dalang* was none other than the workers themselves.

42. Meppy notes that she was given severance payment based on one year of work despite working for only ten months. This is not because of the employer's generosity, but because it was required by law.

43. It seems that even until April 1993 (the last date of entry in her notebook is April 6, 1993), she had yet to find any factory job.

44. Toer was detained without trial from October 13, 1965, to August 16, 1969 (in various prisons). After that, he was sent to the New Order's notorious gulag on Buru Island and imprisoned until November 12, 1979, when there was a general release of all political prisoners from Buru Island, and he was detained in Magelang until December 21, 1979.

45. Marsinah was last seen on May 5, 1993, when she went to the Military District Command (Komando Distrik Militer, Kodim) in Sidoarjo to check the whereabouts of her thirteen coworkers who were illegally detained after their strike at the factory on May 3–4, 1993.

Part 2

NEGOTIATING NEOLIBERALISM

Following the collapse of the New Order authoritarian regime in 1998, democratic institutions were established and worker rights were legally guaranteed. The transition to democracy, however, was accompanied by an economic liberalization that posed new challenges to labor. Although deregulation had already been introduced in the early 1980s, Indonesia's economy remained relatively structured along the corporatist model of development, and therefore the transformation from state-led development to market-oriented reform during the first few years after democratization was significant. Particularly after the 1997 Asian financial crisis, reliance on foreign investment was crucial for the country's fragile economy.

As the flow of foreign direct investment rose after 1998 and its share of the nation's GDP steadily grew,[1] it has played an increasingly important role in generating wage-earning jobs for local labor. Such employment creation in the formal sector is imperative for Indonesia to maintain economic growth based on its policy of export-oriented industrialization. Although the share of manufacturing jobs in total employment is now relatively stable, the country's labor pool remains mainly composed of unskilled and semi-skilled workers, making it difficult to attract investment from high-tech firms. Meanwhile, since the late 1990s, competition from other newly industrializing countries in the region, such as Vietnam dan Cambodia, has put pressure on Indonesia's comparative advantage of cheap labor. In the face of regional and global competition, the Indonesian government in August 1998, a few months after the collapse of the New Order regime, launched the Labor Law Reform,[2] which favored flexible employment and changed the employment structure to reduce employer costs, thus limiting worker benefits.

Since the Reform's implementation, workers commonly report that factory jobs, especially in the light industries, are rarely available on a permanent basis. Rather, short-term positions are continuously renewed (or extended, depending on the company's rules) for years, and come with no benefits. Although workers are paid a minimum wage, many also strive to receive a piece rate (in the garment sector) or a daily rate (in the textile sector) to earn extra income. These rates are not paid out, however, if workers do not reach requisite daily targets of production, thus creating situations in which workers provide labor without compensation. Entrapped in such employment conditions, workers endure wild fluctuations in income and uncertain futures, making life extremely precarious. Yet with limited employment options, many young women in Indonesia still see factory work as one of the few sources of relatively stable income available to them.

Female factory workers face additional difficulties due to the gender roles imposed on them. Many cannot escape from domestic responsibilities—the unpaid work of childrearing and caregiving that society demands of them. At the same time, they are also expected to financially contribute to supporting their families. In the workplace, their labor, like men's, is subject to the logic of a global factory regime that prioritizes the company's profits over their legal rights. Menstruation and pregnancy create a perception that women are less reliable. Women also often encounter sexual harassment at work, which threatens their job security and makes them more vulnerable to exploitation. Thus, while globalization has enabled female workers to attain (formal) employment in the "global factory," it also poses challenges to their livelihood and welfare.

Some sectors of Indonesia's economy have experienced liberalization since late the 1990s, and market intensification after 1998 has brought tremendous changes to the daily life of the country's population, including factory workers. At the same time, post-1998 decentralization has changed the political structure of the state, providing more opportunities for citizens to freely express their concerns and interests. Workers' freedom of association is now legally guaranteed, and unlike during the New Order regime, members of the police and military are forbidden from intervening in labor disputes.[3] Under pressure from the forces of neoliberalism, the government has loosened its overt interventions in the market and now institutionally accommodates the flow of foreign investments. Meanwhile, workers' real wage between 1998–2001 fell. As the income gap widens, it was only in 2004 that the government launched the *Sistem Jaminan Sosial Nasional* (SJSN or National Social Security System) to provide a basic social safety net and healthcare services for all in an effort to establish a new social contract.

These changes in the economic and political landscapes of post-1998 Indonesia have pushed workers to (re)define the strategic purposes and priorities of their organizations and to cope with the realities they face. Workers must now find ways to negotiate with the destructive (as they experience them) forces of today's neoliberalism, such as the privatization of national industries, deregulation, a race to the bottom in labor standards, and a flexible labor market. At the same time, the expanded political space offers new opportunities, albeit limited, for workers to act. Workers cannot escape from these forces and as we see in the two chapters that form part 2, their responses are also shaped by both the economic and political conditions of their time.

Chapter 3 analyzes a number of short essays penned by women unionists on the issue of sexual harassment in the workplace. Chapter 4 analyzes the writing of the single mother Salsabila (a pseudonym), on her struggle working in the factory. These two chapters highlight the diverse literary expression of female factory workers in post-1998 Indonesia and are based on their working experiences under the global factory regime. Unlike their predecessors who entered the labor market in late 1970s to early 1990s, these female workers spent more time in school, attaining levels of education beyond the basic six years of primary schooling. As noted in the introduction, the New Order regime established these new education standards to create a pool of semi-skilled workers. Beyond reading and writing, their schooling enabled these authors to better express themselves through written expression, beyond oral culture. In addition to becoming literary producers, members of the working class are now also reading consumers. In that sense, working-class authors, as discussed here (part 2), write not only to freely express themselves, but also in order to share common concerns with co-workers who read their writings. They also use writing as a means of spurring action on those concerns, for example, to campaign against sexual harassment and advocate for maternity protection.

The purpose of the writings, as discussed in the following two chapters, is to inform fellow workers, as readers, of the common issues they are facing together under the challenges of neoliberalism. It is important to note that their writings are printed in union publications that developed out of the freedom of association enjoyed by workers in post-1998 Indonesia. After decades of silence, female workers can now freely write and use union publications to spread their message so that definitive actions can be taken to ensure a safe and equitable workplace. They thus form part of a collective struggle for equality and social justice.

While freedom of association in post-1998 Indonesia has guaranteed workers the right to form and join unions as they like, at the same time school-based education allows workers to write and compare notes as part of their organizing activities. In other words, their writings give meaning to the practice of their freedom of association. Workers learn from each other by sharing their experiences, strategies to unionize, and actions. As such, they not only articulate to each other the challenges of neoliberalism, but also begin to confront those challenges collectively. These writings remind workers that while they may have specific concerns in their own workplace, what they are facing is part of the broader global factory regime and they are therefore bound to the same call for freedom and must come together.

Significantly, as these writings are penned by female workers for female workers, they raise issues that are often ignored by union activists or male-dominated union organizations. In so doing, they alert fellow female workers and readers more broadly to specific challenges that female workers every-where face under a neoliberal labor regime. In this way also, the writings are a call to unite together for their common cause. This does not mean that the authors are excluding male workers and union activists who are sympathetic to their cause or may read their writings. Rather, these writings highlight how the challenges that women face in the workplace are important not only for female workers, but for all workers, and that their struggle is an important and distinct part of the broader working-class negotiation with neoliberalism.

NOTES

1. Sjöholm (2016: 3) notes that "FDI as a share of GDP in Indonesia increased from 7 percent in 1990 to 15 percent in 2000 and almost 30 percent in 2014."

2. The Labor Law Reform promulgated a set of three laws, namely: Law No. 21 Year 2000 on Labor Unions, Law No. 13 Year 2003 on Manpower, and Law No. 2 Year 2004 on Industrial Dispute Settlement. See Tjandra 2009, 2016 and Mizuno 2020.

3. While cases of police or military intervention in labor disputes still exist today, they don't happen very often compared to that during the New Order regime.

Chapter 3

Articles of Contention

Since 2000, the International Labour Organisation (ILO) has identified the elimination of sexual harassment and violence as a "priority gender issue in social protection."[1] It acknowledges the iceberg phenomenon of women experiencing various forms of sexual harassment in the workplace. In Thailand, although many women workers admit that they experience sexual harassment at work, they rarely complain because they know that any legal protections are not actually implemented, and hence they "fight back only in case of the worst form of harassment, such as sexual assault."[2] In Sri Lanka, Hancock notes that although many women workers report having experienced or witnessed sexual harassment in the workplace, "(n)one were prepared to take legal action."[3] Even when women workers do report sexual harassment, it does not ensure their safety. Based on her survey among female workers in the hotel industry in South Korea, Cho notes that women workers "faced the retaliation and criticism that seemed to follow their refusal to be sexually available."[4] Numerous studies indicate that women workers have no incentive to speak out and little to no protection if they do. This silencing of women workers shows how pervasive and dominant patriarchal values are in shaping society and how women workers are expected to submit themselves to these values. When they speak out against sexual harassment, they break not only social chains but also social norms. As such, many women workers are not willing to take the risk of speaking out.

Indonesian women workers also face sexual harassment in the workplace, and like their sisters elsewhere,[5] many are reluctant to report an incident or speak out when they experience or witness harassment themselves. Scholars have studied this situation to unpack the social and cultural reasons behind it. While the diversity of cultural values in Indonesia may provide a background to further investigate these reasons, many women workers do report that they feel uncomfortable (in some cases, humiliated) by unwanted attention and/ or (sexual) advances of their male supervisors and employers.[6] Especially if they stay in the workers' dormitory (provided by the company), they are constantly monitored by their supervisors. The low rate of Indonesian women reporting sexual harassment in the workplace could be also because women see they neither have the access to nor the support of organizations that defend their interests. Women workers do not report harassment even to their union, because the unions are dominated by men, and they suspect that if they do report an incident, they will not get the help they need.

Based on that reason alone, we understand that the politics of *malu* has its claws deep in the minds of women (workers). It obliges women to keep their experiences private, including those of sexual harassment. It even suggests that it is women who "ask" men to harass in the first place by being unable or refusing to follow their gender roles in society. In that situation, women are forced to accept sexual harassment as "normal" or a consequence of their "mistake," and something that should not be made an issue of. The politics of *malu* imposes a culture of silence in which it is often taken for granted that women (workers) will not report or speak out. This in turn creates a culture of impunity for the perpetrators, reinforcing existing power dynamics. Women workers may see sexualized attention from their supervisors as "a compliment" because the politics of *malu* advises them to do so; they are following expectations to be a woman beautiful enough to attract the attention of a man, but who remains submissive. Male-dominated unions reflect the broader culture that advises them to act within the politics of *malu* to accept harassment either as a compliment or as a shame, but either way not to say anything about it to anyone, even other women. This dominant culture is compounded by women workers' vulnerable position in the current flexible labor market that is created by neoliberal economic policies. Hence, the precarious position of women workers in society and in the labor market makes it difficult for them to speak out when they experience or witness sexual harassment.

It is against this dominant culture that a number of union activists and women workers in Jakarta are tackling the issue of sexual harassment in the workplace, setting themselves free from the politics of *malu* to speak out. They are not content with their working situation. More importantly, they refuse to stay silent in the face of employers' failure to take preventive measures in the workplace, as required by the government, to guarantee their safety. Instead, they write down their experiences as a protest and work together to end sexual harassment.

This chapter discusses how women workers write down their stories of sexual harassment as part of their efforts to end it. It is structured around the activities of the Federation of Workers across Factories (Federasi Buruh Lintas Pabrik, FBLP),[7] a workers' group that organizes women workers in the Kawasan Berikat Nusantara (Nusantara Bonded Zone), the only Export Processing Zone in Jakarta.[8] FBLP claims approximately 5,000 members from eight factory-level unions in the zone.[9] It has six full-time staff (five female and one male) to coordinate its activities, which include preparing a union publication in which women workers write their stories.

This chapter begins with an overview of post-1998 Indonesia, which is characterized by workers' newfound freedom of expression and freedom to organize. Unlike during the New Order period, since 1998, workers have been free to join any union they wish, and unions develop publications to organize members. FBLP's publication, *Suara Buruh* (Workers' Voices), includes articles written by women workers on conditions in the zone, labor disputes, and, also, cases of sexual harassment—a topic that is completely absent in most other union publications. This chapter suggests that the publication provides women workers an important, if not the only, venue to share experiences, alert other women workers to sexual harassment, and encourage each other to speak out against it.

By writing about sexual harassment, women break the culture of silence around it. As the issue has gained attention, the government, with the assistance of the ILO, issued a circular with guidelines on the prevention of sexual harassment in the workplace. The guidelines, however, have had little impact on conditions for women in the zone. It is in this context that FBLP developed a "framing strategy"[10] to extend their activity beyond print media to spread their message and achieve definitive actions to ensure a safe workplace.

FREEDOM TO ORGANIZE, FREEDOM TO EXPRESS

During the New Order, union publications were restricted to reflect the ideological thrust of the regime, which emphasized "industrial harmony." The regime established and sponsored its own version of a union publication—the monthly *Media Pekerja* (Workers' Media).[11] The monthly was the mouthpiece of the regime's policy of "Pancasila industrial relations," in which workers were controlled and confined within the regime's narrative of economic development. Workers could not exercise their rights to seek, receive, or impart information on social and political issues, especially on matters that were important to them as workers. They also could not exercise their right to speak out or express their opinions or aspirations on the factory floor, in the community, or at the national level. Throughout the 1980s, the political climate did not allow workers to express their grievances; it was further darkened by the tight control of the regime on workers' organization. Thus, the labor movement, just like other social movements of the time, had no freedom of expression.

Despite the tight controls on labor, by the early 1990s, a number of urban NGOs (and middle-class activists) had established alternative media, such as pamphlets, flyers, and zines that questioned the regime's economic policies, including on labor. It was part of their efforts to raise workers' political consciousness. Also, it was during 1990–1995 that labor unrest mounted in many industrial cities in Java and Sumatra (see chapter 2). In order to avoid regime censorship and control, these media were published underground and reproduced via photocopier for distribution. Anonymity was required, and most writings in the publications did not bear an author's name, including reports or articles written by workers.[12] Many of these alternative publications did not last long, in part due to the need to avoid being identified by the regime. Problems of budget constraints, limited circulation, and the scarcity of contributions from workers also made it difficult to survive for any length of time.[13]

Since *Reformasi* in 1998, workers have been guaranteed the right to organize, and they have established a variety of organizations. Unions now actively perform a wide range of activities to reclaim rights and interests once suppressed under the New Order regime. At the same time, as part of the democratization of the nation, media freedom is acknowledged and there is no longer censorship by the state.[14] After decades of silence, workers are now free to write and develop their own media. It is within this context that a number of unions (factory-level unions and national federations as well) have established a media arm as part of their structure. The task of this arm is to publish papers (newsletters, magazines, newspapers, and so on) to reach out to union members, accommodate their voices, and share information that is important to them as workers. Media freedom provides opportunities for labor to express their concerns and represent their movement in public. Thus, union papers are seen as an important tool for the movement's organizing efforts.[15]

Indeed, union papers are important mainly for internal communication and for reaching out to members and potential members. Content wise, as expected, they report news from labor's perspective. Most of the columns are about contemporary labor issues, and they report labor-related news that often goes unreported in commercial media. Through informative narratives, they bring readers' attention to the workers' common struggle for economic justice, devoting their pages to describe (and discuss) workers' plight in the context of globalization, which is characterized by job insecurity and the spread of contingent work. Union papers not only inform their readers about labor-related news, they also offer a space for workers to debate social, political, and economic issues that affect them. They convey analogous messages of class consciousness and unionism. This fact alone is not unexpected, as unions will inherently promote their institutional raison d'être and encourage workers to join. In that way, union papers offer direct access to examine the development of the collective consciousness of the working class and its rhetorics.

Unlike during the New Order period, union activists and workers alike now do not need to hide; they write down their own names as authors in union papers. It is relatively safe for workers to express their concerns without fear of state censorship or punishment.[16] While news and articles written by activists or union leaders are dominant, rank-and-file members are also encouraged to write for union papers. Articles by workers are important to show credibility of the paper to readers, that it is written by "one of us." Union papers provide rank-and-file members the chance to contribute their thoughts and ideas on various issues, within the union structure. Male authors are dominant in many union papers, and, as we will discuss below, female workers rarely have a space or column of their own.[17]

All union papers rely on the cheap printing services that have bloomed since 1998 in many cities in Java. The printing cost depends on the number of copies, the type of paper, and the number of colors used on one page. Union papers usually have three to four colors on the front page (as a strategy to attract readers), but black and white inner pages. Union papers are published randomly, often depending on the union's financial capacities. Some are intended as monthlies but are quite often published bimonthly or quarterly.

While unions have been developing their organizational muscle through print media, major changes have been unfolding in the media landscape. The liberalization of the media industry has brought significant changes to the production and distribution of information. The media industry is facing a new set of challenges that forces players to prioritize business objectives. Major media players have intensified the restructuring of their respective businesses to gain control of a larger market share of information, especially with the widespread use of digital and social media. In this context, despite press freedom, alternative media finds it difficult to operate and function as a source of information for marginalized groups. Union papers have limited capacities to deliver daily news to workers and they cannot compete with major media players to inform the public about the labor movement and its activities.

Union activists point out that mainstream commercial media (both newspaper outlets and TV stations) tend to echo and share the opinions of business groups opposed to collective actions by workers—especially union-organized rallies, demonstrations, and strikes.[18] In defending their own economic and political interests, major media groups rarely offer a sympathetic perspective of workers' growing activism. Thus, labor does not receive favorable coverage in most major media. Mainstream media tends to portray the labor movement as an obstacle to the objectives of building the post-authoritarian country through economic development. Although this situation is not unique to Indonesia,[19] the Indonesian labor movement is still developing its institutional capacities under the newly gained freedom to organize. It has to face a media environment that is hostile to its efforts to promote workers' collective demands and more importantly, to gain public support for its struggle. Unions therefore find it difficult to navigate and focus their efforts, not only to develop their own media, but also to penetrate mainstream commercial media to reach the wider public.

Among the many union papers is *Suara Buruh*, a four-page newsletter published by FBLP. It has a circulation of 1,000 copies per issue, which is relatively small compared to other print media published by national-level union federations.[20] It is published irregularly—sometimes monthly and sometimes bimonthly—indicating that FBLP faces both the challenges of print media in the time of digital technology and the challenges of union publications, which include budget constraints, manpower capacity, and limited circulation.

It is important to note that FBLP is organizing workers in the Kawasan Berikat Nusantara (Nusantara Bonded Zone), the only export-processing zone in Jakarta, which has a restrictive environment for unions to operate. Textile and garment companies are dominant in the zone, and, like in any other export processing zone in the region, they prefer to hire young women workers as a global capital strategy of "exploiting women's weak labor market leverage in order to lower labor costs and increase attachment."[21] A number of union activists have been penetrating into the zone to organize workers, with varying results.[22] Although workers are guaranteed the freedom of association, many in the zone are not union members. This is partly due to the fact that many workers are employed on short-term contracts. Hence, workers prioritize their immediate need to secure a job (regardless of the working conditions). It is in this environment that FBLP activists are organizing workers in the zone through regular meetings to improve working conditions and campaigning for women workers' rights.[23]

Similar to the *Dabindu* periodicals produced by garment workers in Sri Lanka's free trade zone,[24] *Suara Buruh* is the work of a collective. It has a regular editorial column, written by Dian Septi Trisnanti, which deals with current social-political issues and the FBLP's position on such issues. It also has a regular column on contemporary women's issues written by a staff member of Perempuan Mahardhika, a radical women's group based in Jakarta.

More importantly, *Suara Buruh* has a special column on specific factory-level issues, which is written by women workers who are members of the FBLP. Such a column is unknown in other union papers, whose articles are primarily written by union leaders and/or press staff (all of whom are usually males), and which generally treat workers as (passive) readers only. Other union papers often do not see women workers as their main audience and dedicate little space for women as readers or for them to contribute their writings, despite the fact that many of these unions have more female members.[25] When women workers do contribute to union papers, they are most often assigned to write on topics that are considered "women's issues and reflect mainstream gender roles."[26] They are not expected to write an analysis of national politics or propose future directions for the labor movement.

Suara Buruh neither assigns workers to write "women's issues" nor limits women's voices in the public. In her writing, Wa Ampi, leader of the factory-level union of P.T. Makalot Industrial, a Taiwanese-owned clothing company in the zone, notes her story of personal transformation after joining the FBLP:

> I am convinced that change is coming. It is not coming from elsewhere. It comes from myself as I become aware. My friend and I are conscientized as we join in the FBLP and become active in it. . . . I learn about solidarity and collective action. I learn to think, to have opinions, to debate and deliver speeches, and to fight injustice. Also, as a woman, I learn about the struggle of women liberation.[27]

Her writing illustrates the shared experience of many women workers of being "conscientized" (*kesadaran*) during organizing activities. Women workers during the New Order period might have had similar experiences (as discussed in chapter 1), but it is during the post-*Reformasi* era, with its freedom to organize and freedom to express, that women workers like Wa Ampi have the courage to write their own names in public, and especially to write for fellow women workers to read. Wa Ampi exemplifies women workers of the post-*Reformasi* period who have higher confidence than their predecessors to voice their concerns, as their political rights are legally guaranteed. *Suara Buruh* gives them the space to write. Thus, unlike other union papers that limit the concerns, interests, and expectations of women workers as readers and as writers, *Suara Buruh* brings women workers to the fore and is proud to promote women workers' voices.

As noted above, for many unions, the issue of sexual harassment is not considered a union issue, but a personal one. Even when it is discussed in union meetings, it never comes to print. Also, as union papers are meant as a tool to organize, the issue of sexual harassment is seen by male unionists and leaders as irrelevant (or worse, an obstacle) to organizing. Hence, many union (male) editors do not see the importance of discussing it or giving the issue print space. In contrast, FBLP recognizes that the issue of sexual harassment is important for organizing women workers, especially in the zone. As such, *Suara Buruh* has become the venue for women workers to write about sexual harassment in the workplace.[28]

ARTICULATING THE WRONG AND ITS CHALLENGES

As part of its institutional objective to empower women workers, FBLP focuses on sexual harassment in the workplace and domestic violence in general.[29] Both issues were previously addressed by the now-defunct Women's Group for Workers' Justice (Koalisi Perempuan untuk Keadilan Buruh, KPKB), a Jakarta-based coalition of NGOs working on gender issues and worker advocacy. As acknowledged by FBLP activists, raising the issue of sexual harassment in the workplace has its own challenges, especially when many women workers do not know where to go to report such cases. Many union organizers also do not have adequate knowledge and experience to handle the issue, and there is little effort from employers to prevent it from taking place.

Added to the specific context of Indonesia, feminist activists around the world note that sexual harassment occurs within a culture of silence. Women workers are culturally incentivized to not raise the issue at all. As such, many victims do not dare to speak about or report what happened because they are ashamed of it and afraid that they will lose their jobs if they complain. The perpetrators are either male supervisors, employers, or fellow (male) workers, and due to their status and/or power in the factory, can wield an upper hand against the victims.

Sexual harassment in the workplace is not an isolated issue. It is directly linked to the poor working conditions in the KBN zone, where factory owners and employers are in a strong position of power due to the expendable nature of workers' labor. Zone jobs on the whole have worse working conditions than jobs outside the zone, and management of the KBN zone applies only minimum efforts to improve those conditions. Osterreich's study confirms that "labor-intensive export oriented-firms [in Indonesia] are less likely to provide what is necessary for decent work,"[30] and the conditions in the KBN zone bear this out. The obstacles to unionizing make it more difficult for workers to make any complaint at work without fear of losing their job. Workers are constantly reminded of their vulnerable position vis-à-vis employers through various forms of violence they encounter in the zone.[31] In a labor dispute in 2005, thugs affiliated with Betawi Brotherhood Forum (Forum Betawi Rempug, FBR), a Jakarta-based paramilitary group, physically attacked striking workers.[32] In recent years, competing violent groups have tried to penetrate the zone.[33] The presence of organized thugs in the zone shows how employers, in their quest to control workers, have taken unlawful steps rather than utilize the existing formal dispute settlement system that was introduced in 2005.[34] Finally, the patriarchal nature of the factory *and* the union add further challenges for women to protect themselves from harassment. Thus, for women workers, working in the zone is full of violence.

It is in this context that Sri, a female worker in the KBN Marunda site, writes her opinion on how women workers see sexual harassment in the zone:

> right now, it is obvious that workers at the KBN Cakung and Marunda sites have experienced suppression, intimidation, sexual harassment, unpaid overtime, and other kinds of violence in the factory. It is not the time to stay silent. . . . As workers, we must get involved in each and every fight. Fight together, do not just be a free-riding bystander.[35]

Sri lists sexual harassment among other forms of violence that women workers endure; she emphasizes it is no less important than intimidation (of the thugs) or unpaid overtime as many male unionists often assume. Sri speaks on behalf of all women workers in the zone who have experienced and/or witnessed sexual harassment and know that their experience is as harrowing as "suppression, intimidation" and as unfair as "unpaid overtime." She calls on them to gather their courage and "fight together." Her call underlines that many women do not have the courage, do not act together, and instead become "free-riding bystanders," waiting for someone as courageous as Sri to stand up (and bear the consequences of breaking the chains of *malu*).

It is important to note that lesbian and transgender workers also experience sexual harassment in the factory.[36] They are not immune from similar unpleasant treatment, unwanted attention, and harassment that heterosexual female workers experience in the factory.[37] In an engaging reportage, Aleksic notes the testimony of Tumini (pseudonym), a lesbian unionist in the KBN and active in the FBLP, who notes that under the patriarchy, male supervisors and employers treat female workers in the factory, regardless of their sexual orientations, as sexual objects, and engage in predatory behavior.[38] Male supervisors and employers do not exempt lesbian and transgender workers from such treatment. In fact, they may see a lesbian/transgender worker as a challenge to their manhood and think they have the right to "cure" her.

Any case of sexual harassment is a power play where one person (often a male with more power) tries to dominate another by embarrassing or degrading her. In the case of a lesbian worker, perpetrators stigmatize her as different, and her private life or sexual orientation is considered a problem in the workplace. Thus, they do not see what they do as something unpleasant (and legally, unacceptable), but as a justified act to correct or normalize the woman's sexuality.

In any case, lesbian and transgender workers, like other workers, "have to swallow" various harassments they experience in the factory due to their position as precariat laborers simply to avoid unemployment. Like other workers, they do not have basic protections against sexual harassment, and when it happens, they have to fend it off themselves and are left to deal with

the emotional impacts on their own. Lesbian and transgender workers, however, may face more challenges, especially when the general society does not
accept their sexual orientation, but instead sees it as a reason to discriminate
and refuses to assist them when they are in need.

Although many women workers are acutely aware of the issue of sexual
harassment and may have experienced unwanted sexual attention themselves, they are in no position to stand up and take a firm stance in the factory. Conditions at P.T. Asian Collection Garment, a Korean garment factory
operating in the zone, provide a good example.[39] Approximately 90 percent
of the factory's 300 workers are female. Workers are paid below the minimum wage,[40] and incidents of sexual harassment are rampant. Despite this,
women are forced to prioritize securing their employment first overreporting
sexual harassment. Atlyserita, a female unionist working in the company,
writes:

> In fact, workers do know that the company forges [workers'] information [to
> avoid tax], there are cases of underpayment, long overtime, unfair treatment,
> and sexual harassment of female workers, but they keep silent as they are afraid
> their employment will be terminated if they start to speak out and question their
> supervisors, group leaders, and especially, the human resources manager.[41]

As Atylserita notes, even when workers experience or know of sexual harassment in the workplace, they are afraid to protest or speak. They are afraid that
they will lose their job if they speak out and they are uncertain about finding
another one. They need to keep their job, despite the poor working conditions
and cases of sexual harassment against them. Her note shows there are two
different yet related issues. First, workers see the labor market is tight, that
younger (women) workers are waiting to take their jobs at lower wages or
without complaining about working conditions. Second, for women workers,
the politics of *malu* keeps them from speaking out and thinking they could
get another job if they leave.

Atylserita does not accept this situation and tries to change it. She describes
her experience of organizing fellow workers on the factory floor:

> We are aware that this is part of our struggle, and it won't be as easy as falling
> off a log, we have to fight for it. Every Sunday we gather and organize, meeting
> to discuss our strategies. We do realize that we have to organize to realize our
> rights.[42]

Workers (males and females) in the factory finally came together to form a
union. They demanded a meeting with the management to discuss their working conditions, including incidents of sexual harassment.

A meeting was held on May 29, 2013, but the management refused to realize the union's demands to improve working conditions in the factory. Knowing that workers now were organized, the management tried to circumvent any negotiation with the union and instead called for the local office of the Department of Manpower and Transmigration to intervene. Workers saw the management's action as a refusal to engage in fair negotiation to address their concerns. They therefore called for a three-day strike, starting on July 28, 2013. On the last day of the strike, the management finally agreed to the union's demands. One of these demands was protection for women workers against sexual harassment; it was the first time a union in the zone made a specific demand related to protection for women workers. Workers returned to work with the hope that conditions would be improved. In the following days, however, the management refused to honor the agreement; none of the workers' demands was realized. Instead, it fired unionists and those suspected of organizing the strike. The union was dissolved, and its struggle to improve working conditions ended.

This case illustrates the consequences of articulating the wrong of sexual harassment in the workplace. Working women of the post-*Reformasi* may have better access to education and more secure political rights than their predecessors of the New Order period, but they live under a globalized labor market that puts them in vulnerable and precarious positions both economically and physically. Under the current flexible labor market, workers are pressured to accept any job available, even if it is short term or temporary. Knowing that so many others are waiting to fill their place, workers are forced to accept poor conditions and not complain about sexual harassment in the factory. Women (or men) who do have the courage to speak out against sexual harassment may lose their jobs, and so they turn a blind eye for the sake of their livelihood. As such, the fight against sexual harassment in the workplace is inseparable from the struggle to improve general working conditions and to restructure the labor market so that workers can decide and have options to find better jobs.

THE LIMITS OF THE GOVERNMENT'S CIRCULAR ON SEXUAL HARASSMENT

On April 15, 2011, the Minister of Manpower and Transmigration, Mr. Muhaimin Iskandar, issued a government circular with guidelines on sexual harassment prevention in the workplace. The circular was addressed to all governors and mayors throughout Indonesia. It states that "issues of discrimination and sexual harassment at the workplace are better prevented to take place."

The circular was drafted with the assistance of the ILO's Jakarta office, under the "Decent Work for All" program.[43] Six years earlier (in 2005), the Ministry of Manpower and Transmigration had issued the Equal Employment Opportunity Guidelines for the private sector. The ministry established an intergovernmental agency taskforce under the program to review and monitor the implementation of the guidelines and produce recommendations for their improved implementation, in particular concerning sexual harassment.

Several consultation sessions were organized with the employer association (APINDO) and representatives of major labor unions (KSPSI, KSPI, and FSBSI) to discuss the issue of sexual harassment in the workplace as input to a proposed "Code of Practice." Subsequently, a national one-day seminar was held on November 23, 2010, in Jakarta as part of the final phase of the program to bring the proposal to the government for implementation. The seminar was attended by around 150 representatives from labor unions, the APINDO, and provincial governments. The guidelines were adopted as a result of the seminar, and they were issued by the Minister of Manpower and Transmigration as part of the circular.

The guidelines provide a working definition of sexual harassment and its forms (physical, verbal, gestural, written or graphic, and psychological/emotional), requirements for preventing sexual harassment, and detailed mechanisms to respond to cases of sexual harassment. One of the requirements to prevent sexual harassment is to include sanctioning and disciplinary action as part of either company policy or a collective labor agreement, or both. The guidelines entrust the monitoring and evaluation of all sexual harassment complaint mechanisms into the hands of the company.

Although the 2011 circular and the adopted guidelines have succeeded in raising the attention of all parties (especially of employers and government offices) to this important issue, several aspects of the guidelines indicate that they will have little impact on the lives of female workers. First, the circular is not legally binding. No matter how detailed and nicely formulated its contents are, it has no power to force employers, for example, to provide the necessary infrastructure to prevent sexual harassment in the workplace; its contents are recommendations only.[44] The very fact that the Ministry issued the guidelines in the form of a circular also demonstrates that sexual harassment in the workplace is considered a low priority; a circular is not part of the hierarchy of legislation in Indonesia's legal system.

Second, the circular considers sexual harassment a crime only if there is a formal complaint or report from the victim. It requires victims to file a formal complaint of the actual case to the police to process, investigate, and detain the (alleged) perpetrator. In this way, it limits the victim from dealing with the incident or seeking recourse through other venues or channels. In one case, a number of women workers from the same factory complained that before leaving work they were all ordered to line up for body searches conducted by a male supervisor. Despite lodging a protest letter, the manager of the factory took no action, and the women had no further channel to resolve the issue.[45]

As such, the circular only accomplishes bringing short-term attention, not awareness or redress, to the issue of sexual harassment in the workplace. This is borne out by the fact that to date, not a single case of sexual harassment in the workplace has gone to either a criminal or a civil court in Indonesia. Prevention of sexual harassment also rarely becomes an issue to discuss, negotiate, or regulate in the collective labor agreements in Indonesia.[46] Female unionists are aware of these problems and they know the limits of the government circular for their campaign activities on inclusive protection against sexual harassment at the workplace.

It is not a surprise that many female workers put little faith in formal "procedures" to deal with an incident of sexual harassment. Rather, they learn from the results of earlier cases in which women followed the procedure. One example is the case of J (pseudonym), a factory worker in the Terboyo Industrial Zone in Semarang (Central Java), who reported the abuse she experienced during 2014–2015 to the police in June 2016.[47] She reported how her supervisor (*mandor*) regularly sexually harassed her at the factory with the help of five male coworkers, who took turns to shield and guard the area where the harassment usually took place. The case was referred to the Women and Children Protection Unit of the Semarang city police office to investigate. Later, the Unit decided that "there is not enough evidence" to support the case, and the investigation was dropped. This case illustrates the frustrating situation for women who do take the courageous step to report incidents of harassment only to face the limits of the legal system and see their case dissolve without consideration of their voice. When women follow the procedure and make a police report, they are constantly reminded of the "shame" they have to bear in the public and in the end, are often forced to accept out-of-court settlements (*musyawarah kekeluargaan*). In this "procedure," women do not have the final word.[48]

The Ministry's circular might have been designed with good intentions to protect women workers and ensure their safety in the workplace. However, its limitations and the "settlement" of previous cases of sexual harassment make women question the very idea of "protection" that it claims to offer. Women are concerned that, instead of protecting victims, the guidelines deter women from speaking out, and impede solutions that are in the best interest of the victims.

As we will see below, FBLP activists are taking a different route to voice their concerns on this issue. They know the limits of the circular and do not have much expectation that it will change the real condition of women workers in the factory. Nonetheless, they see the circular as a tool to advance their organizing efforts. As part of their "framing strategy," they refer to the circular in their rhetoric to make their demands sound "legitimate" (as based on the guidelines) and to garner support from local government officials (in reminding them of their duties to follow the guidelines).

BEYOND PRINT MEDIA: VISUAL CAMPAIGN

Through their organizing efforts, FBLP activists have succeeded in bringing public attention to the issue of sexual harassment in the workplace. By raising it in their print publication, they refuse to sit in silence and wait for assistance from a third party. *Suara Buruh*, however, has limited circulation. It is a means of internal communication among its members and is available only within the zone; it therefore does not reach the broader public. Recognizing this limitation, FBLP activists are trying to improve their advocacy and campaign efforts.

Activists have achieved two important changes. First, they persuaded the management of the zone to install anti-sexual harassment banners and signboards at several locations inside the zone.[49] They referred to the 2011 circular as part of their rhetoric to demand and justify the installation and organized an official event on November 25, 2016, the UN's International Day for the Elimination of Violence against Women, as an unveiling of the installation.[50] By framing the event as such, they succeeded in pushing the zone management to comply with their demand.[51] The event was attended by officials from the Minister of Manpower and Transmigration, representatives from the employer association, and activists from women NGOs.[52] Hence, it was well reported in some major newspapers.

They have also established links with national women's NGOs, such as the Women's Legal Aid (LBH APIK) and the Coalition of Indonesian Women (Koalisi Perempuan Indonesia, KPI), that have worked to promote national legislation on domestic violence and sexual harassment.[53] They see their advocacy for a safe workplace as part of the women's movement in general. In fact, their voices provide a solid grounding for narrating women's experiences in dealing with violence. In their leaflets, they drew up a list of "violences" as experienced by female workers at the workplace. These are sexual harassment, physical violence, verbal violence, and maternity rights infringements.[54]

Subsequently, as a follow-up to the event, since January 9, 2017, activists have established the "Posko Pembelaan Buruh Perempuan" (Help desk to defend Women Workers) inside the zone. The Posko occupies half of a security station at the rear entrance of the zone. It is attended by FBLP activists (two persons, in rotation) from Monday to Friday, usually starting at around

4:00 p.m. to 6:00 p.m., as this is when they can easily meet workers who are leaving the zone after finishing their work shift.[55] The Posko aims to bring the issue of sexual harassment closer to women workers in the zone so they can speak out against it without being afraid of the associated social stigma.[56] The Posko has become a meeting point for women workers in the zone to share news and coordinate activities among themselves.

The banners, signboards, and the Posko work as a campaign to constantly remind everyone in the zone of the issue of sexual harassment at the workplace, and taken together, they have changed the zone's visual landscape. As women working in the zone easily notice the banners and pass the Posko on their way in and out of the zone, they are made aware of their rights and know where to go when they experience or witness harassment.

Second, FBLP activists made a twenty-two-minute documentary film, "Angka Jadi Suara" ("The Day The Voices Raised"), to further raise awareness of the issue of sexual harassment in the workplace.[57] The film records the situation inside the zone and the issues that women workers are facing there.[58] It includes scenes of various testimonies by women workers about their actual working conditions in the factory, a candid scene of a male parking-lot attendant (in the zone) pinching female workers at the factory gate on their way out, and a scene of the (male) secretary of the zone management blaming the (female) victims when activists had a meeting with him to raise the issue of sexual harassment in the factory.

The film was released in late April 2017. It has been screened at a number of art houses across Java, and was also shown at the Komnas Perempuan (National Commission on Violence Against Women) in Jakarta on June 8, 2017, as part of a broader national campaign on the issue of sexual harassment against women.[59] Reviews of the film in major national newspapers have been positive.[60] More importantly, the film was also being screened in labor union offices and shelters where workers gather regularly.[61]

The film serves two different yet related purposes, for the labor movement and for the public. For the labor movement, the film gives women workers as victims of sexual harassment a voice about how they have experienced sexual harassment at the workplace, dealt with it, and found support in the FBLP. It also gives women workers as an audience a reflection that they are not alone; that many other women workers have similar experiences at the workplace. Thus, the film works as a visual catharsis for women workers to work together against sexual harassment at the workplace, especially for those in the zone.

For the public, the film has gathered interest in the issue of sexual harassment in the zone, because it presents a different angle of labor issues than the one commonly reported in the media. As discussed earlier, the media often projects an imbalanced view of the labor movement and its activities, even when workers are simply demanding the implementation of their legal rights. The film invites the public to acknowledge that workers are facing grave problems at the workplace, including sexual harassment, and that they have tried various ways to settle those problems before organizing a protest, strike, or mass rally that may disrupt the public. It allows the public to understand the core issues beneath the workers' public protests or rallies, including that many women workers are actually afraid to speak out against sexual harassment and are unable to find support when they need it. Thus, the film works as a visual campaign to highlight a labor issue that is often left unreported in the national newspapers, and solicits the public to support women workers who are trying to change their situation. In doing so, not only has it brought public attention to the issue of sexual harassment in the workplace, but it has also emphasized that such harassment is a public issue, not a personal problem.

The film also allows its middle-class audiences (in particular, middle-class women) to relate to the similar situation of being unable to speak up against sexual harassment that they too have experienced. The film demonstrates how working-class women are enabling themselves to speak out, despite the pressing social and economic constraints and fewer resources that they have compared to middle-class women. While working-class and middle-class women may share similar points of reference in terms of their gender roles as women, working women's class identity sets them apart to speak out against sexual harassment in the workplace. They have opened the floodgates of public awareness and formal complaints against sexual harassment, unintentionally enabling middle-class women to take advantage of the moment to free-ride on the movement to claim protection for their individual selves.

ORGANIZING IN THE ZONE AND BEYOND

In the context of post-1998 *Reformasi* guarantees of freedom of expression that have allowed the labor movement to develop its print media, the FBLP produces *Suara Buruh*, a publication in which women workers write about issues important to them. Although union papers in general provide essential readings that articulate the conditions of the working class, many give no attention to the issue of sexual harassment in the workplace. Union papers as a forum for the working-class seem to ignore its female members. At the same time, many women workers who are harassed refuse to speak out or come forward in the public, as they fear retaliation and the loss of privacy. This multilayered silence creates a hegemonic environment in which women come to see sexual harassment as something they must endure or try to ignore. As FBLP has come to recognize the complexities of gendered labor, it focuses on women's issues and centers its activities on supporting women workers to organize. In this context, *Suara Buruh* is a critical venue for women workers to share experiences, notify women workers of their rights, and offer advice on what women can and should do at their particular workplace when they are harassed or witness harassment. It gives women workers, unconstrained by the politics of *malu*, the confidence to speak out against sexual harassment at the workplace. They write down and share their stories of sexual harassment. In their articles, they reject becoming powerless victims and instead, claim their rights to a safe workplace. Thus, *Suara Buruh* is a testament of women workers' hopes for gender equality more broadly and their common aspiration to end sexual harassment in particular.

Despite various limitations, FBLP activists are actively seeking new strategies to organize and defend their members' interests. By framing their demands in the language of the government's circular on sexual harassment prevention, they push for change in the zone. Beyond print media, they have established a help desk for women workers to report incidents of sexual harassment cases and have made a documentary film to engage with the general public. These activities illustrate how FBLP both addresses the actual needs of women workers in the zone while strategically raising awareness about sexual harassment in the workplace and workers' rights more generally among employers, the government, and the broader public. By doing this, they also try to change the sociocultural perception that women are victims to be blamed and that women's experience of sexual harassment is a shame to women's integrity. By working together for public awareness, women workers are securing their right to self-autonomy over their own bodies.

The main challenge of awareness within the labor movement itself, however, remains. As women workers are not fairly represented within the union structure, their concerns are often sidelined as women's issues and not considered union issues. Women's common concerns about sexual harassment at the workplace are often ignored or not properly addressed. Sexual harassment between coworkers raises even more challenges. Yet union support to end sexual harassment in the workplace is essential not only to secure the rights of women workers, but also for the survival and expansion of the unions as well. In that way, unions need to change, too. In South Korea, for example, where male unionists, similar to Indonesia, dominate the leadership, the Korean Confederation of Trade Unions (KCTU) has "enacted its own Code to Prevent Sexual Harassment."[62] We are yet to see the long-term result of this initiative, but it is a good step toward institutional safeguard in the union. The fight against harassment is one of the keys to bring women into the union, and increase their participation in union activities. At the same time, joining the union can give women a collective voice to prevent harassment in the workplace.

Studies from other countries suggest that unionized women gain advantages in the fight against sexual harassment, as they can use the union structure to report and seek redress when they experience or witness it, especially in cases where employers and/or supervisors harass workers.[63] Women can use the process of collective bargaining to secure protections against harassment, and use the union platform to network and raise awareness. In the KBN zone, however, the majority of women workers are not in unions. This is a serious challenge for FBLP (and other unions as well) to fully function and protect their members in the zone, especially in the face of the casualization of labor that has put women workers in a more vulnerable position. The fight for a safe workplace is far from over, but FBLP, despite its limited resources, has made a defining contribution to enable women workers in the zone to speak out against sexual harassment, and *Suara Buruh* has a share in it.

NOTES

1. See ILO (2000). The ILO's Committee of Experts, in its 1996 Special Survey on Convention No. 111, defines sexual harassment as

> any insult or inappropriate remark, joke, insinuation and comment on a person's dress, physique, age, family situation, etc.; a condescending or paternalistic attitude with sexual implications undermining dignity; any unwelcome invitation or request, implicit or explicit, whether or not accompanied by threats; any lascivious look or other gesture associated with sexuality; and any unnecessary physical contact such as touching, caresses, pinching or assault. (ILO 1996)

See also Haspels et al. (2001).
2. Ubon (2002: 30).
3. Hancock (2006: 38).
4. Cho (2002: 24).
5. In South Korea, as Barraclough (2012: 5) notes, "They [women workers] were condemned as unfeminine while also exposed to extreme sexual harassment in the factories and on the streets of industrializing Seoul."
6. Tjandraningsih (2000: 264).
7. FBLP was established in 2009 as Forum Buruh Lintas Pabrik (Forum of Workers across Factories), a network of small groups of workers in the zone. It was organized under the National Front for Indonesian Workers' Struggle (Front Nasional Perjuangan Buruh Indonesia, FNPBI), a minor labor federation with leftist tendencies. Although FNPBI is registered as a labor federation at the Ministry of Labor, its national leadership is held and dominated by young activists (many are former university students). Due to internal discord in the FNPBI, a number of FBLP activists consolidated its members to operate independently in 2010. In 2011, FBLP was formally registered as a labor federation at the local labor bureau of North Jakarta city (Dinas Jakarta Utara). In 2013, FBLP changed its name from "Forum" to "Federation."

8. The KBN is Indonesia's first industrial zone. There are three industrial sites within the KBN: Cakung (on the main road of Jalan Raya Cakung-Cilincing) with 176.7 ha; Marunda with 413.8 ha; and Tanjung Priok with eight ha. Although its area is smaller than the Marunda site, the Cakung site is the main industrial site for KBN's facilities and institutional support. In 2006, the Cakung site catered to 104 establishments (75 were operated by foreign investors). In 2009, it catered to 98 establishments (79 were operated by foreign investors, 65 percent of which were Korean companies). In 2016, it catered to 104 establishments (78 were operated by foreign investors).

9. Interview with Dian Septi Trisnanti, February 2, 2013.

10. See Snow (2004); Mills (2005).

11. Farid (1997: 130) describes the contents of the publication this way:

The paper focuses mainly on bureaucratic, organizational issues, Indonesian law and there is some coverage of international labour issues. The paper has not defended workers' interests, nor has it covered the vast numbers of strikes that have erupted since 1990. When the paper does report on strikes, it does so in a manner even more distant from workers than the commercial press.

12. Due to the anonymity, it is hard to confirm if a report or article was actually written by a worker and not a student activist or NGO worker.

13. For example, *Cerita Kami* (Our Stories), a bulletin published intermittently by the Jakarta-based activist group, Yayasan Maju Bersama, during 1990–1995; *Sumbu* (Suara Demokrasi Rakyat, The Voice of People's Democracy), a bulletin published by the Semarang branch of Solidaritas Mahasiswa Indonesia untuk Demokrasi (Indonesian Students' Solidarity for Democracy, SMID), the only leftist student organization during the New Order period, lasted for two years (1994–1995).

14. In terms of press freedom, Indonesia is one of the freest countries in Asia. Nonetheless, violence against journalists is still an issue.

15. It is important to note that there is a wide range of union publications published by various kinds of unions with different political outlooks and organizational affiliations. Union publications are far from monolithic.

16. Chapter 4 discusses the case of Salsabila as an exception to this rule.

17. For a comparison on labor journalism from a women's perspective, see Faue (2002) on the activism of Eva Valesh in the US labor movement.

18. See Mufakhir (2012).

19. In the United States, scholars have critically reviewed and noted that media coverage of labor issues is biased. See Bruno (2009).

20. For example, *Koran Perdjoeangan*, a monthly published by the Federation of Indonesian Metal Workers (Federasi Pekerja Metal Indonesia, FSPMI), has a circulation of 5,000 copies per issue.

21. McKay (2006: 176).

22. Although the National Union of Workers (Serikat Pekerja Nasional, SPN) claims dominance in the zone, many of its experienced organizers are losing their jobs or move out of the zone. Another union federation in the zone, the Federation of Indonesian Labor Unions (Federasi Serikat Buruh Indonesia, FBSI), also has been experiencing a decrease in membership since 2001.

23. With a one-year financial support (2012) from Cipta Media Bersama, a donor NGO under the Ford Foundation, FBLP's activists manage a community radio project, Radio Marsinah, that targets workers in the zone as its main audience.

24. On the *Dabindu* periodicals, Perera (2014: 85) notes, "Writings are contributed by named and sometimes unnamed garment factory workers and mediated by the interventions of volunteer editors."

25. For example, *Lentera*, a newsletter published by Serikat Pekerja Nasional (SPN) of P.T. Panarub Industry (an export-oriented footwear factory in Tangerang), whose members are mostly women, has "Women's Column" (Kolom Perempuan) as it assumes male workers as its main readers.

26. For example, *Koran Perdjoeangan*, in all of its first forty issues (from April 2007 to September 2011), has only three women workers who have contributed to its regular "Opini" (Opinion) column. They are: Endang Widuri (2008), Prihanani (2009), and Siti Komariyah (2011a, 2011b).

27. Ampi (2011: 5).

28. Some cases of sexual harassment in the workplace are reported in national and local newspapers, especially when it is considered "unusual" or "socially unacceptable." They are most often reported in a sensational manner to attract the public.

29. The issue of domestic violence among women workers is even more challenging to deal with, as it is often blanketly considered "family business." It is difficult for FBLP activists to approach some women workers who are rumored to experience abuse or violence at home. One former victim, Sri Jumiati (2015), spoke out about her experiences of despair and isolation at the workplace because her former husband was suspicious of her developing friendships or getting close to any male workers in the factory. After more than ten years of living in fear, she finally decided to gather her courage and end the cycle of abuse. It was only after that initial brave step she made that FBLP could intervene by providing basic counseling and temporary shelter for her.

30. Osterreich (2013: 290).

31. In a similar situation in Bangladesh, Rahman and Langford (2012: 98) note that "most of the union drives were ruthlessly suppressed by local musclemen employed by the factory owners or by the state police, both of whom often used physical torture against union activists."

32. Interview with Jumisih, February 2, 2013. For the politics of FBR as an ethnicized violent group, see Brown and Wilson (2007), Okamoto (2015), and Bakker (2016).

33. The yellow flags of Forum Betawi Rempug (FBR) and the red flags of Pemuda Pancasila (PP) can be easily spotted along the streets in Cakung. Both groups have laid territorial claims in the Cakung area. During 2013–2015, there were a number of conflicts between the two groups. On January 9, 2013, a group named Society Cares Industry (Masyarakat Peduli Industri, MPI) held a short rally at the back gate of KBN. The North Jakarta police (Polsek Jakarta Utara) reports that at around 3:00 p.m., thirty-five men under the leadership of some Ahmad Hisyam came together at the back gate of the KBN. Although they did not wear the FBR uniform, many of these men were also members of the local FBR (North Jakarta branch). On March 1,

2013, thugs attacked workers of P.T. Hansoll Indo, a Korean garment factory, who were on strike to demand minimum wage implementation.

34. For the formal system, see Tjandra (2016).

35. Sri (2012: 10–11).

36. Female homosexuality is prevalent among workers in the zone. There is no exact number on how many female workers identify themselves as lesbians, but Dian Septi gives a rough estimate of 15–20 percent of the all women workers in the zone (interview on February 9, 2013). The term *buchi* (from the English term "butch") is commonly used for female homosexuals. Although same-sex relationships are not unknown, they are not apparent in public. Discourse on lesbianism is generally still considered a controversial topic in Indonesian society, although a number of rights groups have tried to initiate it. For a general observation on working-class butch/femme community in Jakarta, see Wieringa (2007).

37. See Linggasari (2015) on testimony of Adon (pseudonym) of being verbally harassed by her boss in the factory.

38. Aleksic (2017: 25) notes Tumini's opinion:

Je pense que ce lien existe sur la question des violences sexuelles au travail, parce que le patriarcat opprime doublement les femmes et les lbt [lesbiennes, bisexuelles, transexuelles]. Le système patriarcal place les femmes en position d'infériorité par rapport aux hommes, donc les relations de femmes à femmes sont également criminalisées.

39. Interestingly, Kemp (2001: 6) notes that "(s)exual harassment was also a significant problem in the Korean factory, where 70 percent of the sample group reported unwanted sexual attention. Such complaints were slightly lower in the Indonesian factory (56 percent)."

40. In late 2012, the company submitted an application to the Jakarta city government for permission to postpone the implementation of the new minimum wage. Permission was, unfortunately, granted. The company was permitted to pay workers below the minimum wage for one year (from January 1 to December 31, 2013). See Keputusan Kepala Dinas Tenaga Kerja dan Transmigrasi DKI Jakarta (Decision of the Head of the Department of Manpower and Transmigration Office of Jakarta) No. 185 Year 2013 (dated January 9, 2013).

41. Atlyserita (2013: 3).

42. Atlyserita (2013: 4).

43. The follow-up "Better Work Indonesia" (BWI) program is funded by the government of Australia through the Australian Agency for International Development (AusAID), the United States Department of Labor, and the Netherlands' Ministry of Foreign Affairs. It started in 2011. For an analysis on how BWI as a transnational regulation reinforces the state's (domestic) labor regulations, see Amengual and Chirot (2016).

44. Nurus Mufidah (2019) argues how the circular as a recommendation fails to make any impact for women workers. Progressive women groups in Indonesia have been pushing the parliament to approve the bill on the Elimination of Sexual Violence (RUU Penghapusan Kekerasan Seksual), which has a stronger legal standing than the circular.

45. Interview with Jumisih, February 2, 2013.

46. One exception is the collective labor agreement between P.T. Parkland World Indonesia 2 with PSP SPN and PK FSBSI P.T. Parkland World Indonesia 2 (for the period of September 2016–September 2018). Article 26 of the Collective Labor Agreement (CLA) states that sexual harassment is a violation even when the perpetrator apologizes, and it is to be sanctioned with a warning letter, and if any security guard perpetrates sexual harassment, his employment will be terminated at once. P.T. Parkland Word Indonesia 2 is a garment/apparel manufacturing company located in Serang (West Java). There are two union federations in the factory: PK SPN (Serikat Pekerja Nasional) and PK FSBSI (Federasi Serikat Buruh Sejahtera Indonesia). The inclusion of sanctions against sexual harassment in the CLA is due to the code of conduct set by international buyers. I thank Indah Saptorini for this information.

47. This case was reported in a number of national newspapers, and many unionists read about it. See https://news.okezone.com/read/2016/06/13/512/1413233/se ring-dilecehkan-bos-buruh-pabrik-di-semarang-lapor-polisi#lastread; https://metrose marang.com/mau-enaknya-saja-pelaku-pelecehan-buruh-pabrik-ramai-ramai-minta -maaf-38145. I thank Hendro Agung Wibowo for this information.

48. On July 4, 2013, FBLP filed a formal complaint with the National Police after members of the police sexually harassed two union female members by squeezing their breasts (*meremas-remas payudara*) as an intimidation tactic to discourage their participation in a rally FBLP organized in the zone.

49. The banners say "P.T. Kawasan Berikat Nusantara (Persero) Bebas Pelecehan Seksual, berdasar Surat Edaran Menakertrans No. SE.03/Men/IV/2001" (The Nusantara Bonded Zone does not allow sexual harassment, as based on the Circular of the Minister of Manpower and Transmigration No. SE.03/Men/IV/2001).

50. The FBLP distributed leaflets to mark the event as important. The leaflet notes the various forms of workplace gender violence that they have uncovered in the zone: sexual violence (eleven cases), physical violence (three cases), verbal conduct (three cases), and maternity rights violations (four cases). It demands that the parliament discuss and enact the bill on the elimination of sexual violence against women (RUU Penghapusan Kekerasan Seksual).

51. The zone management might have seen the event as useful to promote an image of the zone as a safe and clean environment, especially to avoid further criticisms and to attract more investors.

52. The FBLP invited members of the Working Group on Women Workers (Pokja Buruh Perempuan), which includes a number of union federations and human rights NGOs, including the Jakarta Legal Aid Institute (LBH Jakarta) and also the Alliance of Independent Journalists (Aliansi Jurnalis Independen, AJI).

53. I thank the reviewer who reminded me about it.

54. In their list, "sexual harassments" include the requirement to show menstrual blood as proof for menstrual leave, unconsented kissing, breast touching, hugs, and other physical contacts, sexting and foced dating by male supervisors and employers; "physical violences" include hitting, kicking, slapping, pinching, tweaking one's ears, and kicking off one's desk/work station; "verbal violences" include intimidation, menace, and insults; "maternity rights infringements" include miscarriage, and the

absence of any facility at the workplace for pregnant workers/working mothers (such as a lactation room).

55. The Posko keeps a logbook of who comes to the Posko and what issues are discussed.

56. Interview with Jumisih, February 2, 2017.

57. It is not FBLP's first documentary about working conditions in the zone. In 2011 they made *Soal upah kami marah* ("We are angry about our wage"), a documentary about their strike and demonstration in the zone during November-December 2010 protesting the minimum wage set by the governor of Jakarta.

58. Interestingly, the film notes that "in two months of data collection [September and October 2015], 25 women workers reported their cases to the Committee [about their experiences of sexual harassment]." I have no other information to confirm the cases, or how, or if, they were settled.

59. The Komnas Perempuan sees the film as part of its agenda to push for the enactment of the bill on elimination of sexual violence against women (RUU Penghapusan Kekerasan Seksual).

60. For the newspaper review in English, see, for example, Szumer (2017).

61. Since December 23, 2017, the film has been available for free on Youtube. See: https://www.youtube.com/watch?v=wX54cYgqr1g

62. Moon and Broadbent (2008: 149).

63. In Turkey, as Britwum et al. (2012: 59) note, "the militant union KESK is seen as gender sensitive and has made gains for mothers in provision for the care of their babies and infants."

Chapter 4

Epistolary Protest

As noted earlier, the female labor force participation rate in Indonesia has been stagnant since the mid-1990s. Women and men do not participate equally in the labor market. Moreover, female workers are mainly concentrated in informal sectors of the economy, where working conditions are often not monitored by the government, and they have limited access to decent employment (or fair wages). When they do find paid employment in the formal sector, their choices of work are limited by neoliberal conditions and relatively constrained by cultural norms. Female participation in the industrial sector remains low. Nonetheless, one study notes that the participation of younger women from urban areas in the labor force has increased in the past few years.[1]

In the manufacturing sector, female workers are often employed as casual labor (under outsourcing or subcontracting practices) and receive less pay for performing the same work as their male counterparts.[2] Their income is often assumed as supplementary even when they are the breadwinners in a household. Many perform manual work. Pervasive cultural norms pressure women to be devoted daughters and when married, obedient wives (and mothers); they are expected to perform work at home, such as cooking, cleaning the home, and care work (children and elderly members of the family). At the same time, they are expected to earn money outside of domestic life. Having to balance these two expectations, many female workers view wage earning as a temporary situation.[3] This puts extra pressure on them to restrain (and in some cases, abandon) their own personal needs or dreams. Such personal sacrifices are taken for granted, as the work they perform in the factory is considered temporary not only by them, but also by their employers. Many women wind up without permanent positions. Their workload and obligation are as heavy as permanent workers, but they do not have the same employment security due to their employment status as temporary workers. For the last ten years or so, temporary employment has become the norm among female workers. Employers often turn a blind eye to the fact that many female workers are breadwinners, and that they often have to face more social obstacles.

The culturally bounded and gendered role of female workers poses tangible challenges to organizing labor, as many female workers tend to prioritize familial obligations above attending or participating in union activities. Also, as their jobs are temporary, women workers have fewer incentives to organize and do not see that they have much power or even can change their working conditions. Contributing to these constraints is the fact that most major unions, whose leaders and officials are predominantly male, rarely discuss legal violations of female workers' rights as such. If such violations do find their way through the union bureaucracy and are put on the agenda in union meetings, they are usually considered as "women's issues" only. Although unions are now guaranteed the right to recruit members, female participation remains relatively low, especially in the unions' governing structures. As discussed in chapter 3, struggling against hostile working conditions and social obstacles—some of which come from their male coworkers and unionists—a number of women unionists have been actively taking matters into their own hands to demand basic protections.

This chapter discusses women workers' efforts to secure their right to maternity protection, particularly at the factory level.[4] Salsabila (a pseudonym), a temporary worker (*buruh borongan*) at a cardboard factory in Bekasi,[5] writes her story of struggle to "obtain" this right—a right that is often reserved only for permanent workers.[6] As a temporary worker, she does not have any job security, like millions of other female workers in Indonesia's many industrial zones who perform manual work on a day-to-day basis but are denied stable employment and, often, their rights as a (female) worker. In the globalized labor market that seeks out the lowest production costs, workers have little option but to accept whatever job is available, even if the working conditions violate prescribed labor regulations, and even if it is temporary. Unlike her coworkers, however, Salsabila's employment status as a temporary worker does not stop her from challenging the injustices of the factory regime that have come to be accepted as normal practice.

Salsabila's essay—in the form of a letter to her son—is the focus of this chapter.[7] She writes about the precarious working conditions of the global factory regime as a temporary worker, and how workers are organizing to demand better working conditions. In it, she gives special attention to the issue of maternity protection, an issue that is often ignored in similar stories of workers' organizing efforts. In that sense, it illustrates how female workers are actively organizing to solve issues that are important to them as women, especially in the situation where women's participation in the labor union is limited.[8] Salsabila stands out among her coworkers due to her activism (she was also later elected as a union steward at the factory level). Just like many other female unionists, she has freed herself from cultural prejudices, and it is in her essay that she assumes her independence. Her employment status as a temporary worker and her living situation as a single mother do not deter her from questioning the authority, both in the factory and in the union hierarchy. It is this quality that makes her story stand out. It is an important example of the struggle of female worker activism in post-1998 Indonesia.

This chapter starts with a historical survey of the issue of maternity protection for female workers in modern Indonesia. Although maternity protection is considered fundamental and is legally acknowledged, in reality it is hardly implemented, as employers have not been pressed by the government, the market, or the unions to do so.[9] The chapter therefore turns to how female workers, in the context of post-1998 Indonesia, have taken on the fight for maternity protection, primarily at the factory level.[10] Salsabila's writing features as documentation of this struggle. To read her writing is to understand her efforts as a single working mother to fulfill expected social duties, to put food on the table, and to advance protections not only for her, but all women. Her epistolary essay shows her courage to speak up beyond the politics of *malu*. Thus, this chapter describes her struggle at the workplace as an integral part of her life as an urban lower-class (working) mother. It also illustrates women's need and ability to work beyond the politics of the union, for although Salsabila's initial struggle for maternity protection led her to a deeper involvement in the union, her primary concern remained defending the rights and interests of female workers, without exception. Beyond conventional union activism, her writing is a means of protest against injustice so that other female workers can take note and develop their own path—regardless of support from the union.

A DEEP-ROOTED PROBLEM

Securing maternity protection has been a persistent challenge for women wage earners in post-independence Indonesia. It is thus important to understand the historical process of how this became a challenge, the factors that have shaped (and supported) it, and the social-cultural forces that prevent it from being overcome.

As early as 1946, union activists recognized that maternity protection was often sidelined, simply because it was considered "women's issues." In her speech to a congress of women activists that year, S.K. Trimurti, a prominent female activist in Indonesia's struggle for national independence and the first

Minister of Labor, warned how issues related to maternity protection were often "left behind":

> there are also some specific issues of female workers, meaning they are experienced and suffered by women only. These specific issues of female workers are often unnoticed by male workers and in their [common] efforts, are left behind. . . . Examples include the lack of protection for a woman's security and dignity in the workplace, the unavailability of child rearing spaces for female workers, and many others.[11]

In the early post-independence years, efforts to tackle this problem included guaranteeing certain protections by law (with the reasoning that by including "specific issues" into the law, women workers would not have to worry that their interests were "neglected," but instead, were guaranteed by the legal system).[12] During the Sjahrir Cabinet (March 1946–July 1947), a new labor regulation was drafted and discussed under Maria Ulfah as the Minister of Social Affairs. Educated in law and in many ways sharing Sjahrir's idea of a *masjarakat sosialistis* (socialist society), she wrote into the labor regulation protective provisions for women workers, including three months of fully paid maternity leave, to be paid by the employer.[13] Her work was later carried on by Trimurti, who became the Minister of Labor in the Cabinet of Amir Sjarifuddin (July 1947–January 1948). A few months after the fall of the Sjarifuddin Cabinet, the draft regulation was promulgated as Law No. 12 Year 1948 (dated April 20, 1948), but it did not come into effect until 1951.[14] It included a number of specific provisions for the protection of women workers, including menstrual leave, maternity leave, and the right for women workers to breastfeed their babies at work. These provisions are guaranteed for all female workers, regardless of their employment status.[15]

Despite their legal rights being guaranteed by the law, however, women workers still could not exercise those rights as they wished. A number of contemporary reports note violations of the labor regulation, including women workers' rights. Praptinah, for example, notes that many companies were violating provisions concerning night work for women workers.[16] Not only were they employing women workers outside permitted hours, some companies did not even have the required permit that would allow them to employ women workers for night shifts.[17]

In another report, Praptini gives a detailed account of how some employers laid off pregnant workers:

> Once an employer knows that a female worker in his factory is in her sixth or seventh month of pregnancy, he will sack her. Although the law does not mention anything about legal marriage, if a female worker cannot show the

marriage certificate, the employer will never agree to provide leave with full wages. While the law is meant as [protection for] female workers who have to bear some pains after delivering a baby, employers reason that such a law would encourage illegal marriage.[18]

As noted above, workers' right to maternity protection was difficult to secure. Employers would identify pregnant workers and terminate their employment before they could even ask for maternity benefits, which, by law, were their rights. This practice sent a message to all workers that pregnancy was not welcome and that getting pregnant could result in losing one's job. For the employer, pregnancy creates a financial burden to the company, so there is no incentive to keep a pregnant worker and every incentive to discourage workers from getting pregnant. Not wanting to provide benefits, employers use the pretext of safeguarding (female) worker's morality to limit maternity protection.

Praptini also notes the difficulty in implementing menstrual leave as one of women workers' rights:

(E)mployers said that since menstruation is "uncontrollable," workers could deceive their employers. Even when employers comply with the Government Regulation....usually they separate between permanent workers and contingent workers. Employers are willing to allow permanent workers a day-off with full wages, but for contingent workers (temporary workers) [there is] none at all.[19]

Her report highlights how, although by law it is a right, securing menstrual leave in practice is dependent on the employer's willingness and ability to limit its implementation. It also shows that even as early as 1951, menstrual leave was wrongly reserved for permanent workers only. Although originally intended to legally ensure any female worker, regardless of her employment status, a time to rest during her period, the provision quickly became a privilege reserved only for permanent workers. Employers used—and continue to use—the right to menstrual leave to divide (female) workers so that permanent workers do not, or at least hesitate to, join hands with their nonpermanent coworkers. The strategy has, for the most part, worked: rather than form solidarity, (female) workers tend to aspire individually to become a permanent worker rather than come together to defend their collective interests as women.

The extreme difficulties in securing menstrual leave and other maternity protection did not improve much throughout the 1950s. Even women working at government institutions as civil servants expressed "their disappointment" in the partial implementation of maternity protection, which gave no consideration to the actual and specific conditions of expectant and new mothers.[20]

We do not have many reports on the status of maternity protection during the 1960s and 1970s, but it is safe to assume that women workers of that time also faced difficulties in exercising maternity protection, as it remained a problem in the 1980s and 1990s, specifically among industrial workers. In their report on the working conditions in an export-oriented tobacco company in East Java, Indraswari and Thamrin note that women workers could not secure their maternity protection, and were asked to quit once the employer knew they were pregnant.[21] Many workers complied with the "request," not knowing that they were legally entitled to paid maternity leave. Another report notes that even when workers knew of their rights, only a few had the courage to demand them.[22] As shown in Meppy's case (see chapter 2), some female factory workers were demanding menstrual and maternity leave as part of strike actions. They were mainly urban workers who had developed contact with legal aid workers or NGO activists who informed them of their rights as female workers. Their demands, however, were often overshadowed by others deemed more pressing (such as securing the minimum wage) or "genderless" issues (such as working hours or work safety). Even today, when women's demands are heard by the union or included in the union's struggle, they are often treated as minor issues. Indeed, unions in Indonesia, as elsewhere, need to bring women's issues on to the union bargaining agenda.

The change of regime in 1998 did not usher in any new enforcement of maternity protection for women workers. Female workers in post-1998 Indonesia continue to fight for the same issues as women workers who came before them did, confronting problems that have not dissipated since the country's independence in 1945.[23] These include the exclusion of non-permanent workers when granting menstrual and maternity leaves, setting limitations on maternity protection (such as granting them only under certain conditions), and persistent efforts to prevent women workers' from exercising their rights—including to breastfeed their babies.[24] Women workers today, even in the absence of unions' support, are not afraid to claim their rights. We shall discuss Salsabila's writing to show how female workers, individually and collectively, are struggling to attain and exercise their rights as women.

NEW STRUGGLE

In the face of decades of entrenched state, market, and cultural resistance, women's struggle to secure their rights is taking on new characteristics and women are mounting new kinds of protest. While women unionists during 1946–1948 aimed to pass laws that would protect the interests of all female workers, women workers of the post-1998 period are using legal instruments to support their demands at the factory level. While it is true that many female workers do not know (and often, are made ignorant) of their rights, a number of women workers are now demanding their rights directly to their employers. Through direct actions in the factory, they also alert coworkers of rights that have been ignored and violated by the employer.[25] Their actions may be individual, but that is because they are instigated from their own personal experiences. Their action may be sporadic, but that is because, in many cases, the union is not supporting them when they speak out.

The sporadic and individual characteristics of this contemporary struggle are best illustrated by the case of Enong (a pseudonym), a temporary worker who was working in a factory in the Kawasan Berikat Nusantara (KBN) at Tanjung Priok, Jakarta's export processing zone, when she suffered a miscarriage and demanded her right to paid leave. Her story was recorded in a research report, as follows:

> In that company, there were four workers who had had miscarriages in 2006. One of them even had it in the factory's toilet. But it was only Enong who demanded [her] right of leave due to miscarriage, and [she] had all her [medical] fees reimbursed, while other workers were only allowed to take rest for a few days and soon had to return to work. [Reflecting] on that case, Enong was of the opinion that workers should demand to the company to follow the law and grant them paid leave after a miscarriage. Workers have been passive because they themselves do not know their own rights to such leave. Also, union stewards do not check if a worker who has had a miscarriage was granted leave or not. They reason that if a worker does not report her case [to the union], they cannot do much [to help].[26]

Enong's case echoes the pattern of employers' violations of workers' rights in previous times: turning a blind eye to them or implementing them only for certain cases and not for all workers. Sadly, the union also did not advocate for female workers' rights or fight against the injustices in the factory. Instead, union stewards excused themselves by saying that technically, they could only act upon a worker's report. Apparently in Enong's case, as was common, male workers dominated the union and ignored the welfare of women workers.

The report indicates that Enong's case was an exception rather than the rule, apparently because other women workers in the factory did not have the same amount of knowledge and courage as she did. Her case is instructive, however, in illustrating how individual women workers are taking matters into their own hands. They know that their employer has been violating their rights and the union will only lend them support under certain conditions. Enong was brave enough to demand her rights. She did it on her own, without the support of the union. She is an example of a female worker who is no longer confined under the politics of *malu* or the politics of the union to speak against the employer's discriminatory treatment of female (temporary) workers.

Similar to Enong, Salsabila also took matters into her own hands by demanding maternity leave on her own and without the union's support. Contrary to Enong who chose to remain silent after her action, however, Salsabila did not keep her story to herself. It is because she shared her case, using it to raise awareness among her coworkers and guide them toward change, that her courageous action prompted other women workers in the factory to demand the same rights for all.

FACTORY WORK AND MOTHERHOOD

Salsabila wrote her essay in 2015 as a long letter to her only child and son, Nazik Almalaika, and hence it is titled "Surat pendek untuk Nazik Almalaika" ("Short letter to Nazik Almalaika").[27] As stated in the first paragraph of her essay, she wishes to convey the story of the struggle that she and her coworkers went through, "from being a temporary worker to a permanent worker, from being denied of our rights to gaining our rights as humans" (p. 189). The main content of her essay is, indeed, about the process of the change in their employment status and becoming able to exercise their rights. Although her essay presents the story of a "successful" struggle (as workers finally got what they demanded), it also includes expressions of her own feelings and thoughts of the important events in that process as she saw or experienced them, and stories of her entry and involvement in the union, and also her disappointments in the final result. All are intertwined with the personal struggle she had to face as a single mother.[28]

The very fact that her essay is written as a long letter to her son highlights the dilemmas she has to face being a widow, a single mother, and a temporary worker. The death of her husband eight months after the birth of her son forced her to face the pervasive societal prejudice against single mothers, especially widows[29]:

When you were eight months old, your father died. Leaving you behind, leaving me behind. I became a widow, and you, an orphan. Honestly, my heart was broken, son. In our society, being a widow is not easily accepted and often, underestimated. It is as if her humanity is lost; becoming half-human. I don't understand why it is so. (p. 200)

Against these conditions, the epistolary form of her essay allows her to describe her feelings and thoughts about her situation, as it contains some confessional tones of the troubles, hardships, and also, intimate fears that she wants to convey. Confession here does not mean she is telling some secret; unlike some epistolary fiction where readers are allowed to learn a private secret or stories of intrigue as representational of truth, there is no particular secret in her essay.[30] Rather, Salsabila's essay tells the truth based on her actual personal experiences.

The epistolary form allows Salsabila to express her feelings and thoughts more genuinely and fittingly than any other form, and better suits her needs in writing. On the one hand, she invites her readers to read the essay as a personal letter in which she can express freely without being (self-)censored. On the other hand, readers assume the role of bearers of her "confession" after having the privilege of previewing her intimate thoughts and feelings. Salsabila as an author does not shy away from sharing these intimacies to her readers (not only her son) in order that they may better understand her activities and the choices she made in her life.[31]

Salsabila's condition as a temporary worker is part of the feminization of labor in the manufacturing sector that has been taking place since the 1980s and has changed the contour of female employment in Indonesia. Many (rural) women see factory work as the only option of formal employment. Although factory work may have allowed them to escape from rural hardships and/or domesticity, it also limited their time outside of work to socialize and perform filial duties. With the intensification of labor market flexibility since the late 1990s that has made permanent employment redundant, many (female) temporary workers have been forced to spend more time in the factory to maintain their independence or to support their households.

Salsabila is not an exception to this phenomenon. As a temporary worker at P.T. Alim Rugi,[32] she was not secure. As the sole breadwinner of the family, she has very little option other than factory work to sustain life. In fact, factory work alone, as she informs us, is not enough. Urban lower-class (working) mothers like her have to find various jobs to supplement their meager wages from factory work. And as a single mother, she has to work harder. In her own words:

Economic problems force me to work harder than any other mother in general. Your birth was possible through caesarean section. I could not afford to pay the 16 million rupiah [that it cost]. I am just a daughter of farm workers who migrated to the city. I am just a temporary worker at PT Alim Rugi. How could I find and get as much money as that? (p. 190)

Salsabila understands perfectly well that as the sole breadwinner she has to bear all the expenses of her household. Her financial hardship started when she was about to give birth: she had to take out loans to pay for the cesarean section she needed to deliver her son. She describes her post-natal financial situation with the increasing living expenses as a (single) mother. Her wages as a temporary worker are not enough to cover her daily living expenses, let alone cover the costs of the original loan. Indeed, she also had to take out new loans:

> At that time, every month my income was not enough to buy milk. You would need 4-5 boxes of milk, about 1,000 grams of powdered milk, diapers, soaps. . . . Every month I had to allocate my income: for gasoline, about 150,000 rupiah, for daily meals, about 500,000 rupiah, for other provisions, about 200,000 rupiah. Among all those expenses, the need for your milk has the biggest [allocation], son. Still days away from the payday, I did not have any money at all. I was forced to borrow money for my [transport] fare to work every day. Yes, you were not given exclusively breast milk, my dear. I will tell you the reasons why next time. (pp. 200–201)

It is obvious that Salsabila faces unbearable decisions as a single mother and, at the same time, a (temporary) worker. She must work to have the money to buy milk, among necessities. Yet, she is not being able to take care of her son due to her work (there is no child-rearing facility in the factory as required by the law). Even if she could breastfeed (and therefore would not need to buy milk), she still needs to work because she is a single mother. The need to buy milk because she cannot breastfeed at work is a common issue faced by many working mothers. It is a major issue for single mothers with temporary employment status, as Salsabila alerts us.

As a temporary worker, she has to toil for long hours, including by taking overtime work to supplement her meager basic wages. Long working hours, however, prevent her from spending time, energy, and care on child-rearing and domestic work. Paid employment as a factory worker is crucial to sustain her life and her son's. After the death of her husband, she is the sole breadwinner of the family. She cannot perform her role as a stay-at-home mother because she cannot neglect her duties as the sole breadwinner of the family. She laments:

> My wage is not enough, son! In a week I work for six days from Monday to Saturday. [From] Monday to Friday [I work for] eight hours, minus one hour for a break. On Saturday, five hours. Sometimes there are long shifts or extended working hours. Sometimes there are also overtime works on Sundays. Sometimes there are overtime works for the whole month. I took those overtime

works, son. In that way, my wage would be better. . . . While working, I also sell my friends' items, either by cash or credit, such as clothes, shoes, and even electronics. From those sales, I get some commissions if the items sell well and the money is handed over to the owner [of the item]. I also took a side job after [factory] work as a saleswoman of sanitary napkins. . . . Because of that, every day I can only go back home late in the afternoon. Those are all for you, Nazik. If I stayed home with you, there would be no milk and diapers for you. (pp. 195–197)

Salsabila has no option but to work overtime and take on side jobs to supplement her income. Long working hours at the factory allow her to gain more wages, but it also keeps her from caring for her son at the most important time of his growth as a baby.

Despite all her efforts to supplement her income by working overtime, doing various side jobs, and limiting her own expenses, there are times when she still cannot cover all her living expenses as a single mother. In that situation, she resorts to fasting. She explains:

Otherwise, I would be fasting. Sometimes, in a week I would fast for five days and not fast on the other two days. This is not the *qhada'* fasting or making up a missed fast due to menstruation, but fasting because of not having money [to buy food] to eat. (p. 198)

In times of financial hardship, fasting becomes one of her physical sacrifices to ensure that her son has enough and proper food.

Her story here illustrates the difficulties that many urban lower-class working mothers have to bear to sustain life in their households. Working hard for their children, they know their income is important to cover the family's expenses. Indeed, in many cases, their wages from factory work are the only source of the family's income. And when it is not enough, they are willing to make sacrifices, including physical sacrifices, by limiting their own expenses, and as Salsabila did, by voluntarily fasting.

Since Salsabila has to work hard and only has limited time to care for her son, she relies on her family to look after him when she is away at work. It is common for working mothers to rely on their parents and other family members (or other substitutes) to help take care of their children. Apart from her parents, her sister also helps take care of her son and performs some household chores:

Mamah Haji is my sister. She has helped taking care of you when I was busy working. She has helped us a lot. She used to work in Saudi Arabia for a long period after finishing middle-high school. Since 2013, she stayed at home. (p. 200)

It is here in the essay that Salsabila fully realizes her absence as a full-time mother. As she has to spend more time outside of home to earn wages, she has to rely on other people (family members) who will act as a mother to her son. Salsabila could not exclusively clean, look after, and cook for her son all the time, but she earns enough income, with her own physical sacrifices, for her son's food, clothing, and shelter. In this respect, she tries to inform her readers (and her son) that despite her absence as a full-time mother, by working hard she is also mothering her son. She notes that "(w)henever I go to work, you cry hard. I feel sad seeing you wailing. I have to go to work and leave you crying. I am happy and proud seeing you grow and healthy" (p. 249).

Salsabila's story illustrates the dilemma that all working mothers, especially from lower-class families, and particularly single mothers have. As a breadwinner in the family (in many cases, the only one), a mother may work hard for her children, but cannot care for them on a full-time basis. Her earning potential requires her to devote her time to paid employment (from factory work and/or other side jobs) and thus, she only has scant hours to spend on childcare and housekeeping—it is painfully clear that it is her job that enables her to sustain not only her life but that of her loved ones. By taking paid employment (and spending more time to earn more), working mothers demonstrate their personal sacrifices and devotion.

Through telling her story of hardships and dilemmas as a working (single) mother in epistolary form, Salsabila is able to convey to her readers (and her son) that she is doing everything she can to perform her duties and responsibilities as a mother, despite her absence as a stay-at-home mother. In that way, her essay is an act of performative mothering. It is performative because she tries to convince her readers that the main reason why she takes on paid employment is in fact to fulfill her duty as a mother. Earnings from her factory work and side jobs provide for the basic needs of her child, which is mothering. Both, paid employment outside and domestic work inside the household are equally important, and neither negates the other.[33] She uses the essay to define (at least part of) mothering as working for wages outside the home. As such, she claims her identity as a working mother, beyond the conventional image of a stay-at-home one. The very act of writing *to her son* is also mothering.

Performative mothering is necessary for readers to understand Salsabila's situation as a working mother, and because the choice she is forced to make is commonly caricaturized as uncaring or inadequate mothering. The ideal image of a mother (as one who stays at home rather than work outside) is ingrained in the politics of *ibu*, or a "proper" mother.[34] Challenging this fixed image, Salsabila demonstrates that an *ibu* does not necessarily need to stay at home. By referring to herself in the essay as *ibu*, she defines mother not only as a woman who has given birth, but more importantly, as a woman who is mothering her child in the best way available to her—in her case, working for wages outside the home. Thus, the essays show that working is part of her existence as a (single) mother and it is important to support the life of her son and her family. As an urban lower-class single mother, she does not have the same power or privilege as middle-class mothers to negotiate her life-work balance. Such mothers do not need to claim mothering nor articulate their hardships to show their devotion as a mother. In contrast, as a lower-class single mother, Salsabila has limited options to claim mothering beyond earning wages outside the home to support her son. Writing an essay in epistolary form provides her the space (and the stage) to claim that mothering and express her devotion as *ibu*.

Like many other urban working mothers from lower-class backgrounds, Salsabila has to toil long hours at work to maintain her life and at the same time, she has limited time to spend with her loved ones—the same individuals she wishes to convey her struggle against life's hardships to. She is not ashamed of her situation; instead, it is the basis of her epistolary essay. The essay allows her to assert her relative freedom to express herself, beyond the politics of *malu* and of *ibu*. Thus, by acknowledging her performative mothering in the essay, readers are able to glimpse not only the harsh working conditions she endures, but also the workers' struggle to improve them, in which she took an active part. The following paragraphs will discuss both of these.

WORKING CONDITIONS UNDER NEOLIBERALISM

Salsabila wrote her essay in the context of the changing landscape of Bekasi. Born and raised there, she witnessed the drastic changes it underwent after it administratively became a city in 1996. Urbanization, coupled with economic growth, transformed Bekasi from a satellite town of Jakarta to a sizeable city of its own. She must have experienced this change as part of her own life story, like many people whose lives are intertwined with the dynamic of their hometown. Nonetheless, in her essay, she describes the changes as a story of economic inequality:

> As a native of Bekasi, which now has rows of factories and industrial complexes, upscale apartments and hotels, we do not get any work except as a temporary worker or a contract-based worker. We have to struggle, son. (p. 189)

She understands that Bekasi is experiencing major transformations (economically, socially, and environmentally), but she, like many other local residents of the city, is left out and cannot gain any benefit from it. She contrasts the changes in Bekasi with her own situation. The fact that she is a temporary worker (like many of her peers) shows that Bekasi's development has been uneven and her (vulnerable) employment status is a result of it. Although she is upset about it, she knows that she "has to struggle" against this inequality—and so will her son, in the future.

Salsabila's life as a factory worker started right after she finished high school at Madrasah Aliyah in Bekasi.[35] She first started working at a food processing company in 2006 as a contract worker for eighteen months. After that, she worked for a toy company, also as a contract worker. Following that, she worked for an electronics company on a twelve-month contract, but she resigned after eight months due to the illness of her first son, Umar, who later died. After that, she found work at a DVD manufacturing company as a daily worker, but she quit after three months due to late payment of her wages. All of these companies operated in Bekasi. We can see that she worked for four different companies in the span of five years, and always as a short-term contingent worker (either contract-based or as a daily worker). Throughout her working experience, she was never offered permanent employment. Like other factory workers in many industrial zones across Indonesia, she faced the nearly insurmountable challenge of securing permanent employment from unregulated companies in the country's manufacturing sector in the age of neoliberalism.

Salsabila's story follows the general pattern of vulnerable working conditions that can be found in many other developing countries. These conditions are exacerbated by strong pressures from the labor market to reduce legal restrictions on the hiring and firing of workers, and the limited ability of inspections to record and penalize companies for violations of labor regulations. Employers have the upper hand in controlling labor conditions, especially after the promulgation of Law No. 13 Year 2003, which allows companies to hire workers through a subcontract/outsourcing system. Although labor rights are guaranteed for all workers, in reality workers with temporary and subcontract/outsourcing status are in a vulnerable position to stand up to defend their rights. Precariat workers like Salsabila have little bargaining power with which to challenge these conditions; if they reject them, other workers are already lining up to replace them.

Interestingly, Salsabila also notes the role of employment agencies in reducing the bargaining power of workers and taking advantage of their labor. Employment agencies offer companies, as their clients, a constant supply of subcontract or outsourced workers—without any legal responsibilities (i.e., labor rights) attached to the employment relationship. She writes about it based on her own experiences:

I worked in that company through a foundation (*yayasan*) after [agreeing] to pay two million rupiah. The payment [to the foundation] was made as follows:

one million rupiah was paid up-front and another one million rupiah would be deducted directly from my wages, beginning with the first wage payment [I would receive]. So, every month, 100,000 rupiah was deducted from my income. It was deducted right before I could even use it. . . . [when] My contract finished, I was offered another contract through the foundation (*yayasan*). I didn't want it. (pp. 193–194)

In Bekasi (and other industrial zones in Indonesia), employment agencies, disguised as foundations (*yayasan*), channel contingent workers to companies that are their clients.[36] Under pressure in the global market to cut costs, many companies (especially in the manufacturing sector) reduce labor costs by getting rid of permanent positions and replacing them with various kinds of nonpermanent jobs. This allows them to pay lower wages and have more flexibility, but perhaps most importantly, allows them to avoid legal responsibilities to provide workers with welfare and social benefits. Employment agencies take advantage of labor's weak position in the flexible labor market to sell a service to the companies. They provide companies with workers on a temporary basis, and in turn companies do not have to hire workers directly. In that situation, workers cannot deal directly with the company, including to claim their maternity protection.

Salsabila's experiences illustrate the general context of the working conditions in Bekasi, which is characterized by the difficulty in finding secure jobs and the exploitative practices of employment agencies. It is quite difficult for workers to apply directly to companies; they become dependent on the agencies to get hired. Salsabila was only hired as a temporary worker and could not escape the webs of the employment agency. She clearly understands that as a temporary worker she is being used both by the employment agency and the employers:

It's not easy to get a job, even when you bribe [an insider], there is no guarantee you would get the job. Besides that, I was tired. Tired, son! For I always get a job only as a temporary worker. After the contract would end, I had to find a job again, to be hired as temporary worker again and then, the contract ends. Continuously like that. Worse is when you are under contract through a *yayasan*, son. (p. 193)

Her experience underscores the precarious conditions of work life in Bekasi for factory workers (who are predominantly temporary and outsourced) and especially, for those who are under contract through an employment agency (operating as *yayasan*). Interestingly, she also highlights the waning power of *nyogok* (bribing an insider) to land a job in the factory. It was once a common practice for job seekers to approach a *mandor* (supervisor) or *satpam* (security guard) of the factory to get a job. They usually paid the bribe in installments that were deducted from their monthly income. This practice is no longer potent, as companies now rely more on employment agencies rather than their *mandors* or *satpams* to supply manpower.

Tired of the poor working conditions under employment agencies, Salsabila tried to look for a job in Bekasi on her own. She submitted job applications to some factories, and P.T. Alim Rugi (her employer when she wrote the essay) gave her a callback. She was offered a job as a *buruh borongan* (temporary worker). To her surprise, she found the whole process was not as difficult as she expected and hence, she accepted the job without much thought, although she noted that at the time she did not really understand what it meant to be a *buruh borongan* at that company. It was only later that she started to grasp the meaning of it:

> Son, you know what, I don't get any copy of the employment contract when I am working at this PT Alim Rugi. It's different from my previous experiences with other companies, where I got a copy of the contract. [Nonetheless,] I started to work, son. My co-workers and I, as newly employed, were trained for a week. Not everyone passed the training, son. They [the factory managers] said that those who did not pass it had poor work performance and were not fast enough. But I passed it. After that, I was assigned to the slitter department. (p. 195)

By now she realized that as *buruh borongan* she would not receive a copy of the work contract—even if such a document existed. As a temporary worker, she could be fired anytime, but she still was expected to keep up her work performance and work fast on the factory line. There was a clear divide between permanent and temporary workers: they were even assigned different colored work uniforms (brown for permanent workers, navy blue for the temporary). Salsabila also did not receive the benefits that the permanent workers did. This division is a common strategy for factories to divide workers and at the same time, discourage interactions between them so they do not develop common interests.

Salsabila describes how her work duties in the factory were physically demanding, but the income was not that much to live on. The heat and humidity inside the factory constantly made her thirsty, and the lack of masks inevitably made her inhale dust during work. According to her description, the factory did not comply with occupational safety and health regulations to give minimum standard protections to its workers. She describes the conditions as follows:

> Day one, day two, a week, a month, and day after day, I finally realized the tiring job as temporary worker and with minimal income. [Besides,] I am always

thirsty because the [factory] site is hot. [My job as a] slitter is to cut long papers into smaller sizes and [as a result] there is paper dust everywhere. Indeed, there are masks. But they are not enough for all. So we have to compete for the masks [to grab it first]. If you do not put on the mask, whatever comes out of your nose or mouth will be black. Even when I wipe my face with any material [to clean it], it would be black. Thick black. (p. 195)

Despite these poor conditions, Salsabila did not complain or leave the job. She knows that she must endure as it is her only source of income to maintain life.[37]

In addition to the lack of safety and health, the main issue in the factory was the lack of maternity leave. Salsabila was not yet pregnant, but as a female temporary worker, she quickly became aware of the unspoken rule in the factory: female workers were expected not to get pregnant.

Some stories were circulating in the factory that made temporary workers afraid of getting pregnant and [thus,] cancel their plan of pregnancy. Many temporary workers have [limited] educational background from primary and middle school only, some don't even have a school certificate and with limited skills and more importantly, it will be difficult to land a job when you are not young anymore. That's why temporary workers are afraid of losing their jobs. (p. 203)

She notes the general atmosphere in the factory that haunted all female workers, that pregnancy would cost their jobs. Female, particularly temporary, workers were expected to show their dedication and stay loyal to their job by making sure not to get pregnant.

It is important to note that a temporary worker found to be pregnant would be sacked from her job without any severance payment, a punishment that was not only unjust, but had serious economic consequences. It was also difficult to return to work after giving birth:

If you were pregnant and after giving a birth you want to get back to work, you will need to make a new job application. We, all the temporary workers, would be accepted back to work with our years of service counted as zero. Temporary workers who are expectant mothers would be considered as resigning from work [and thus] not given any severance payment. (p. 202)

Hence, the decision by temporary workers not to get pregnant was not made out of free will, but was imposed on their bodies by the factory regime.

Salsabila had her own experience regarding this unspoken rule. As a temporary worker, she knew that she would not get any maternity leave, and she knew that it was not fair. She notes her frustration as follows:

Then, what rights did I get, son? Nothing, no rights as a human and as a woman who by nature would have to discharge dirty blood monthly, and as a pregnant mother for nine months and later give birth to a son or daughter as the next generation, like yourself. Even for miscarriage, there was no right. Nothing! When I was pregnant and giving birth to you, Nazik, I couldn't exercise the right to leave. Because I was a temporary worker! That's the reality, son! I couldn't exercise the right to leave. It was then a custom in the factory where I work that non-permanent workers didn't have the maternity leave rights. It was only permanent workers who had such a right. (p. 202)

The above quotation shows how angry Salsabila was with the unfair conditions. Although temporary workers worked alongside their permanent coworkers and some even performed the same tasks, they could not exercise the same rights. The factory imposed an employment status on them that limited their rights and put them in a more vulnerable position. Female temporary workers could not take maternity leave, although the law states that workers, regardless of their employment status, should enjoy the same rights.[38]

Facing this unfair condition, Salsabila insisted on exercising her right to maternity leave. When she entered her eighth month of pregnancy, she realized she would not be able to work as hard as she was required to and she would need to take a leave. She consulted some coworkers, her team leader in the factory, and one of the union officers. It seems that none gave her a satisfying answer about her right to maternity leave. Nonetheless, with much confidence, she went to the factory's office, took a copy of the application form for maternity leave, and after filling it out herself, she submitted it. With that, she had challenged the unspoken rule on maternity protection for temporary workers and by using her own experience as a test case, she demanded the same rights as permanent workers, without hesitation.

Her path, however, was not easy. Her application had still not been processed by the requested start date of her leave. Nonetheless, she took the leave (as designated, for forty-five days, until January 5, 2013). When her leave was approaching its end, she phoned her team leader to confirm her return to work, but she was ignored. Although she was allowed to enter the factory premises on her return date, she was not assigned any work and instead, after a brief meeting with a male supervisor, she was told to go back home, as the office no longer had any record of her work or her leave application.

She persisted. The next day, she went to the factory again to check with the office of human resources about her work record; the record was still available in the office database. With that fact, she claimed her right to return to work after the leave. The administrative office could not refuse her claim and she was allowed to return to work as usual. As she recalled it, another male supervisor even made an excuse about why they allowed her to come back:

"It's just because I felt pity on you as you just delivered a baby that we have to accept you back despite that a temporary worker should never have had maternal leave," said Sugiono. After that, I went back working as usual. (p. 217)

Whatever the reason (or the excuse) was, the company knew it could not forbid female workers from taking maternity leave (as it would constitute an illegal act), yet company staff still misinformed her of her legal right to maternity leave. Meanwhile, Salsabila, like most female workers in the factory, did not yet know about her legal rights (she only learned that maternity leave was a legal right later on). Thus, her claim to return to work was based on the fact that the company still kept her work record, not based on her right to take maternity leave. Nonetheless, her persistence saved her from losing her job after taking the leave. She did not give up after being told by a male supervisor to return home on her first day back to work. Against the social expectation of a woman to be *malu* at the workplace, she had nothing to lose and thus was not afraid to confront the office and return to work.

Foreseeably, yet unintendedly, her experience set an example for other temporary workers who became unafraid to get pregnant and take maternity leave. Salsabila notes that after she returned to work, a number of temporary workers openly showed that they were pregnant deliberately to inform their supervisors of their condition and their intention to take maternity leave:

About three to four months after working in the repair department, I saw some [female] temporary workers [feeling] dizzy, a sign of being pregnant. For example, sister Esih, sister Acem, Omah, and Devi from the stitching department. Yanti, Kokom and Dede from the slitter department. Ucu and sister Eli from the repair department. There was always some news about a temporary worker who got pregnant. [You may wonder] what made these mothers have the courage to get pregnant, as they were fighting against the old custom in the factory. Finally, some pregnant temporary workers asked [me] how to take maternity leave. For example, Mrs. Sukaesih from the stitching-conversion line. She was afraid and not confident to do the [application] process by herself. "I would have been sweating," [she said]. I slowly explained how to take the leave; whom she needed to get signatures from, explained what is the procedure in the leave form, explained the re-start date of working, helped her write and fill in the leave form, and accompanied her to take the leave form to the staff office. (p. 217)

Temporary workers, some from the same department and many others from different departments and who she did not know personally, were no longer afraid to get pregnant. They were "fighting against the old custom in the factory" and thus, eager to exercise their right to maternity leave, a right they had just "discovered." The once guarded gate that differentiated permanent and temporary workers was opened. This small step of gaining maternity leave gave the temporary workers a sense of worth; they were equal to permanent workers, and there was no reason to treat them differently. From this, they realized that they could seize other rights and benefits that were once off-limits. From her essay, we see that Salsabila understood this possibility, and it drove her closer to union activism in the factory.

FACTORY-LEVEL STRUGGLE

Union activism was not in Salsabila's thoughts when she insisted on taking maternity leave and fought for her return to work. It was the *"grebek pabrik"* (factory raid) that took place in a number of factories in Bekasi's industrial area, during the eight months from May to October 2012, that led her to the union. The "raid" was most often conducted spontaneously, and combined factory occupation with an on-site strike by the workers (including, sit-downs). It forced employers and management to negotiate with workers and make immediate decisions to agree with the workers' demands. It was used to press employers to comply with labor regulations, especially in relation to subcontract and outsourced workers.

Factories in Bekasi had been reducing their number of permanent workers and replacing them with subcontract and outsourced workers; many were hiring such workers beyond what the labor regulations legally prescribed, both in the types of jobs and length of employment.[39] Agitated by their employer's reluctance to end subcontracting/outsourcing practices, temporary workers demanded that they be hired as permanent workers. Some factory-level unions assisted and organized these workers in their common struggle for economic justice.[40] The "raid" in Bekasi was considered a successful strategy to force employers to the negotiating table and ensure workers' job security.

As we have seen, poor working conditions and lack of job security were endemic in the factory where Salsabila worked. It was during the time of the "raids" in Bekasi that the union in her factory demanded that all temporary workers (*buruh borongan*) be hired as permanent workers. Salsabila took part in the demonstration in the factory that led to the negotiation in which the employer agreed to all the demands of the union, especially to employ all workers as permanent workers only. "There was a hope," she writes, that temporary workers would be able to exercise their rights without being discriminated against (p. 220). But, the employer did not give in easily, and had prepared some counter steps to ignore the agreement and weaken its significance. First, temporary workers were targeted for forged job applications so that their employment record registered them as new recruits.[41] Salsabila notes that a number of her coworkers fell into this trap and despite their years of long employment as temporary workers in the factory, they could not be employed as permanent workers.

The employer also refused to adjust the company's wage system. Although now employed as permanent workers, their wages remained based on a piece rate. In other words, their income did not improve. Salsabila explains the overall outcomes of the employer's counter steps, in particular noting that the workers were not even paid for their overtime work (on the dubious reason that an employer is allowed to ask permanent workers to do overtime work without payment):

> [The employer] reasoned that there isn't any clause on wage determination in the collective bargaining agreement [so], all temporary workers who [although] have been employed as permanent workers still receive their wage based on piece rate (*borongan*). Thus, what the workers got were a letter of employment as permanent workers, and the benefits like other permanent workers, such as: paid maternity leave, miscarriage leave, menstrual leave, attendance incentive, transport allowance, and uniform. Their wage is still based on the units produced, and [they] do not receive overtime payment as it should be. (p. 221)

As such, the "raid" might have succeeded in forcing the employer to hire temporary workers (*buruh borongan*) as permanent workers, but it was an illusive victory because it came with no substantial changes to their wages or job security. The employer's agreement with the workers' demands during the "raid" seems to have been simply to tame the workers so they would end the action as quickly as possible.

Salsabila's description shows that temporary workers, like her, understood well the employer's refusals and counter steps against their struggle. Due to their vulnerable position, they might not have been able to resist the employer's countersteps on their own, but the union was willing to support their struggle. It did not take long for Salsabila to become active in the union; she joined their activities, especially demonstrations and rallies in late 2012 to press for workers' demands during the regency-level (*kabupaten*) negotiations on the minimum wage. In fact, she notes that it was during one of those rallies that she had her first experience of class solidarity ("*saling peduli satu sama lain*," p. 222) among workers from different union federations and across industrial sectors.

It was in this context that Salsabila came to realize the power of the union. Although she had fought for the right to maternity leave for all female workers in her factory, she did it all alone. The "raid" in her factory and participation in subsequent worker demonstrations and rallies in public spaces inspired her to commit herself to union activism. The collective power of the union could help achieve other objectives, especially on the issues that mattered most to all temporary workers: job security and wages. This was even more important to her when she realized that a number of temporary workers were now employed as permanent workers, but their wages were still based on a piece rate. As such, when the union called for demonstrations and rallies to demand fair wages, she did not hesitate to join in. When their demand was met, she writes what she thought about the collective struggle and the importance of the union:

> The demonstration, after days, bore fruit. The result was that the 2013 minimum wage of the Bekasi regency rose from 1,491,000 rupiah to 2,474,000 rupiah. I was happy. I would benefit from the triumph of the collective struggle of the united workers. . . . All workers would benefit from their collective struggle. Could you imagine, son, if there wasn't any union in the company, who would press the management? Or, what if there was a union, but it was a yellow union? (pp. 226–227)

Salsabila sees that the union has important roles in defending workers' interests, especially on fair wages and securing a minimum wage for all workers regardless of their employment status. She knows it is part of the union's broader struggle for social justice for all workers, especially for temporary workers (*buruh borongan*) like her, and more generally, subcontract/outsourced workers who did not have a union to defend their interests and support their struggle.

Upon the government's formal decision on the minimum wage, the ensuing struggle for the workers was to ensure that the employers would implement it indiscriminately. In her writing, Salsabila provides a chronology of this factory-level struggle. The temporary workers had some hope that the employer would pay the minimum wage as regulated by the government. Given their vulnerable position, however, it would be difficult to push the employer to do so; their problem was a common issue faced by temporary workers elsewhere. To break this vicious cycle, Salsabila tried to gather the temporary workers so they could talk and discuss their problems together. As she was the only temporary worker actively involved in union actions, she took the initiative to bring this issue of wages to the attention of the union stewards so that the union would help defend their legal rights. It was not an easy task:

> I thought hard what went wrong and what should be done, so temporary workers could organize, and how the union stewards and the rank-and-file could sit next to one another. I feel there is a wall that separates them. Thus, even if the stewards and rank-and-file meet, it would be difficult. As I know, rank-and-file are respectful yet they are shy (*segan*) toward the stewards and often do not

know what the stewards do. The stewards are all permanent workers, are all male, have years of experience in unionism, and are keen-witted. [Thus,] The rank-and-file hesitate to sit together next to them, and don't even have the courage (*berani*) to ask questions. (p. 239)

As Salsabila notes, the union is a closed shop whose members are permanent workers; temporary workers could not join. The male stewards who all had years of union activism under their belts were a sharp contrast to the temporary workers who were predominantly female, had neither the experience nor technical knowledge in union organizing, and many of whom did not even know about union activities.

Interestingly, Salsabila describes the general psychological characteristics of her coworkers (the temporary workers) as "respectful yet shy" (*segan*) and "don't have the courage" (*tidak berani*). This description is not necessarily due to their gender roles (as female), but more to their lack of experience (in union action) and rhetorical skills (speaking out) in defending their rights and interests. She might have reflected on it because of her own personal experience in defending her right to maternity leave: to have self-confidence and to gather courage to voice (against injustice), to be *berani* on her own. She sees this issue of confidence and courage as critical so that they, too, can be free from the politics of *malu*.

After coordinating with some of her coworkers, Salsabila finally succeeded in organizing a meeting among temporary workers and the union stewards on May 31, 2014. It was so well attended by the temporary workers (100 persons of 115) that she "felt fully satisfied and very overwhelmed" with the meeting and its result (p. 244). A subsequent meeting soon followed. The union later agreed to bring their issue of wage disparity to a negotiation with the employer.[42] With that, Salsabila began collecting her coworkers' wage slips and work records as supporting evidence for the union.

The negotiation between the union and the employer was tough. While the union pushed for a common wage system for all workers (based on the minimum wage), the employer insisted on postponing any change in the wage system, citing recent financial difficulties. It took three more meetings between the union and the employer to come to an agreement. Despite its claims of financial difficulties, the employer did not have any legal ground to keep paying (temporary) workers below the minimum wage and thus, finally agreed to change its wage system to be based on the minimum wage. It managed, however, to make the union agree to a clause stating that workers are expected to meet production targets without exception.

The agreement was heralded as a success. All workers now had a wage based on the legal minimum wage, as Salsabila reflects, "due to the workers' struggle, and not given" by their employer (p. 249). Temporary workers and those who are later employed as permanent workers could now exercise their legal rights as workers and would receive compensation for their labor based on the minimum wage. It seemed their two-year struggle had finally paid off and they could feel secure about their rights and wages as long as they were employed in the factory. But it was not long before the workers realized the condition of the agreement between the union and the employer—an increasing production target:

> Our wage is finally based on the minimum wage, as our status is now as a permanent worker. But the production target keeps increasing. Every day [we have to produce] 7,000 pieces of small box, 4,040 pieces of mixed box, and 3,500 pieces of big box. It's a high target, son. As it is so high, some senior female workers started to complain. "As it is now, if all of us have to work to reach this high target, I won't be able to do so. I would prefer to stay as temporary worker than to work like a robot. I am old already. My strength is not like those who are young." I also worry about this high target. [Thus] I reported this complaint to the union stewards. (p. 247)

As the union that represented them agreed to the production clause, the workers did not have any other option than to follow it if they wanted to keep their job as a permanent worker with full rights and receive a minimum wage-based wage. Many workers now "started to complain" by comparing their current job conditions to those before the change; they wondered if they had lost their relative freedom as a temporary worker by being bounded by the production target as a permanent worker.

This situation created a new problem for the workers and the union. Although Salsabila reported this issue to the union, there was no change in the production line and workers were expected to meet the production target as set by the employer. Workers were happy that the union helped negotiate their wage, but they felt it made a mistake in agreeing to the clause without any prior consultation with them. Noting this dilemma, Salsabila felt there was nothing more she could do to change this situation. As she later made her way to become one of the union stewards, she realized she was entangled in the union's politics and had little capacity to make change in the factory.

BEYOND UNION ACTIVISM

Salsabila participated in a number of union activities for over one year (during 2013–2014), including demonstrations for fair wages and general meetings. She organized the first meeting between temporary workers and the unions' stewards and took a union assignment to coordinate the female workers' education program—although, as she honestly notes, she had no prior experience to do so. Compared to other female (temporary) workers, she did not hesitate and was not shy (*malu*) to be involved in union activities. She showed her enthusiasm for the union through her participation, which was beyond that of an ordinary member. In turn, perhaps because the union regarded her as a promising cadre, she was elected as a union steward. She might not have intended to leave such an impression on the union, as she saw her activism as something "natural," and not as a demand. Her experiences must have given her a belief that the union offered a hope to defend workers' rights and interests.

It is important to note that Salsabila was the only female member of the union's council of stewards and the only member who was a temporary worker (*buruh borongan*) at the time she was elected. On the one hand, it shows that her activism was acknowledged and she had proven her commitment to the union. The union understood that she was a key person that deserved to represent (temporary) workers in the factory, especially when it was facing new challenges due to the employer's strategy to undermine the struggle of temporary workers. On the other hand, it also illustrates that the union was male-dominated and had not previously done anything for temporary workers (who were mostly female workers).

In her writing, she notes that she was not welcomed at first by some male stewards; they doubted her commitment to union activism because she was a woman, who they thought would be less committed and not able to do union works,[43] and because of her status as a temporary worker. Nonetheless, she took her duties as a steward seriously. She devoted her time, in particular to organize temporary workers and raise their concerns. Through her union work, she acknowledges that she learns "new things and gain(s) a lot of experiences." However, it was also her union work that forced her to challenge many of the employer's arbitrary decisions at the workplace, and ironically, some of her co-stewards viewed her outspokenness as a threat to the union's "harmonious relationship" with the employer. She describes this delicate situation as follows:

> Since I became one of the union's stewards, I learn new things and gain a lot of experiences. However, I am also sad and upset, son. The company and the union are drawing a sanction on me for this month. I can't really tell you what has happened, son. Maybe, next time. You know, I am the only female among the nine members of the union's stewards; not only I am new in the union's stewardship, but also, I was a non-permanent worker then. Nazik, as a male, [please be reminded] never to look down on women with the pretext of protecting, giving the best [to them] or any other excuses that show you are more powerful. (p. 249)

Although she did not disclose the actual event and reason of the sanction against her, she indicates that it was due to her activism. It seems that she was seen as outspoken (*berani*). If that is the case, she must have been warned by her (male) co-stewards and "in the pretext of protecting" they were, in fact, patronizing her. She was expected to follow what she was told to do, simply because she is a female. For her, that attitude was "looking down on women" (*merendahkan perempuan*).

At the time of writing the essay, she was still struggling with this issue. Her concern about the increasing production target (as set by the employer) may have been the starting point, but as things went further, it proved to be only the tip of an iceberg. She realizes that she is facing a bigger problem than just that of the increasing production target. She had turned to the union for institutional support. Although it had once defended workers' rights for employment security and fair wages, it now could not do much to organize any meaningful action to counter the employer. As an individual worker, Salsabila did not have the power to negotiate with the employer. As the only female steward, she was shackled by the patriarchal attitudes shared among the co-stewards that patronized her. It made her realize that the union, despite its institutional power, was limiting her struggle for equality for all workers in the factory. Under sanction by the employer and yet receiving no support from the union, she expresses her protest to her son, in hopes of changing attitudes in the next generation.

DEFENDING RIGHTS, CHANGING THE WORKPLACE

In her writing, Salsabila narrates her experiences as a factory worker and a union activist. Like many others in the industrial area of Bekasi, she is trapped in a flexible labor market that provides her with only casual employment in a nonpermanent position. As a single (working) mother, she has to toil for a living; she cannot risk losing her job, despite the difficult working conditions. Still, she brings herself to stand against the factory regime that denied her maternity protection due to her status as a temporary worker. She was the first temporary worker that had the courage to challenge this denial, and she did it by herself. It was her persistence that finally granted her the right. She did not keep her struggle to herself, but instead, helped her coworkers to exercise the same right and thus, started raising awareness among the temporary workers as a collective. Her individual struggle fomented a change at the factory level. For herself, this was the start of her involvement in the union. She was elected as a union steward; she was the only female and the only temporary worker on the steward council. Just like other female unionists who came before her, she set herself free from the politics of *malu*, climbed the ladder, and learned the ropes in the union. Her path as a steward was not easy, yet she did her best to represent and defend the interests of female (temporary) workers. Her writing is a testament of her struggle.

Writing her essay as a long letter to her son, Salsabila bridges her public and domestic lives. Like many other working mothers, she has to balance both worlds. She is aware of the difficulties in performing her duties both as a mother and as a union activist. As a widow, she is the sole breadwinner in the family and thus, she has to keep on working (and take various side jobs) to sustain her family. She has only limited time for her son due to obligations at work and must rely on family members to assist her to take care of her son. Unlike upper- and middle-class women, work for her is not merely a means to express herself or an extension of ambition, but the means of survival for her family. In work, she claims the act of mothering; her wages allow her to financially support her family despite her absence.

Salsabila's struggle for maternity protection stands as an important story of working women's activism in post-1998 Indonesia. Although legally recognized in 1948 and guaranteed since 1951, employers have not respected maternity protection, and male unionists often ignore them as part of the union's struggle. Female workers have had to fight for them on their own. Post-1998 Indonesia provides the space for female workers to voice their concerns and interests, and a number of them, like Salsabila, have the courage to defend their rights, even without the support of a union. We have seen how Salsabila fought for maternity protection on her own and as a result, other female (temporary) workers now can exercise the same rights as permanent workers. Salsabila's subsequent struggle for employment security and fair wages illustrates common obstacles that female workers have to face in their struggle for equal rights. Employment security is a luxury for many workers in post-1998 Indonesia, but especially so for female workers. Female (temporary) workers, like Salsabila and her coworkers, often must accept their employers' decisions or lose their jobs. Although post-1998 Indonesia has provided some basic institutional protections for workers who enable female workers to form and join any union they wish, there is limited space for them to raise their concerns as female workers. Thus, her writing can be read as a protest not only against the neoliberal conditions of the global marketplace that reinforce gender stereotypes, but also the patriarchal nature of the labor movement.

NOTES

1. See Schaner and Das (2016).

2. Although the gender gap in wage employment has steadily shrunk since 2000, the median wage rate for women is still less than that for men. Sohn (2015) notes that female workers earn about 30 percent less than men, in both paid work and self-employment.

3. See Athreya (1998) and Warouw (2008), based on their fieldwork in Tangerang, an industrial city on the outskirts of Jakarta. Athreya (1998: 53) notes that many workers tend to "go back to their native village." Warouw (2008: 105) notes that they "have no intention of becoming fully integrated into their factory employment."

4. The ILO's Convention No. 183 and Recommendation No. 191 (2000) identifies five core elements of maternity protection at work: maternity leave, cash and medical benefits, health protection at the workplace, employment protection and non-discrimination, and breastfeeding arrangements at work.

5. Bekasi is an industrial town located on the eastern border of Jakarta. Administratively, it is part of the West Java province. It has been developed as an industrial town since the late 1980s, when Jakarta's city limits left little space for the establishment of a factory within its borders. Due to its proximity to Jakarta and its importance as an industrial hub, Bekasi is part of the Greater Jakarta metropolitan region (*Jabodetabek*).

6. Salsabila (2015). Her essay is approximately 13,000 words long.

7. Letter writing as a genre is common in modern Indonesia, as early as the publication of R.A. Kartini's correspondence with her Dutch friends and patron in the early twentieth century. Many Indonesians are well aware of it, although they may not have read Kartini's letters completely. For the English translation, see Kartini (1921). I thank the reviewer who reminded me about it. Pramoedya Ananta Toer's *Nyanyi Sunyi Seorang Bisu* (1995) includes a collection of letters to his daughter describing his imprisonment on Buru island.

8. On a similar situation in the Philippines, Britwum et al. (2012: 57) note that "unions with bargaining teams led by men tended to focus more on wage increases and other direct economic measures in the collective agreement and were less likely to see gender-/women-related proposals as important."

9. Britwum et al. (2012: 57) note a similar situation in Turkey.

10. Jeon (2008: 13) notes that

(d)emonstrations in the late-Suharto regime failed to reshape unions into independent workers' organisations, despite an increase in the number of factory level strikes during this period. In the post-Suharto era, workers have been able to form their own unions, and to carry out "organisation-led resistance" at a factory level.

11. This keynote speech was later published as a newspaper article. For S.K. Trimurti and her important roles during the early period of the Indonesian Revolution (1945–1949), see Trimurti (1980), Soebagijo (1982), and Soeprapti (1958).

12. See Elliot (1997). See also Soetjipto (1947) for a short story on this issue.

13. By the early twentieth century, maternity leave was common in many European countries on the grounds of protecting mothers and infants. Nonetheless, in France, as Stewart (1989: 189) notes, it "never covered the large contingent of

nonwage workers, including peasant wives." This development in Europe must have informed the legal drafting of Law No. 12 Year 1948. According to this Law, maternity leave was mainly for industrial workers and as in France, did not cover nonwage workers.

14. See Law No. 1 Year 1951 (dated January 6, 1951) and Government Regulation No. 4 Year 1951 (dated January 6, 1951).

15. Article 13 of Law No.12 Year 1948 guarantees menstrual leave, maternity and miscarriage leaves, and breastfeeding periods for all female workers.

16. See Praptinah (1951).

17. Her report covers a number of companies: a coconut factory in Menado (Celebes), a fiber factory in East Sumatra, and weaving factories in Pasuruan and Tegal. Praptinah does not question the patriarchal ideology behind the women's night work provision. She emphasizes how employers have violated the provision; implicitly, she agrees to the provision. It was only in the 1960s that feminist studies began to focus on women's night work provision; see, for example, Stewart (1989). On ILO's conventions on women's night work, see Politakis (2001).

18. Praptini (1951).

19. Praptini (1951).

20. See SOBSI (1957).

21. Indraswari and Thamrin (1994).

22. See Singarimbun and Siarin (1995).

23. Perempuan Mahardhika, a radical women's NGO in Jakarta, reported in late 2017 that 50 percent of its research respondents in KBN Cakung felt insecure about their jobs and their pregnancy. Although the majority of the respondents could take maternity leave, many who cannot take leave have to conceal their pregnancies, as they fear losing their job (which is on short-term contract).

24. Yulia Sari (2016), based on the 2012 Indonesian Demographic and Health Survey, finds that full-time working mothers are 1.54 times more likely unable to practice exclusive breastfeeding than unemployed mothers. Lo Bue and Priebe (2018: 405) also note that "a clear competition exists between maternal employment and breastfeeding." Many factory workers cannot breastfeed their babies as they want to because breastfeeding rooms are not commonly available on the factory's premises and many are not allowed to bring babies to work.

25. In a study of workers' health in an export-oriented electronics factory in Purwakarta (West Java), Andriani and Assalam (2020: 41) note that "some workers were reported to have consecutive miscarriage during their time of employment. . . . Some other workers also reported having menstrual aberration and difficulty in getting pregnant." In many cases, workers do not have access to medical services. In at least one case, the number of miscarriages and stillbirths experienced by women workers in a foreign-owned ice cream factory during 2019–2020 sparked a protest. See "Factory work blamed for fetal deaths," *Jakarta Post* (March 5, 2020).

26. Maimunah (2008: 97).

27. Salsabila's son was two years old at the time of her writing. Preserving her story as if in a time capsule, she hopes her son will read it in the future. Like "Salsabila," "Nazik Almalaika" is also a pseudonym.

28. Throughout the essay, she recounts her story in the first-person mother ("ibu") and refers to her son as "anak" or "sayang." I translate her first-person reference of "ibu" as "I" and "anak" and "sayang" as "son."

29. On the social stigma of widows in Indonesian societies, see Parker et al. (2016).

30. On epistolary novels, Altman (1982: 61–62) notes that

> Any confidential exchange is motivated by psychological need, and the letter writer's own emphasis on that need. . . . [T]he continuation of correspondence constitutes a practical narrative necessity for the epistolary novelist, but his characters also charge the chain of communication with psychological necessity whenever the desire for self-expression, self-justification, revelation, or admiration becomes a major propelling force behind the narrative.

In Jane Rhys' postcolonial short story, "Fishy Waters," the letters confirm what the public already suspected and heard about and so readers hear the insider's voice. In Mariama Bâ's *Une si longue lettre*, as Reyes (1994: 198) notes, "the epistolary narrative consciously extols the impression of reality that has not been censored."

31. Sjahrir's *Indonesische overpeinzingen* (1945) could have been the first epistolary essay in modern Indonesia. It also contains elements of personal feeling and intimacy, next to political aspirations to allow the intended reader (Maria Duchateau, his future wife) to understand his activism. It is important to note, however, Sjahrir's *Indonesische overpeinzingen* is, in fact, a collection of real letters that was published years after they were written.

32. The company's name is not real; it is her invention. In fact, it is a pun as it literally means "honest loss" to highlight how honest workers working there were treated unfairly.

33. Ruddick (1995: 40) notes that "feminist writers distinguish the experience of mothering from the oppressive, confining, isolating institutions of motherhood that spoil that experience for so many women."

34. See Suryakusuma (1996); Sen (2002); Blackburn (2004).

35. Madrasah Aliyah (MA) is secondary school-level religious institution (for students 15–18 years old). It is part of the Indonesian national educational system, under the Ministry of Religion.

36. Many employment agencies operate as a *yayasan* (foundation), instead of a "Limited liability company" (Perseroan Terbatas), to evade paying taxes and making a public accounting report. Based on his research on employment agencies in Tangerang, Juliawan (2010: 50) concludes that

> (e)mployment agencies function in a way that separates labor from its owner (the worker) and sells it to client companies as a factor of production. In so doing, PEAs [private employment agencies] radically alter the social relations and institutions that are the backbone of a society, transforming them into a profit-making nexus and socializing them into market relations governed by the imperatives of efficiency and competition.

37. This situation has two attributes. On the one hand, limited choice of employment and difficulty in getting a job must have forced her decision to stay in the job,

regardless of the working conditions that were endangering her own safety and health. On the other hand, taking the risk of her own safety and health at work affirms her performative mothering. Her "willingness" to stay in the job shows her dedication as a mother to her child.

38. Law No. 13 Year 2003 guarantees paid menstrual leave (articles 81 and 93), maternity and miscarriage leave (article 82), and a breastfeeding period (article 83) for all female workers, regardless of their employment status.

39. Law No. 13 Year 2003 regulates that subcontract/outsourced workers can only be employed for certain types of jobs and for limited terms of employment.

40. National-level labor unions, whose members are permanent workers, were taken aback by the novel strategy of temporary workers that was actually developed at the factory level and outside of their institutional arrangement. Many unions, however, opted to protect their members' employment and status as permanent workers and thus failed to see the potential of subcontract/outsourced workers to become union members.

41. This strategy is known as *pemutihan* (literally meaning whitening). Under various pretexts (in some cases, with financial compensation) the employer does not acknowledge the employment record of temporary workers and thus, as prescribed in the labor regulation, is allowed to keep them employed as nonpermanent workers.

42. Although paying a worker below the minimum wage is illegal and such offense can directly be reported to the authorities (the local office of the Ministry of Labor) for legal penalty, the union suggested to negotiate this issue first (with the employer) to avoid further conflict in the factory. It seemed that the union, whose members are permanent workers, did not want to "upset" the employer too much in supporting the temporary workers' demand. As the "raid" as a strategy began to lose ground and the employer's counter steps gained success, the union now took a cautious approach to dealing with the employer so as not to lose what the workers had already gained.

43. Ockey (2004) and Hirai (2008) note a similar situation in Thailand.

Part 3

LIBERATING SELF

Although domestic workers have migrated from Indonesia since colonial times,[1] similar to several developing states in Asia, Indonesia established state institutions to encourage its citizens to work overseas in the 1970s.[2] In order to support its developmental agenda, the New Order state created a specific image of overseas workers, and domestic workers in particular, in its official discourse. On the one hand, such workers are considered fragile subjects who need the state's paternalistic protection, while on the other hand, their economic value is indispensable to supporting the country's development. This image production has led to a popularized view of overseas female workers as representing both the nation's pride and its shame. The public image of overseas domestic workers in particular was mediated through newspaper reports that emphasized certain types of portrayals—an image that was consumed by (potential) overseas workers, too. This image and such fixed portrayals have not significantly changed even since the 1998 *Reformasi*, which brought about some institutional changes related to migrant labor placement procedures.

Since 1998, the government of Indonesia has imposed several moratoriums on the deployment of workers overseas, for instance to Malaysia (in 2009) and Saudi Arabia (in 2011). Although such moratoriums claimed to protect workers, they were imposed only *after* public outcries about alleged abuses, including sexual abuse, perpetrated against domestic workers while they were overseas. While there are some genuine efforts to improve protections for overseas workers (and to eradicate human trafficking), persistent limitations of the state's capacities to implement and monitor its regulations consistently require overseas workers to find their own means to survive and endure hardship.

It is important to note the feminization of labor as a salient characteristic of Indonesia's labor migration.[3] More than 70 percent of the annual number of officially documented Indonesian overseas workers are women, and they are predominantly young (below the age of twenty-five). Considered unskilled labor, they mainly work as domestic helpers. Although Gulf countries had been the primary destination for these workers since the 1970s, beginning in the late 1990s, the number of workers heading to the more developed countries of East Asia (Singapore, Malaysia, Taiwan, Hong Kong, and South Korea) has been steadily increasing. Many Indonesian domestic workers now prefer Hong Kong to the Gulf countries, for better payment, treatment, and other various personal reasons. Indeed, Indonesians working as live-in maids and/or caregivers have penetrated the labor market in Hong Kong to such a degree that as of 2017, nearly 45 percent of the 360,000 registered foreign domestic workers there were Indonesians.

It is also necessary to understand the status of overseas domestic workers within the New International Division of Labour (NIDL) of twenty-first-century global capitalism, which relies on the "desire" of these women to work overseas. As Cheah writes:

> What drives the temporary emigration of FDW [foreign domestic workers] is not only their ideological constitution as good wives, daughters, mothers, or sisters—although this is an important factor—but, more crucially, the crafting of their interests as subjects of needs by biopower, just as the ground for the importation of foreign workers is prepared by the crafting of their employers by similar governmental technologies. . . . Whatever the role of ideology in making the wills of these women migrants, they also go with the firm desire to improve their lives, because this is how their needs and interests have been shaped by governmental technologies.[4]

Indonesian women do work overseas to earn higher incomes and better their lives. Yet while the image of overseas domestic workers as "economic heroines" is based on some truths, this reason is often singled out as the dominant narrative since it fits well with the state's project of promoting labor emigration to support developmental projects (including, to solve domestic unemployment).

In reality, however, economic reasons alone are not the only factor pushing these women to take the risk of working abroad in difficult jobs.[5] In the stories presented in part 3, Indonesian domestic workers give an honest depiction of the complex and multifaceted reasons—aside from financial considerations—for working abroad. These reasons range from a passion for adventure and aspirations for personal freedom, to escaping social duties at home and forgetting painful past events (such as failed relationships and marital breakup).

Despite their own reasons, migrant workers are most often valued based on economic calculations alone. Their employers quantify their labor as an expense. Agents constantly remind them that their employer expects them to work only and not to have a life outside work. Meanwhile, the Indonesian state values their remittance more than their thoughts, aspirations, and sensibilities. The underlying assumption is that, regardless of their reasons for working abroad, they must only contribute economically, not socially or politically—both in destination countries and in Indonesia. Although their labor is indispensable, their aspirations are not acknowledged.

Disproving the notion that their only contribution is economic, part 3 presents both fiction and nonfiction literary products of overseas domestic workers (journals in chapter 5 and short stories in chapter 6). These writers have been prolific both individually and collectively. Between 2005 and 2016, more than two dozen notes, novels, diaries, and short stories by overseas workers were published—all written in the Indonesian language. Several individual poems have also been published in local and national newspapers throughout Indonesia. Despite the volume of work, only a few reports of these writing activities and no serious study of overseas worker stories have been published. Their works have not been properly acknowledged and, sadly, are neglected by literary communities.

Indonesian women working (or who used to work) in Singapore and Hong Kong are writing their stories of migration in various literary forms and on many different topics. They are prolific and creative in penning their stories. They defy a conventional public image that assumes they are uneducated or do not "have the culture of writing," an issue discussed in chapter 5. Constable notes that employers in Hong Kong often treat domestic workers "like children who might be tempted to stay out late, mix with bad company, and get into trouble."[6] Their literary works challenge such stereotypes and patronizing treatment and illustrate the broad range of aspirations, thoughts, and feelings held by overseas workers. They also demonstrate how these authors do not let their domestic work stop them from developing and expressing themselves.

Their stories are diverse and portray various themes; they are written in distinct styles and display a keen personal interest in reading and writing. It is undeniable that the opportunity to work overseas provides workers with life experiences unknown to them back home. Their work and life in urban capitalist cities in East Asia have inspired them to write stories; many only started to write when they began their two-year stint abroad. It appears that among destination countries, Singapore and Hong Kong in particular have provided an enabling social environment and cultural support for them to write.[7] Nonetheless, their literary skill is the result of their own craft.

Chapter 5 discusses how overseas domestic workers, through their journals, confront the narrative of their suffering that is often propagated in the public and in the media. Chapter 6 discusses how overseas domestic workers use fiction as a literary tool to showcase their creativity, and in so doing, liberate themselves from the public image and social construction imposed on them. Both the journals and fictional stories are media for overseas domestic workers to express and convey their personal and work experiences, thoughts and feelings, and fantasies and hopes. Their writings are part of the fearless speech of the Indonesian working class.

NOTES

1. During the Dutch colonial times, a number of native-Indonesian *zeebaboe* (sea nannies) went along with their masters to the Netherlands for fixed periods of time (see Poeze 1986). Max Blokzijl wrote the *kroncong* song "De Zeebaboe," which tells the story of Adinda, who took the six-week journey by boat with her Dutch master to the Netherlands (see Mutsaers 2014).

2. See Hugo (2006); Killias (2018).

3. Hugo (2006: 83) notes, based on Indonesia's official data from 1977 to 2003, that "the dominance of women involved in official international labour migration and it is apparent that domestic workers make up the majority of this flow."

4. Cheah (2007: 97).

5. On motives for migration, see Oishi (2005, especially chapter 5). For Eastern Indonesian women, as Williams (2007: 132) notes,

the appeal of traveling and working abroad – apart from the money – was the opportunity to escape from family constraints and live in a different community overseas for an extended period. Some simply wished to experience different spaces and places, which in their words was '*memperluas cakrawala*,' which literally means to expand their horizons.

In the case of Bugis migrant women workers in Malaysia, Idrus (2008: 168) notes that

[s]earching for brighter futures (*massappa'dallé'*) for *passimokolo'* carries not only a sense of economic purpose (as labour migrants), but also, for single women, the non-economic intention of finding a husband . . . . Working in Malaysia is about earning and consuming, not about saving or sending money home.

6. Constable (1997: 546). On how legal technologies have wrought tremendous impacts on domestic workers, see Cheah (2010).

7. On the involvement of local NGOs and the Catholic Church in Singapore to provide for the needs of the foreign domestic workers, see Arotçarena (2015) and Devasahayam (2016).

Chapter 5

Journals for Rights

Indonesian overseas domestic workers express their experiences abroad through various media. Letter writing was once the only and primary means of communication to family members and close friends, even up to the late 1990s. This was due to the expensive nature of international telephone calls, which were only used for emergencies.[1] Friends or acquaintances returning home would often pass on letters to family members. While the content varied, the letters mainly described a worker's life and work abroad and conveyed messages of their safety and promise to return home once their contract was finished. Today, letter writing has been replaced by the extensive use of the internet, mobile phones, and social media.[2]

Some overseas workers keep diaries, finding consolation in keeping track of the entries.[3] As a private record, a diary allows workers to express their thoughts and feelings for personal consumption and reflection. Some workers compose poems, either for themselves (kept in diaries) or for family members (written in their letters).

Published poems, on the other hand, express workers' thoughts and feelings to the public.[4] Most poems are free from literary conventions (such as meter or rhythmic structure) and instead emphasize the content and message. Readers are invited to interpret these poems as a way to understand workers' difficult lives as foreigners away from home. Poem-writing competitions for overseas workers have been regularly organized by local and regional NGOs in Hong Kong, Singapore, and Taiwan (since 2014) and in Malaysia (since 2015) and they have attracted a considerable number of submissions.[5] A number of Indonesian domestic workers participate in these events; many see it as a venue not only to share their feelings and experiences but also to gain recognition for their cultural activism and to set an example for others to follow.

These various written expressions (in the form of letters, diaries, and poems) are normally intended as a private record or for limited circulation among friends or relatives to maintain personal communication. When they are published, however, they are necessarily made public, and therefore serve a different purpose. From these published writings, the public is able to step into the shoes of overseas workers, see from their perspectives, and listen to feelings that are often left unsaid (or are not allowed to be expressed in public). Published letters are a window to workers' plight and thus enable readers to sympathize with their struggle for decent work. By publishing (either through competitions or submissions to newspapers and magazines), workers want to show that they are "productive" beyond their wage-earning job, and they are not "wasting" their time abroad. Publishing for the public also gives readers a chance to think beyond stereotypes and assumptions. Several organizations have also used workers' writings in campaigns to gain public support and force the Indonesian government to change its policies vis-à-vis sending female workers abroad.[6]

This chapter will examine two published journals, or *catatan*, written by Indonesian women who worked overseas: Rini Widyawati's *Catatan Harian Seorang Pramuwisma* (*Journal of a Domestic Helper*) (2005) and Astina Triutami's *Aku Bukan Budak* (*I am not Slave*) (2015).[7] Their works illustrate the conditions faced by many overseas workers, from the beginning of their journey to go abroad, to their work and social life in a land with a different cultural orientation than their own (in this case, Hong Kong), and finally upon returning home. Both were written and published after the authors finished their stints as domestic workers.

Although both Rini Widyawati and Astina Triutami went to work in Hong Kong for different reasons, as described below, they share similar backgrounds to many other overseas domestic workers. First, they both had a low level of formal education and therefore found it difficult to secure a job in Java. Domestic work is often considered unskilled work and unlike factory jobs in urban Java, it does not require a high school diploma. Both authors are also from low-income families (although they are not the poorest of the poor) and had to start working at a young age.

After finishing primary school in 1992, Widyawati (born in 1979) worked for Ratna Indraswari Ibrahim, a well-known local author in Malang, East Java, as her typist. Realizing that she only had limited job opportunities in Indonesia after the 1997 Asian financial crisis, she registered with an overseas employment agency in her town and got a job as a manual worker in an electronics factory in Malaysia for two years (1999–2001). After returning home for a brief period, she went to Hong Kong as a domestic worker under a two-year contract (2002–2004).

Triutami (born in 1988) had a different life path. At fifteen years old, after finishing junior high school (Sekolah Menengah Pertama), she lived on her own and went to work as a shop attendant in a clothing store. She did not stay long at this first job, joining some friends to form a music band and perform as a busker in Bandung (West Java). After two years living as a busker, she got a job as a ticketing agent in a travel agency. It was at this time that her father became ill and she had to take care of him full-time and thus, quit her job. After the death of her father, at nineteen years old (going on twenty), she entered the labor market only to find that she had extremely limited options due to her educational attainment.[8] It was then that she registered as an overseas domestic worker with an employment agency. She notes that the agency changed her age to twenty-one, as the minimum age requirement for overseas workers was twenty years old. After passing several tests during a month-long placement process, she finally secured a two-year contract to work in Hong Kong as a domestic worker. She arrived in Hong Kong in February 2009.

In their journals, both women give a vivid picture of daily life as a domestic worker and provide detailed practical and factual information on work and life in Hong Kong. They inform readers about the work assignments and house chores that they were expected to perform. Their work was demanding and they rarely had their own time. However, unlike in the Gulf countries, domestic workers in Hong Kong are entitled to have one day off per week. Both Widyawati and Triutami made use of this day off by spending time on their own and sometimes hanging out with fellow Indonesian domestic workers. They tell personal accounts of what they saw and experienced at work in their employers' apartments, including their employers' habits, and the social activities they joined in Hong Kong.

These two journals differ from journals written by male workers. A number of Southeast Asian men have published their accounts of working abroad. Ventura, a Filipino worker in Japan, published his notes about working as a manual day-laborer in Japan.[9] Sharif Uddin, a Bangladeshi construction worker in Singapore, published a collection of short essays (dubbed as a "diary") about his experiences written during 2008–2016.[10] Ventura and Uddin's accounts focus on male characters working in public spaces and are written from a male perspective. Although Widyawati and Triutami are working overseas, they are confined to the domestic sphere. As such, they are able to observe (and record) life in "private" spaces. Rather than specific eventful episodes, their journals recount everyday encounters of working in a foreign home. They are living together with their employers, yet are treated as strangers and subordinates, and they note this contradiction in their writing. In public spaces, when domestic workers gather and socialize among each other during their days off, they are identified as one single entity, regardless of their diverse identities (as mother, single, married, lesbian, adventure seeker, devout Muslim, etc.). The authors describe how social interactions in Hong Kong are shaped by pre-conceived notions of their work, nationality, skin color, and sexuality.

This chapter begins by placing the two journals within the literary context of the *catatan* in Indonesia, which was developed during the latter period of the New Order regime. Reading these journals as *catatan* makes us understand how these workers as authors speak of broader social change aspirations. Although their journals list the problems and difficulties the authors faced during their work in Hong Kong, they invite readers to see their work and personal lives in their full complexities, beyond the narrative of suffering that is often portrayed in and by the media.

This chapter sees both journals as examples of literary products that alert fellow—and potential—overseas domestic workers about the ups and downs of working abroad, and, importantly, about their rights as workers. They want to raise awareness among domestic workers about their rights so they might be able to demand those rights at work without fear. Based on this perspective, this chapter shows how domestic workers in Hong Kong, with an understanding of workers' rights, are taking control of their own lives, breaking social barriers, and taking actions toward change based on their own power and resources.

CATATAN AND ITS POLITICAL SIGNIFICANCE

Catatan as a literary form originally referred to a personal account or life story. The most representative example of this is Pospos' *Aku dan Toba*,[11] which recounts the author's personal development from childhood to adulthood with a sense of reminiscence and "looking back." His *tjatatan* (*catatan*) is often considered one of the very first autobiographies in modern Indonesia. A *catatan* is not an autobiography in the Western concept of it, however. Although a *catatan* may be autobiographical, it is more limited in its scope than a conventional autobiography. Similarly, although often translated as "diary," many published *catatan harian* are not diaries or journals in the strictest sense of the word. Not only do they lack a chronological telling, they are often written after the events of the work, making many *catatan harian* more like a post factum note. The blurring of forms between *catatan* as an autobiography and *catatan harian* as a diary or journal is understandable in that Indonesians use various historical and cultural trajectories to chronicle their lives, recollect their past, and preserve their memories in a more fluid manner than most Western authors do. Both forms allow the author to narrate his or her life story with a certain degree of literary freedom while injecting personal opinions of certain historical events that she or he was involved in or witnessed. Thus, both *catatan* and *catatan harian* can (and should) be treated as life-story literature and readers should, as Reid says, "accept them [the authors] as real people with real responsibilities and real decisions to make."[12]

While *catatan* as a form remained firmly rooted in Indonesian literary tradition, it was not until the early 1980s, during the height of the New Order regime, that *catatan* were cast in a new light with the publication of Ahmad Wahib's *Pergolakan pemikiran Islam* (*Upheaval in Islamic Thinking*) (1981) and Soe Hok Gie's *Catatan Seorang Demonstran* (*Annonations of A Demonstrator*) (1983). Both Ahmad Wahib and Soe Hok Gie were born in the same year (1942) and wrote, individually, a number of thought-provoking articles as university student activists and young scholars. Both were prolific public intellectuals of their time (in the late 1960s, during the early years of the New Order regime). Both died young: Soe when he was twenty-six years old (in 1969, one day before his twenty-seventh birthday) and Ahmad Wahib when he was thirty years old (in 1973). It is important to highlight that their *catatan* were actually an anthology of their published articles on many social-political issues and their personal thoughts. They were edited and (re)published posthumously to fit the social and political context of the time of their publication. The titles *catatan* and *catatan harian* were added by the publisher, the Institute for Social and Economic Research, Education and Information (Lembaga Penelitian, Pendidikan dan Penerangan Ekonomi dan Sosial; LP3ES), a Jakarta-based NGO that advocates for social change through its research and publication arms.[13]

Both *catatan* were well received by the reading public. Many young activists during the New Order regime could easily relate to the many issues that both authors raised in their articles, and related to the authors as (young) persons of integrity, something they wanted to emulate in their own activism. Both Soe and Wahib symbolized an ideal (male) activist able to keep his integrity without being "contaminated" by the political bargaining that characterized the New Order regime. The political context of the time of their publication reflected the consolidation of authoritarian power under Soeharto after the 1977 legislative election, and the 1978 "normalization of campus life" policy (*normalisasi kehidupan kampus*) that was meant to sterilize universities throughout Indonesia from political activism and prevent university students from becoming regime dissidents. In that sense, both *catatan* became political texts for a generation that was looking for inspiration (and idols) within the suppressive political conditions of the New Order regime. With the publication of both accounts, *catatan* as a literary form not only narrated the author's life story; it now contained political aspirations as well.

After the publication of both accounts, *catatan* were written not only by young activists and political dissidents but also by regime supporters. For example, in his *Catatan seorang WNI* (1988), Junus Jahja uses the *catatan* to unflinchingly support the New Order. Junus Jahja was a Chinese *peranakan* who converted to Islam (in 1979) in an effort to advance the New Order's assimilation policy (*kebijakan asimilasi*). Under the policy, expressions of Chinese culture through language, religion, and traditional festivals were suppressed; ethnic Chinese were expected to assimilate within their social surroundings, practice their cultural heritage within the private sphere only, and show their "Indonesian-ness" in public.[14] Jahja's *catatan* set out to illustrate that the New Order had successfully addressed the "Chinese problem" (*masalah Tjina*) through its assimilation policy, and that the policy was, after twenty years of implementation, without a doubt the most desirable solution for every ethnic Chinese in Indonesia. By doing so, he highlighted how *catatan*, as a form that includes political commentary, can be used by both regime dissidents and supporters.

The political nature of *catatan* endured after the fall of the New Order and the democratization process that began in 1998. It remains the most common form of narrating one's life story combined with political views and continues to be used by authors of various political backgrounds and orientations. It is considered the best form to express one's political stance. As in the past, it is still used by those who disagree with mainstream political thought. We can see this in *Catatan dari Penjara* (*Notes from Prison*) (2006), written by Abu Bakar Ba'asyir, a Muslim cleric who espouses an ultra-conservative interpretation of Islamic teachings and whose Jemaah Islamiyah has been linked to Al-Qaeda. The book is meant to be his instrument of political *da'wah* to reject (Western) democracy and instigate political *jihad* toward a true Islamic caliphate.[15] The book has not been banned by the Indonesian government, illustrating that *catatan* as a form accommodates different political agendas, especially as liberal democratic institutions are taking root in post-1998 Indonesia and freedom of expression is legally guaranteed.

Former political prisoners of the New Order regime are also writing *catatan*.[16] Long denied the right to share their stories and express their thoughts in the public, political prisoners are now taking the opportunity, under newly guaranteed civil and political rights, to speak out about the many injustices they suffered under the New Order. The flexible nature of the *catatan* allows former political prisoners not only to write their life stories, but to also share their experiences as important lessons for the public to learn from. In the context of post-1998 Indonesia, their *catatan*, collectively, can be read as a record of human rights violations as well as a literary remedy of past injustices inflicted by the authoritarian regime. The publication of their *catatan* presents evidence of how their rights were violated (by the state) and indicates that the time has come for the state to acknowledge, compensate, and apologize for those violations.

Widyawati's *Catatan Harian Seorang Pramuwisma* and Triutami's *Aku Bukan Budak* can be read in the same vein as other *catatan*—as political notes of one's life story. They allow readers to better understand the authors'—and therefore overseas domestic workers'—position in society and the political meaning of that position. Their *catatan* also provide important contributions to the discussion of the development of *catatan* in the context of Indonesian literature, for two reasons.

First, both Widyawati and Triutami write their *catatan* foremost as domestic workers and as women. This is important because, as indicated by the examples above, most *catatan* are written by male authors who use the form as a way to publicize their political views and highlight their activism in the public sphere. In contrast, neither Widyawati nor Triutami aims to showcase her activism or achieve broad political change with her *catatan*. Unlike the male authors, who describe enduring physical and emotional tortures precisely for their political stands, these women describe the everyday experiences and indignities of simply being an expendable commodity in the regional labor market. Rather than directly calling for specific political changes, their *catatan* provide fellow workers with information to protect themselves, and fellow members of society with insights that may lead to better treatment of workers.

Despite these differences, Widyawati and Triutami's *catatan* share an important characteristic with the *catatan* written by political prisoners. They do not merely list past injustices and violations of rights, but rather describe their suffering as an expression of their political demands and aspirations for change. While former political prisoners demand restorative justice from the state, overseas domestic workers, as we will discuss below, demand equal rights and legal protection within the state's existing structure. While both the political prisoners' and domestic workers' experiences are important as historical episodes in the nation's memory, their political aspirations and demands are the important elements that bind their writings together as *catatan*. As a personal record, similar to letters, their journals narrate their lives and the injustices they experience abroad and in Indonesia.[17] As a *catatan*, however, they represent the broader struggle of female domestic workers in dealing with the problems they face, and their collective efforts to articulate those problems to raise public awareness. They write about violations of rights as well as aspirations for state protection, better treatment, and equality. Their *catatan* therefore move the form beyond incorporating a "political manifesto" to oppose a specific political system, to providing information to precipitate change within an existing political system.

Second, both Widyawati and Triutami's *catatan*, like the suppressed stories of former political prisoners, provide a platform for stories that have been hidden or neglected. The political prisoners' stories were "hidden" because they could not be published during the New Order regime. They only came to light after the fall of the regime and democratization. Widyawati and Triutami published their stories after they finished their stints overseas and went back home. Yet, their stories remain marginalized in mainstream publishing. As noted above, *catatan* can accommodate various authors from different backgrounds and political orientations. With its flexibility, *catatan* as a form also allows overseas domestic workers to blend their personal life story with personal and societal aspirations and express them in their own creative way.

While Widyawati and Triutami's accounts may not have as direct a political tone as the male authors' *catatan* do, they carry the same weight of attentiveness to problems that require political action. Although they are writing in the context of democratic Indonesia, unlike their male counterparts, these women authors do not have the access to enter and join political debates at the national level. Widyawati and Triutami are working women; their situation (and experiences) as female overseas domestic workers therefore form the basis of their *catatan*. This perspective serves as a window to the larger context of their life stories: the political economy of Indonesia as a low-income country that pushes them to work overseas, the weakness of Indonesia's legal institutions that make them easy prey for employment agencies to exploit their labor, the failure of Indonesian diplomacy abroad to protect their rights at work, and the limited economic prospects for them to become financially independent even after their long stints abroad.[18] Their accounts therefore adhere to the traditional usage of political commentary based on personal experiences in *catatan*. As we will see in the subsequent paragraphs, however, their life stories as female overseas domestic workers set a different tone of political *catatan* in a post-1998 Indonesia, which, with its democratic institutions, guarantees freedom of expression. Thus, these working women authors are using *catatan* to push marginal voices into political debates, expanding the form to include those who are not only neglected by their government, but also those marginalized by the economy and society. Finally, through the *catatan*, they also articulate and publicize their aspirations.

BEYOND A NARRATIVE OF SUFFERING

Overseas domestic workers are often associated with the hard life and sufferings they have to endure at work. Stories of overseas domestic workers being trafficked, exploited, and abused (physically and emotionally) are easily found in the media, which often sensationalizes this kind of news to garner readers' attention.[19] Concerned NGOs (both local and regional) also often bring cases of worker exploitation to the public's attention, carrying out extensive investigations of all stages of the employment process, including pre-departure, employment, and return to Indonesia.[20] Their reports alert the public to the structural problems of the employment process that treats workers as commodities.[21] However, government agencies quite often turn a blind eye to these problems and refuse to acknowledge them. In most cases, the government intervenes only after a public outcry about a particular case. Such an outcry is often coated in a nationalistic language that equates the case with an offence to the nation's pride and sovereignty and accuses the government of failing to protect its people. Similarly, politicians (local and national) often only highlight the plight of overseas workers to boost their public credentials and gain votes. Despite either good intentions or strategic decisions to protect workers and amplify their voice, these three public institutions (the media, NGOs, and government agencies) are producing (and reproducing) the public image of overseas domestic workers as poor and weak subjects who are destined to suffer at work—and unable to defend themselves.

Many domestic workers, ironically, also share this public image and project it themselves. Being isolated and suffering at work is often taken as the grand narrative about overseas workers' time abroad. In their respective journals, both Widyawati and Triutami note this strong image, which they also once shared. Widyawati describes her feelings upon arriving at the Hong Kong airport for the first time, as follows:

> Who knows if I'll die in this land, . . . like other domestic workers whose cause of death is unknown. Who knows if I'll commit suicide when I feel lonely living on my own with problems that come continuously from family and employer, as some of my neighbors said who once worked in Arab countries, Malaysia and Singapore.[22]

Widyawati, like many other first-time domestic workers, learned about the abuse and exploitation of workers from stories passed on by immediate friends and neighbors. These stories may function as cautionary tales about the dangers of working abroad, and particularly of being a domestic worker, as they are more vulnerable to specific types of exploitation. As Widyawati notes, these stories plant gruesome images in the mind of the listeners, who often take them as a matter of fact.

Meanwhile, when Triutami learned that her chance of finding work in Indonesia was very slim (due to her education background) and that her

options were limited to going abroad as a domestic worker, she describes her
feelings as follows:

> On my way, I thought about the news that I often saw on TV about overseas
> workers. I shuddered and shivered thinking that I would go abroad as a domestic
> worker and would unluckily end up working for a wicked employer or one who
> often sexually harasses domestic workers. That would be scary.[23]

Triutami, like Widyawati, is fearful of the abuse and exploitation of domestic workers at the hands of employers and employment agents. Just like
Widyawati, she was initially hesitant and afraid to work abroad because of
the strong public image of overseas domestic workers associated with suffering. She would prefer to avoid working overseas, but the tight domestic labor
market for low-skilled workers pushes her to take the journey abroad.

Interestingly, while Widyawati picked up stories from her neighbors,
Triutami notes the role of TV in distributing the narrative. The ten-year gap
between both accounts shows how the contents of the narrative have not
changed much despite the different means of sharing it and the development
of communication technology over the decade. The narrative of suffering has
captured the public's mind (including the workers'), and it endures as the
grand narrative that defines the kind of job that low-skilled female workers
must be willing to take rather than becoming unemployed. Although workers
have a range of experiences during their time abroad, the narrative of suffering is a convenient means of corroborating stories of personal dedication
and sacrifice, and thus further cements stereotypical images of women in the
broader culture and psyche.

Some scholars working on issues of regional migration and employment of
domestic workers also embrace this narrative of suffering and emphasize it in
their analysis. On his study of short stories by Indonesian domestic workers,
Piocos notes:

> I frame my discussion of the affective dimension of labor migration of Southeast
> Asian narratives by studying how the effects of suffering in Indonesian domestic
> workers' stories are produced and in turn, function as discourses.[24]

Although Piocos understands the pitfalls of emphasizing the narrative of
suffering in his reading of the short stories,[25] he does not continue to interrogate the very meaning of it. In failing to do so, he exposes the danger of
"suffering" becoming a hegemonic narrative that may prevent workers from
telling—and living—their stories from a different framework, and that even
if or when workers dare to do so, their stories may still be read within such a
narrative as a way to normalize and discipline them.

Both Widyawati and Triutami's accounts offer insights beyond the narrative of suffering. Both do write about their own feelings of isolation and loneliness as well as the suffering of fellow domestic workers. For example, Widyawati describes in detail the story of Sutiyah, a fellow worker who is not treated well by her employer:

> I know how miserable Sutiyah is babysitting two kids and cleaning up the house. She especially suffers during winters. Her boss has never bought her any lotion even after noticing her hands are red and sometimes, bleeding. . . . Although she has been here for years, she looks as if she has never changed her clothes. Her boss, indeed, doesn't like seeing her wearing any new clothes, or any clothes beside the ones that were first given to her.[26]

Before coming to Hong Kong, Widyawati heard about the suffering of domestic workers as stories told by friends and neighbors. But now that she is in Hong Kong, she has her own experiences and she learns more detailed information about the situation of her fellow workers. This knowledge, however, does not paralyze her into a passive subject that is unable to resist, overcome, and survive the situation. Instead, these stories make her aware of her rights as a worker.

Widyawati and Triutami tell us how they learn from these stories, understand their own limitations, and seize opportunities to make their situation better. Widyawati expresses her transformation and the importance of sharing with fellow workers:

> I realize I have a space for my own: humanity; our stories of sadness and happiness are not a subject we discuss with employment agencies, either in Hong Kong or Indonesia, not even with our government. Instead, they are for our fellow workers. Only with fellow workers, we can share our pain, our fears.[27]

Although they may have limited resources and capacities, domestic workers are not passive subjects; they do not give in and surrender to their suffering, but rather struggle to resist and overcome it. Through their personal agency and the collective support of other domestic workers, Widyawati and Triutami survive their work overseas and are encouraged by sharing their experiences for others to read about.

By going beyond the narrative of suffering, we gain a more nuanced reading of their *catatan*, which allows us to acknowledge the workers' personal struggles in their lives and work in Hong Kong.[28] We see how Widyawati and Triutami as authors share their life stories to help their readers (fellow domestic workers) understand the situation they face together as domestic workers in Hong Kong. Thus, both *catatan* do not merely describe the suffering of domestic workers (as cautionary tales); they provide lessons for their readers to learn about their rights as workers. This in turn enables them to demand better working conditions and defend themselves against any inhumane treatment.[29]

SHARING PROBLEMS, LEARNING ABOUT RIGHTS

In their *catatan*, both Widyawati and Triutami raise two important aspects of working conditions in Hong Kong: the minimum wage and working hours. They know their substandard incomes and long working hours (sometimes, without day offs) are not exceptional; many domestic workers in Hong Kong (and elsewhere) share these conditions. They consider these twin issues the root cause of their suffering at work and use them to illustrate the common situation among workers. As they explain these issues in their *catatan*, they express workers' shared experience of suffering, and, more importantly, their collective need for legal protection.

It is important to note that both wages and working hours are regulated in the employment contract. Hong Kong's Immigration Department has regulated (since 1974) that the standard employment contract for all foreign domestic workers is limited to two years. Although there is a Statutory Minimum Wage (SMW) in Hong Kong, the city government excludes domestic workers from SMW coverage.[30] This policy continues to this day, on the grounds, among others, that domestic workers "have a distinctive working pattern" from non-live-in workers and "enjoy in-kind benefits."[31] The policy establishes a two-tiered minimum wage structure with the SMW for all non-domestic workers, and the much lower Minimum Allowable Wage (MAW) for all domestic workers.[32] Although the monthly wage that domestic workers receive in Hong Kong is relatively higher than that of other countries in the region, it is not enough to cover basic needs in the city. Consequently, underpayment of foreign domestic workers is a widespread problem in Hong Kong.

Both Widyawati and Triutami, like thousands of foreign domestic workers in Hong Kong, experienced this persistent problem, and share their stories and thoughts about it in their journals. There are two common concerns about underpayment: first, that Indonesian domestic workers are paid less than workers from other countries (viz., the Philippines and Thailand), and second, that wages are declining over time. Widyawati expresses these concerns as follows:

> I know that our wages are below the standard wage. . . . In fact, my wage is decreasing. When I came here, I was earning HK$2,000 [monthly]. But now it is just HK$1,800 with 5 months of no wages at all.[33]

By comparing Indonesian workers' wages with the "standard wage" (the actual wage received by workers from other countries), Widyawati highlights an injustice shared by all Indonesian domestic workers.[34] In Hong Kong's labor market, Indonesian domestic workers are considered unskilled labor (by the employment agents) and hence, their wages are set lower than the MAW. They are classified as cheap labor. Yet, they are required to do the same work as domestic workers from other countries who receive better wage.

Widyawati also underlines the decreasing amount of nominal wages she receives. Her experience is consistent with a seven-year decline in the MAW from 1996 to 2003.[35] When Widyawati first came to work in Hong Kong in 2002, the MAW was HK$3,670 (as set in 1999). This was HK$190 lower than the previous MAW of HK$3,860 set in 1996.[36] In 2003, the Executive Council of Hong Kong again set the MAW at HK$3,270, a HK$400 decrease. This decrease affected all Indonesian workers whose wages were already lower than the MAW.

Many Indonesian workers, as Widyawati notes, do not receive any income during an initial period of work, which lasts at least for five months. Agents claim that this exorbitant "wage cut" is meant to repay the costs of air tickets and job placement fees. In reality, this scheme traps workers into keeping their employment contract regardless of their working conditions or employer treatment, and makes them dependent on their agents and employers who have an upper hand to exploit their labor. In some cases, employers pressure workers to end the contract before actual wages are paid, forcing them to find a new employment contract and start again with a new wage cut. In that situation, workers have no option other than returning to their agent, creating a vicious cycle of exploitation.

The issue of underpayment is directly connected to the issue of working hours. There is no standard working hours for domestic workers. And since workers are required to live in their employers' house, they are on call twenty-four hours a day. Most have to work from early morning until late nights, and they often do not have regulated break times or time for themselves. Many workers work more than ten hours a day.[37] Clearly, domestic workers are overworked, are expected to work long hours, and are often unable to refuse their employers' demands. Sadly, their long working hours are not fairly compensated by the income they receive (which is below the MAW). Widyawati writes about this:

We are working 24 hours a day. . . . At night, our employer's children wake us up to accompany them to the toilet. The same also if we work for the elderly; at night, we have to take them to the toilet and clean up their mess. Do they think HK$2,000 is too expensive? It's not even enough to cover our meals for one month; we can only afford vegetables and fish. Again, it is, honestly, not enough for us.[38]

Widyawati stresses the connection between being underpaid and being over-worked as their common problem at work, speaking directly to her readers. Noting that their wages are "not even enough to cover meals for one month" she draws her readers' attention to how they have been treated unfairly both in terms of their low income and that they cannot refuse their employers' demands.

Triutami also writes about the common problem of underpayment and overwork among her friends. It is obvious that working conditions in Hong Kong have not improved during the ten-year period between Widyawati and Triutami's journals (2005–2015). Triutami describes her work assignments, which were not written in the employment contract, and warns her readers that the contents of the contract were completely different from her daily reality:

> Apparently, I had to clean two houses every day. Unbelievable! I was shocked. . . . As far as I knew, this arrangement was against the law. I know for sure that a domestic helper isn't allowed to work in two different houses. Also, a domestic worker isn't allowed to perform works that are not written and agreed upon in the contract. . . . Why does the contract say that I have to take care of a baby? I suddenly felt cornered with this reality. And I didn't have the right to speak against it.[39]

Triutami's case illustrates two important issues. First, how employment agents and employers deceive workers by showing them a false contract and making them accept any working condition, regardless of whether it is against the law. Second, how workers are made to do chores at two different locations and thus are overworked.

Widyawati does not mention these two issues in her *catatan*, either as part of her own experience or that of people she knew. It could be that these practices were not yet common before 2005 (when her book was published). When Triutami first came to Hong Kong in 2009, it seemed that her employment agent already knew what to do to conceal this illegal practice (provide a false contract). While Widyawati points to being on call for twenty-four hours a day as overwork—and that this is a common condition among domestic workers—she also alerts her readers to the tactics that agents and employers use to violate the law and exploit workers more effectively. In this regard, she exposes how the issues of underpayment and overwork include illegal practices that force workers to do chores that are different from the contract.

It is interesting to note that Triutami refers to the "law" when describing her situation. She knows that what the agent is doing is "against the law" even though she is in in Hong Kong for the very first time. This indicates that workers are getting more information about their rights. It is worth noting that over the years, the Hong Kong government and concerned local NGOs (in Hong Kong and Indonesia) have produced various publications to inform workers of the law and give them practical tips on how to report any labor rights infringement. Widyawati writes, however, that employment agents (and employers) never forget to confiscate such publications from workers:

> There is a rule that forbids us to bring certain things in to our boss's apartment, including contact addresses and others. The agency also checks our luggage to see what we are going to bring inside. . . . We aren't allowed to carry with us the book from the Labour Department, which is given to us when we enter Hong Kong. Undeniably, it is an important book for us; for at least, when we feel lonely, we know that we are protected.[40]

Confiscation of these publications reflects the common interest of agents and employers to keep domestic workers unaware of their rights and hence, docile and totally dependent.[41] Domestic workers are aware of this and have various ways to evade the censorship routine of agents and employers. One of these ways is by writing about work conditions in fictional stories (as discussed in chapter 6). Such stories are a means of resisting surveillance and control over their private lives. Both Widyawati and Triutami describe such control in their writing. They tell us how, as live-in domestic workers, their lives are fully regulated by their employers from morning to night. They do not have their own private time, without being interrupted by their employers. Widyawati explains how she tried to keep her own time:

> In between chores, when I was on my own, in my loneliness in the 13th floor apartment, I wrote secretly. If my employer found out, he would say that I was not working but writing letters to my boyfriend.[42]

Keeping a diary (*catatan*) was Widyawati's way of keeping her own time, and in that way, her *catatan* is evidence of her resistance against her employer's control and surveillance. It is particularly important because, as she informs us, she had only one day off per month—although the law in Hong Kong stipulates that domestic workers should have one day off per week. Since private time was precious to her, she spent it by writing her *catatan* (hiding it from her employer's eyes).

Meanwhile, Triutami tried to make the best of her private time in Hong Kong by applying to short courses at a local college, after noting that she had one day off each week to spend on her own. However, once her employer found out about her application to the local college, they angrily terminated her employment contract at once. She recounts the event, as follows:

They were very angry when they found out that I would continue my studies in Hong Kong—although, there is no law against it. . . . I asked why
they terminated my contract, even though I didn't do anything wrong. Their
answer was something like this: "You are a domestic helper! You came to
Hong Kong to work, not to study!" I was totally stunned by that, and with
trembling hands I signed the letter of termination; it was wet from my tears.
When I packed my clothes, granny [her employer's mother whom she had to
take care of] came over and shouted, "I've never seen an Indonesian maid
studying English. And even reading newspapers, too!" She continued on like
that, grumbling about it.[43]

Although Triutami must have known and anticipated that most employers in
Hong Kong would avoid hiring a "smart domestic worker," she didn't expect
that her plan to study would result in the termination of her employment
contract.

Both Widyawati and Triutami's accounts here illustrate how employers
control the working hours of domestic workers beyond what is allowable by
law and monitor what workers do in their own time as a way to dictate what
workers can and should do. Putting aside employers' preference not to hire
"smart workers," the issue here is how employers believe that they own a
worker's time (despite paying poorly for it) at work and outside work.

By raising the twin issues of underpayment and overwork, Widyawati and
Triutami clearly alert their readers to the dire situation that shapes their life
and work in Hong Kong. They show how underpayment makes them suffer
and puts them in a weak position vis-à-vis their agents and employers. Their
readers can easily relate to this, as they may have experienced it, too. In this
way, readers are able to see that their situation is not a particular one, but, in
fact, shared by thousands of other (Indonesian) workers in Hong Kong who
face common problems laboring under an exploitative system. Furthermore,
readers can understand that their suffering at work in Hong Kong is a result
of underpayment and overwork—in other words, a violation of their rights
to fair treatment and to rest. By pinpointing the cause of their problems,
Widyawati and Triutami's *catatan* move improving workers' situation
from something beyond their reach into the realm of something that can be
changed when they have the courage to speak up, as what Widyawati and
Triutami try to do with their *catatan*.

Their *catatan* highlight the importance of legal protection for overseas
domestic workers. Indonesian workers realize that their government has not
been able to provide minimum protections to ensure their safety and well-
being overseas. They reason that this is the root cause of their plight, as
Widyawati explains:

we need a clear-cut law so we can articulate freely, without any fear, our rights to our employers, like other workers of different countries who are more protected [by their government].[44]

There is little doubt that "other workers of different countries" here mainly refers to Filipina workers. It is a common belief among Indonesian workers that their Filipina sisters are rarely harassed by employers due to protections provided by their government. Whether this belief is based on certain facts or imagined, many Indonesian workers refer to it when lamenting their situation as part of the narrative of suffering.

How Indonesian workers came to share this belief aside, there is a purpose in their self-comparison with Filipina workers. The Philippine government promulgated the Migrant Workers' Law in 1995, and as early as 2001, its Department of Foreign Affairs implemented a "migrant empowerment program" in cooperation with the ILO.[45] In contrast, the Indonesian government had neither formulated nor developed any legal protection for domestic workers overseas until 2004.[46] While the scope of protection and related programs administered by the Philippine government is limited (some may argue that in reality, it has little impact), the Philippines does set a standard for its embassies and consulates to guarantee legal protection (including consultation and legal defense) for overseas domestic workers, especially those in Hong Kong. This is a basic service that the Indonesian consulate in Hong Kong has often failed to provide. Furthermore, as Setyawati notes, "a national agency responsible for the reintegration of workers, like the Philippine NRCO [National Reintegration Center for Overseas Filipino Workers], is absent in Indonesia."[47]

The absence of the government's legal assistance for Indonesian domestic workers has been raised by local and regional NGOs for years. A coalition of local NGOs in Indonesia submitted a report on the condition of overseas domestic workers to the UN Special Rapporteur on the Human Rights of Migrants (UN SR-HRM) in 2002 and 2003.[48] Responding to mounting pressure from the NGOs, in September 2004, the Indonesian government signed the International Convention of the Protection of the Rights of All Migrant Workers and Members of Their Family, and in 2006, the Special Rapporteur on the Human Rights of Migrants, Dr. Jorge Bustamante, visited Indonesia.[49] The Convention was ratified in May 2012 after languishing for more than four years in parliamentarian sessions. This development in providing legal protections for domestic workers shows that the Indonesian government, under democratic conditions, is aligning its institutions with some international standards. Many overseas domestic workers, however, are still waiting for the implementation of the standards.

Providing legal protection includes protection for workers during the pre-departure period and upon return to Indonesia.[50] UN bodies and local NGOs have urged the government countless times to address exploitative practices, to no avail. Both Widyawati and Triutami record their personal experiences of how recruitment agencies in Indonesia exploit workers, especially those who are vulnerable and uninformed of their rights. The lack of government monitoring and the absence of penalties in the case of infringement have made the matter worse and many workers have to bear the price.

The most crucial issue, however, is when workers are returning back to Indonesia. In 1999, the government established a separate gate at Jakarta's airport known as "Terminal 3" to separate out and process returning workers from other travelers entering the country, and to arrange transportation back to their hometowns.[51] In the name of protection, returning workers were segregated and expected to comply with the state's control of the movement of people across the national border. In reality, however, workers were subjected to extortion and harassment by the very apparatus that was supposed to protect them.[52] It shows that "protection" was used to justify the extortion and harassment workers had to experience and endure.

Despite numerous direct complaints from returning workers and protests from local NGOs, the government continued to enforce the separate gate policy. In 2002, it appointed the Central Cooperative of the Police (Pusat Koperasi Kepolisian Mabes Polri), the business arm of the police, to manage the returning process of domestic workers at the airport.[53] It was apparent that the economic benefits of managing returning workers were more important than the state's duty to protect workers. Following protests from local NGOs on this arbitrary appointment, the government delegated the management back to the Minister of Manpower.[54] The security apparatus, however, was kept intact. In 2007, the government established "Terminal 4," which operated much like the previous Terminal 3. It opened in February 2008, and workers immediately found that it was no different. It became known among workers as the "thieves' den" (*sarang penyamun*). Triutami also had to enter "the den" when she returned to Indonesia:

> I was required to go through Terminal 4 Selapajang, the thieves' den. It is an isolated gate and all migrant workers are assigned to go through it. Instantly, I remembered stories from some friends who had bad experiences [of being harassed] and don't want to return to Indonesia through Soekarno-Hatta airport anymore.[55]

Triutami then proceeds to detail how she was extorted and harassed, as if to warn her readers of the real situation behind the government's promise to protect them. Although she holds contempt against the whole process at Terminal 4, Triutami sees it more as a problem of implementation and "unprofessional officers"[56] rather than an inherent problem with the system itself. Women workers are made to believe that they need protection, while in reality they are treated as objects.

After constant protests from the NGOs, the government decided to end its separate gate policy in 2012.[57] In August 2014, the Corruption Eradication Agency detained as many as eighteen officers of the Terminal 4 (including a number of police and army officers) for alleged extortion of returning workers.[58] The government, finally, decommissioned Terminal 4 in that year. There is no separate gate for returning workers anymore; they can choose their own means of returning home.

On November 27, 2017, the parliament passed Law No. 18 Year 2017 on the protection of Indonesian overseas workers. Although this Law establishes some important changes in the placement process for Indonesian overseas workers (such that placement should be free), it does not have any specific provisions to prevent exploitation of domestic workers. The Law assumes that all overseas workers are the same, ignoring the particular nature of domestic work that makes female overseas workers more vulnerable to abuse, being paid substandard wages, and having to work limitless hours. In response to this, NGOs have been advocating the government to ratify ILO Convention No.189 on domestic workers, which specifically addresses the unique challenges of domestic labor.[59] It is not yet clear how responsive the government will be to the demands of female domestic workers for legal protection. In the meantime, Indonesian domestic workers in Hong Kong are organizing themselves to claim their rights.

ORGANIZING AND ITS CHALLENGES

Indonesian workers are disappointed by their government's limited capacity to protect them abroad. Despite constant criticism, over the years the Indonesian consulate in Hong Kong has changed little to respond to workers' needs for basic services, including reducing placement fees and providing legal assistance.[60] In light of this inaction, workers have started to organize.

In Hong Kong, Filipina domestic workers began organizing much earlier than others, and it is from them, through acquaintance and friendship, that Indonesian domestic workers have been encouraged to form their own association. Since the mid-1990s, overseas workers, with the support of local NGOs, have established organizations that provide counseling and legal assistance on employment issues for overseas workers in Hong Kong. Generally, these organizations are formed based on nationalities. For instance, United Filipinos in Hong Kong (UNIFIL-HK) caters to the needs of Filipino workers, while Friends of Thai (FOT) assists Thai workers. These organizations come together to work on common issues, such as campaigns against pay cuts and advocacy against racial discrimination at work. Many Indonesian workers learn about these support organizations (only) after they are caught in troubles regarding their working conditions and realize the need to organize among themselves.[61] In 2010, Eni Lestari, the chairperson of the Association of Indonesian Overseas Workers in Hong Kong (Asosiasi Tenaga Kerja Indonesia di Hong Kong), admitted that her organization was relatively new compared to organizations of workers from other countries, and that "Filipinas, Thais and Sri Lankans had been organising for years."[62] Needless to say, Indonesian workers are relative newcomers when it comes to organizing to more effectively defend their interests.

Nonetheless, inspired by the experiences of fellow workers from other countries, Indonesian workers in Hong Kong have made some significant strides in organizing in recent years. Some committed worker-activists, like Eni Lestari, joined hands and formed a formally registered organization among Indonesian workers. Workers are beginning to recognize that organizations have succeeded in defending their interests and are advocating for public support for their cause.

Despite this progress, however, many workers do not consider organizing as imperative. It is important to note that many Indonesian workers just beginning their two-year contract for the first time in Hong Kong quickly learn—after being told by their agents or employers who inspect their luggage and confiscate books on workers' rights—that organizing is not welcome. They may lose their job if agents or employers know about their participation in such activities. Since organizing is cast in a negative light, and may result in substantial negative consequences, workers tend to be reluctant to join in any organizing activity—even if they might be interested in it. This explains why only a handful of Indonesian domestic workers are actively joining workers' rights organizations in Hong Kong.

The hegemonic power of the market entrenches this situation. Indonesian workers are forced to accept whatever work is available no matter how bad the working conditions because they know they have weak bargaining power in the market. Considered unskilled and not fluent in speaking Cantonese (and/or English) compared to workers of other nationalities, employment agencies put Indonesian workers at the lower end of the pay spectrum in the labor market in Hong Kong. Although many workers strive to upgrade their skills and take language lessons, only a few are able to surmount existing barriers and break the stereotype to change or upgrade their employment contract and earn a decent wage at work. Those who do succeed tend to attribute it to their own personal determination rather than to any result of collective struggle by an organization.[63] Therefore, Indonesian workers, unlike workers of other nationalities who draw support easily from their own organizations, are conditioned to resolve workplace issues on an individual basis without the support of an organization to defend and secure their minimum rights as an overseas worker.

In their *catatan*, both Widyawati and Triutami point to a much deeper challenge to changing workers' perception of organizing. They note that many workers are *willing* to be underpaid:

> Many workers are willing to accept in their second-term, for example, two days off per month and a monthly wage below HK$3,000. They reason, "That's enough already. I won't need to have a day-off every week." . . . That's [the answer of] an obedient worker.[64]

Triutami observes a similar situation: that many of her fellow workers are willing to accept underpaid work. She reminds her readers, whom she believes must have heard of such cases (or even be one themselves), that by accepting underpaid work, they are complicit in their employer's violation. She expresses her resentment:

> I can't stand those who are willing to accept underpaid contracts. [They are] Very dumb. Far away from home to work for two years. With open hands, they support their employers in violating the laws paying a maid below the minimum wage. I imagine their employers would be laughing hard on their goose-feather beds as they whoop, "Ha ha ha, Indonesians . . . not only poor, they are also dumb. So happy I can save my money. What a dumb maid!"[65]

Although Widyawati and Triutami wrote their *catatan* ten years apart, both confirm that many Indonesian workers tend to accept pay even below the MAW, indicating that not much has changed over the years. They prefer to keep quiet and not raise any complaint about their working conditions (including being underpaid), even when they know it violates the laws and they must suffer the consequences. As such, although they know organizing is important, they avoid it. They want to keep their job, regardless.

This willingness to accept underpay presents the greatest challenge to organizing Indonesian domestic workers in Hong Kong. Despite payment below the MAW, no pay for five months or more, limitless working hours, and other difficult working conditions, Indonesian overseas domestic workers are willing to keep their jobs. They are willing to suffer at work until they are fired. They will bear the hardship in order to send their earnings to their family at home as part of fulfilling their obligations as a "good daughter." Under this patriarchal ideology, they know they have to endure the suffering and show their dedication to the family. If they complain about the working conditions or join a workers' organization, they will be out of job and they will not be able to fulfill their familial obligations.

RAISING AWARENESS, DEMANDING RIGHTS

Indonesian overseas domestic workers, like workers of other nationalities, use various means to convey their experiences of living and working abroad to family members, friends, and the general public. They write letters, compose poems, keep diaries, and publish books. After democratic changes in 1998, more domestic workers, especially those who (used to) work in Hong Kong, have published a number of writings. Among these are the journals of Widyawati and Triutami, written ten years apart after each author finished contracts in Hong Kong as domestic workers. Widyawati and Triutami's books offer two examples of how working women are advancing the genre of the *catatan* while using it as a platform to advocate for worker rights. They illustrate how overseas domestic workers express their concerns and aspirations, what options they have to voice those concerns and aspirations, and challenges of doing so.

The *catatan* has been used by various actors in modern Indonesia to express their political thoughts and ideals. Under the authoritarian regime of the New Order, the *catatan* was instrumental for political dissidents to express political narratives different (although, not always alternative) to the state's. Since 1998, as Indonesia establishes democratic institutions, the *catatan* as a literary form has continued to function as an important instrument. With *catatan*, former political prisoners tell the public about their experiences of injustice under the New Order, reclaim their rights, and demand rehabilitation. As political *catatan*, Widyawati and Triutami's journals offer a reading beyond the narrative of suffering that has framed the life experiences of domestic workers as powerless victims and has limited their modes of expression. Widyawati and Triutami's *catatan* inform the public about their life and working experiences abroad and raise awareness among domestic workers about their rights as workers. They illustrate how Indonesian overseas domestic workers have strived, despite hardships and difficulties at work, to learn about and defend their rights. In doing so, they have moved *catatan* from an instrument of direct dissent to a tool to precipitate change within existing systems, while at the same time enhancing women's agency.

More Indonesian workers in Hong Kong now understand their rights, including to a decent wage, normal working hours, day offs, and fair treatment.[66] Inspired by the efforts of fellow workers of other nationalities in Hong Kong, they have also established an organization to help garner public support and better defend their rights. Some issues (such as placement fees and wage cuts) are still unresolved, but the language of rights has enabled workers to earn better wages and social protections. Workers' organizations, however, remain unable to build a collective consciousness among workers. Domestic workers are atomized in the labor market due to fear of losing their jobs and the temporary nature of their contracts, which prevents them from investing more time and energy into organizing as a collective class. Despite all these obstacles, Widyawati and Triutami's *catatan* declare that overseas domestic workers are not powerless victims. By writing their own stories, they are claiming their rights and their own destiny.

NOTES

1. See Aeniah (1998), Krisnawati and Mardzoeki (1999), and Salma et al. (2010). For many Southeast Asian overseas workers, letter writing was the dominant form of communication. See, for example, Koetsawang (2001) on Burmese workers' private letters and De Guzman's (2008, 2011) analyses of letters written by Filipino workers to family members and NGOs.

2. For example, see Camposano (2018) on the use of Facebook among Filipino male migrant workers in South Korea.

3. For example, the case of Cambodian manual workers in Japan (in *Mainichi Shimbun*, October 19, 2010).

4. See, for example, Adepunk et al. (2008), Ally Dalijo (2010), and Aliyah Puwanti et al. (2010). In the context of Southeast Asia, see Hossine (2016), a Bengali overseas worker in Singapore who writes poems; Belen Esposo Repollo (2015), a Filipina domestic worker in Singapore who notes that "writing poetry is her way of overcoming homesickness and longing for her loved ones." Repollo was the only domestic worker among the thirty contributors of an anthology that claims to offer a "glimpse into the lives Filipinos in Singapore."

5. See, for example, Premanathan and Tshiung (2017).

6. For example, Salma et al. (2010), a five-year report of Women's Solidarity (Solidaritas Perempuan), a Jakarta-based women's NGO, on its advocacy activities on female overseas workers' issues, includes eleven letters from nine overseas workers (working in Kuwait, Abu Dhabi, and Singapore) to their family members as an appendix.

7. Although Widyawati's book is titled *catatan harian*, it is not a diary or journal in its strictest sense, because it was not written chronologically and was composed only after she finished her stint in Hong Kong and returned to Indonesia.

8. Triutami (2011: 38).

9. Ventura (2006 [1992], 2007). On Ventura, Hau (2004: 268) notes that he "devotes more spaces to recounting episodes of violence and mayhem rather than the

uneventful everyday, and contributes character sketches of 'interesting' or noteworthy people."

10. Uddin (2017).

11. Pospos (1950). See also Rodgers (1995).

12. Reid (1972: 3).

13. LP3ES, established in 1971, was well known during the 1980s–1990s for its quarterly journal, *Prisma*, that provided space for liberal/critical articles on democracy and development in Indonesia. Eldridge (1995: 95) notes that "(d)uring its early years, FNS [Friedrich Neumann-Stiftung, a German NGO related to the Freie Demokratische Partei, a liberal center-right party] gave sufficiently substantial assistance to LP3ES to enable it to concentrate on its work without spending time raising money."

14. On the assimilation policy, see Coppel (1983).

15. In a similar vein, Imam Samudra, an Islamist extremist who was involved in the 2002 Bali bombings, wrote a memoir of his life and political thoughts. Although Ba'asyir's charismatic influence is more extensive and deeper than Samudra's, both of them have limited vocabularies in their common quest for political change in a diverse Indonesia after 1998. Shiraishi (2011: 281) notes that "what I find striking about Imam Samudra is the thinness of the language with which he makes sense of his own life, mission, and journey."

16. See, for example, Atmoko (2011) and Moeljono (2013). It is important to note that former political prisoners are using various mediums to express themselves and are not limited to *catatan*. For example, Putu Oka Sukanta writes novels. See Sukanta (2004, 2012).

17. "Surat Tapol kepada TKW, Cucunya" (A Letter from Political Prisoner to His Granddaughter, A Migrant Worker), a short story by Martin Aleida (2017), highlights this commonality between ex-political prisoners and a migrant worker in narrating their lives and struggle for humanity.

18. A World Bank study (2006) shows that worker remittances are primarily used to pay debts and meet daily needs (such as school fees for children or siblings), and they may not have a significant or permanent effect on the lifetime income of a household. Upon their return home, the savings of these workers can only support them for a few months and in less than a year, they need to get a job to survive.

19. Many male migrant manual workers also experience abuse in the workplace. See, for example, Yi et al. (2018) on the horrifying working conditions of distant water fishing (DWF) that employs many young migrant workers as fishermen.

20. See Eko et al. (2008), Tagaroa and Sofia (n.d.), and Umar (2010).

21. Although their official monthly wages could be ten times higher than the wages of domestic workers in urban cities in Indonesia, they have to shoulder "overhead" costs such as agency and placement fees that can deplete up to ten months of wages and hence, they are made to pay these fees in installments for the first few months of their employment. The first seven to ten months of employment are so crucial that workers often choose to keep quiet and persevere, despite experiencing abuse and labor rights infringements, in order to pay back these fees.

22. Widyawati (2005: 2).

23. Tirutami (2015: 39).

24. Piocos (2016: 92).

25. Piocos (2016: 107) notes that

> I am also aware that by focusing on the theme of suffering, I am at the risk of portraying Indonesian women, in general, as passive, pathetic preys of globalization devoid of any form of agency. However, . . . by telling their story and expressing how they feel about their experiences, they affectively mediate, in terms of what else to do, the narrow possibilities of resistance that their cruel subjections could allow.

26. Widyawati (2005: 37–38).

27. Widyawati (2005: 178).

28. On reading Chistiakova's autobiography as a typical working-class narrative of suffering during the Soviet times, Rotkirch (2004: 154) reminds that, "it is crucial to remember that such rhetorical use of self-sacrifice and passivity does not imply actual passive behaviour."

29. It is interesting to note that both Widyawati and Triutami use various terms, interchangeably, to describe their employment status: "babu," "TKW," "buruh migran," and "domestic helper." It is beyond the scope of this present chapter to discuss if any of these terms has significant impacts on the workers' perceptions of their employment status and working conditions, and their understanding of their rights.

30. Since 1973, the SMW has been set every two years.

31. Hong Kong's Legislative Council Brief on Minimum Wage Bill (2009: 5) notes,

> Having carefully considered all relevant factors and circumstances as well as the views of stakeholders, we propose to exclude all live-in domestic workers, local or foreign, from the coverage of the SMW (statutory minimum wage). Our major considerations are, namely, (a) the distinctive working pattern of live-in domestic workers; (b) their enjoyment of in-kind benefits not usually available to non-live-in workers; (c) the possible significant and far-reaching socio-economic ramifications; and (d) the fundamental erosion of the long-established FDH policy. (See http://www.legco.gov.hk/yr08-09/eng lish/bills/brief/b24_brf.pdf.)

32. Leubker et al. (2013: 80) note, "When introducing the new minimum wage that will take effect on January 1, 2013, Malaysia followed Hong Kong's example and exempted domestic workers from the coverage on similar ground." The government of Singapore also does not prescribe a minimum wage for foreign workers.

33. Widyawati (2005: 112).

34. "Standard wage" here means the Minimum Allowable Wage (MAW).

35. Hong Kong's Economic Development and Labour Bureau (Labour Branch), in its report on Adjustment of Minimum Allowable Wage (MAW) of Foreign Domestic Helpers (FDHs) (2003: 2), notes that

> the reduction of the MAW by $400 (or 10.9%) from $3,670 to $3,270 with effect from April 1, 2003, is to reflect the downturn in Hong Kong's economic and employment situation since the last review of the MAW in February 1999.

The report does not mention (and evidently, did not consider) that many domestic workers, especially from Indonesia, receive wages below the MAW.

36. Widyawati did not mention this earlier wage cut. She was most likely unaware of it.

37. Amnesty International (2013: 10) notes that the vast majority of Indonesian domestic workers it interviewed in Hong Kong "worked on average 17 hours a day."

38. Widyawati (2005: 120).

39. Triutami (2015: 254–255).

40. Widyawati (2005: 112–113).

41. Eni Lestari (2010) also notes that Hong Kong's government has "translated the employment ordinances into Indonesian and hands us pamphlets about our rights when we go through immigration. [but] Lots of agents confiscate the booklets along with migrants' passports as soon as they leave the airport."

42. Widyawati (2005: xii).

43. Triutami (2015: 396–397).

44. Widyawati (2005: 112).

45. See Ofreneo and Samonte (2005).

46. On October 18, 2004, the parliament passed Law No. 39 Year 2004 on Placement and Protection of Indonesian Workers Abroad.

47. Setyawati (2013: 274). It does not mean that the Philippine government has never failed to provide protections for its workers abroad. The (mis)conception among Indonesian workers is that the Philippine government performs better than their government.

48. The 2002 report is titled "Indonesian Migrant Workers: Systematic Abuse at Home and Abroad." The 2003 report is titled "Indonesian Migrant Domestic Workers: Notes on its (*sic*) Vulnerability and New Initiatives for the Protection of their Rights." These reports are available in Indonesian, published by Komnas Perempuan and Women's Solidarity (Solidaritas Perempuan) with financial support from the Ford Foundation and DGIS.

49. Dr. Bustamante visited Indonesia during December 12–21, 2006, at the invitation of the Indonesian government. On International Migrants Day (December 18), he spent time with a coalition of over sixty NGOs in Jakarta. See "Report of the Special Rapporteur on the Human Rights of Migrants, Jorge Bustamante, on his mission to Indonesia, 12–20 December 2006" (dated March 2, 2007).

50. Sukamdi et al. (2001: 132) note,

Indonesian government does not respond to the problems raised by female international migration well. It does not have a protection policy which covers the recruitment process. . . . This means potential migrant choose the private agencies to help them migrate abroad, even though they are expensive. Potential migrants rely more on information from family, and friends than from formal information sources.

51. See Decision of the Minister of Manpower No. 204 Year 1999.

52. In her study of Terminal 3, Silvey (2007: 277) concludes,

The state has planned, built and managed the terminal to serve as a funnel through which the bodies and incomes of returning overseas workers are renationalised and reterritorialised. . . . Terminal 3 represents one site within which the state participates in the social reproduction of inequality across transnational space.

53. See Decision of the Minister of Manpower No.173 Year 2002 (dated September 24, 2002).

54. Etik Juwita (2006) writes a short story on workers' experience of returning home in fear due to this special gate policy.

55. Triutami (2015: 345).

56. Triutami (2015: 352).

57. See Regulation of Minister of Labor and Transmigration No. 16 Year 2012 (dated September 26, 2012).

58. See https://antaranews.com/berita/453000/kpk-bubarkan-bpktki-selapajang-pa scapemerasan-tki (Accessed on September 7, 2017).

59. Hirano (2017) discusses the nature of Convention no. 189 and its possible implications for Indonesia's labor policy.

60. See, for example, the short story "Potret Susi" by Ratna Khaerudina (2010) on how workers find the Indonesian consulate in Hong Kong unresponsive to their call for help.

61. See Asato (2004) on the efforts of the Indonesian Migrant Workers Union in negotiating placement fees.

62. Lestari (2010).

63. Interestingly, Triutami (2015: 332) notes that

luck is one of the main factors to explain the success of Indonesian domestic workers. No matter how dedicated workers are at their work, no matter how fluent they speak Cantonese, no matter how good their personalities are, there are still unpredicted factors that are inevitable to face and that's where luck plays its role, and it is beyond worker's control.

64. Widyawati (2005: 65).

65. Triutami (2015: 331).

66. It is interesting to note that domestic workers in Latin American countries are fighting for equal rights in ways similar to domestic workers in Hong Kong. Blofield (2012: 62) argues that

legal reform appears not to be correlated with the citizenship status of the domestic worker labor force. In Argentina, Chile, and Costa Rica, three of the richer economies in South and Central America, a growing share of domestic workers are Andean and Nicaraguan, respectively.

Chapter 6

Fictions of Freedom

On the morning of November 1, 2014, the lifeless bodies of Sumarti Ningsih and Seneng Mujiasih were found in the apartment of a British banker living in Hong Kong. Rurik George Jutting (age twenty-nine) had dated these women (ages twenty-three and twenty-nine) before murdering them.[1] Both had come to Hong Kong as overseas domestic workers, but their incomes were so meagre (around US$500–530 per month) that at some point during their stint, they began moonlighting as sex workers to earn extra income. Seneng Mujiasih had overstayed her domestic worker visa by three years, while Sumarti Ningsih entered Hong Kong on a tourist visa after previously having been a domestic worker for three years (2010–2013). Like millions of others, they had dreams of success in Hong Kong and were willing to take risks to better their lives and those of their family. Both women were breadwinners of their respective families, and had been devotedly sending remittances home. Yet far from achieving "success," their dreams ended in the hands of an upper-class foreign male.

Although the heart-breaking news of this double homicide case shocked their families back home, the two women's lives in Hong Kong were not necessarily uncommon among those who live in the island city. Characterized by fluid interactions across boundaries of race, class, occupation, and citizenship, Hong Kong provides the space and opportunities for people of different backgrounds, including domestic workers, to make initial contact, blend in, and collide across the social spectrum of its diverse society. Despite being easily identifiable as of a certain social status due to their occupation, even domestic workers partake of these opportunities.[2] Within the limits of social governance in the city, moonlighting as a sex worker is a common option for domestic workers (not only from Indonesia, but also from the Philippines and Thailand) to make extra income to send home. Dating upper-class foreign men (mostly, Caucasian)—either as a client or a lover—is seen as acceptable street wisdom, if not a golden ticket, to alleviate economic burdens in life. The life circumstances of Seneng Mujiasih and Sumarti Ningsih are not unfamiliar to domestic workers in Hong Kong; others face similar situations and they share their stories among each other.

Beyond the social marker of "domestic worker," however, anthropologists remind us that these female workers embody many overlapping identities: as a working woman, a mother far from her children, a single woman, a worker with digital literacy skills, a low-paid worker capable of standing on her own and defending her economic interests alone, a foreigner who often gets lost in cultural negotiations, a member of Muslim community that holds Friday prayers together, and so on.[3] These overlapping identities are constantly (re) negotiated and (re)shaped against the realities the workers face daily in Hong Kong, and are central to their existence in the city.

This chapter is an attempt to understand these overlapping identities, and the lives, of overseas Indonesian workers through a reading of their own literary narratives, specifically, works of fiction. It focuses on Tarini Sorrita's *Penari Naga Kecil* (*Little Dragon Dancer*) (2006a) and Maria Bo Niok's *Geliat Sang Kung Yan* (*Writhes of the* Kung Yan) (2007b), two pioneering anthologies of short stories penned by overseas Indonesian workers. It also reads a number of works by other worker-authors that were published more recently.[4]

The chapter starts with a description of the background of overseas workers' writing activities and the social meaning of the cultural shift to writing fiction, to highlight the characteristics and the challenges of their work in Hong Kong. Their literary works of fiction represent an important break away from the conventional practice of letter writing among migrant workers (see chapter 5). Writing fiction provides a public forum for domestic workers to describe their life, work, and hopes, freeing them from the politics of *malu*. In the hands of these domestic workers, as this chapter will show, fiction as a literary form is proven to be a strategic instrument for self-expression in their search of freedom(s).

The act of writing fiction as taken by these women shows that, regardless of the limited free time they have, they believe writing to be worthwhile and through writing, they wish to convey their messages to others. This in turn helps create a forum of readership among fellow domestic workers who treat reading, in one way or another, as a solace from their manual labor. With this in mind, this chapter reads both *Penari Naga Kecil* and *Geliat Sang Kung Yan* in terms of "seriality"[5] to understand the condition that has shaped their writing activities in Hong Kong.

Given the underprivileged status of the authors as domestic workers, these short stories are a product of their experiences in formulating personal feelings, social observations, and practical understandings of the urban capitalist world, and their daily struggle and personal dreams to resist, but also to become part of that world. Maria Bo Niok's use of the term *kung yan* (domestic worker)[6] in the title of her work resonates a sense of solidarity with her intended target readers (fellow overseas Indonesian domestic workers, especially those in Hong Kong) who can easily associate her writing with their own personal experiences. Undeniably, the writings explored in this chapter appeal to fellow overseas domestic workers, who can identify with the content and seek lessons and suggestions from each other through it.

The stories illustrate how Indonesian domestic workers manage life, seek leisure and romance, and share their experiences despite the challenges that capitalism and globalization pose to their lives and perceptions. By writing, they overcome social and cultural pressures that supress or forbid them to express themselves freely in other outlets. Their works of fiction are important materials to enrich our understanding of the contemporary conditions of labor migration in East Asia, from the perspectives of workers—in particular, women workers—themselves.

It is also important to note that these writers are actually reading and responding to (and interestingly, promoting) the works of their fellow working sisters, and thus the issue of intertextuality is central to their writings.[7] While they write based on their personal experiences of living and working abroad, their stories are more than self-expression; they are artistic representations of the world of working people. In the absence of the state's protection and amid the waves of an emerging collective social awareness as foreign domestic workers, these workers have developed a form of self-liberation through the vehicle of writing fiction to collectively claim their own autonomy.

OVERSEAS DOMESTIC WORKERS AS AUTHORS OF FICTION

The literary path taken by these female overseas workers is shaped by various factors, yet one important quality of this path is that they learn to compose short stories and novels by themselves. They do not have any prior training in creative writing or writing experience that might have prepared them with some literary techniques or vocabularies to entertain readers. Instead, they learn to write by self-practice and studiously laboring over drafts for publication.[8]

Tarini Sorrita's *Penari Naga Kecil* and Maria Bo Niok's *Geliat Sang Kung Yan* are important examples of the kind of narrative prose being produced by overseas domestic workers through years of self-practice in narrating stories.

For them, life abroad not only offers experiences that they could not have had back home in Indonesia, but more importantly, provides opportunities—however limited—that have shaped their lives toward a different understanding of the world around them. Fiction as a literary genre has become an effective tool that workers like them use to give meaning to their new lives and work abroad. It provides a space for them to freely combine facts and fantasies, to move between anonymity and having some public profile, and to convince their readers about some important issues while at the same time entertaining them.[9]

Both Tarini Sorrita (nom de plume of Tarini binti Saban bin Jungkir, born in 1971) and Maria Bo Niok (nom de plume of Siti Mariam Ghozali, born in 1966) attained primary education, but did not begin writing until they worked overseas.[10] Both had to do manual labor from an early age and indeed, their working experiences were the main sources of their learning about the world. Interestingly, both of them note that their "highest education" is the sum of experiences they have had in life (*pengalaman hidup*).

Prior to Hong Kong, Sorrita worked as a street vendor, a golf caddy, and an administrative assistant for a marketing office. Bo Niok ran her own petty stall selling rice and birds in a traditional market in her hometown, Wonosobo, Central Java.[11] After her failed marriage, and being a single mother, she decided to work abroad to support her children and family.[12] Both Sorrita and Bo Niok became seasoned overseas domestic workers, working in more than one country before Hong Kong: Bo Niok worked in Taiwan for two years and Sorrita in Singapore for four years. While this shared background (coming from a poor family, having a limited education, being an urban manual laborer, and eventually an overseas domestic worker) is common among millions of Indonesians, these two authors are always seeking opportunities to improve their life through their own efforts, and they view writing as a liberating way to transcend the limitations of their social background. As such, their works break the chain of silence among overseas domestic workers and open the door of opportunity for others to express themselves beyond the politics of *malu* and to enter the world of literature. Indeed, their works have encouraged fellow Indonesian overseas domestic workers to start writing, and many, especially those in Hong Kong, have followed their path to write.[13]

By writing and publishing, these workers are also participating in the Indonesian public sphere, where literature and mass media (as well as film, radio, and television) are important mediums for public debate and exchange. Despite NGO campaigns and media attention on the stereotypical hardships experienced by overseas workers, the lives of foreign domestic workers have never been explored in depth in any Indonesian novel. Overseas workers almost never become the subject of Indonesian literature, reflecting their absence from the minds, and horizons, of the middle- and upper-class authors and themes that dominate.[14] Overseas domestic worker-writers, therefore, add heretofore absent female and working-class perspectives to Indonesia's public discourse.

As we have seen in chapter 5, in contrast to the (re)production of their public images as poor, weak, and uneducated subjects who are unable to defend themselves, Indonesian domestic workers in Hong Kong are taking an active step to describe their own world through their writings. They create a context in which they can freely narrate their personal lives and experiences to share among themselves, but also for the general public to read.

In fiction, these writers discuss their vulnerabilities as overseas domestic workers and share their fantasies and hopes as women. Unlike upper- and middle-class women authors, they do not write fiction as a leisure activity or for a literary experiment.[15] Instead, they use fiction to share life stories among themselves in a creative and meaningful way, beyond conventional forms of non-fiction. Unlike non-fiction, where the worker/writer assumes the first-person position (see chapter 5), fiction allows domestic workers to see and write from different angles and perspectives, to move between realities and fantasies, and more importantly, to entertain their readers. As authors, they know that short stories attract and keep the interest of readers with similar backgrounds (who are also young, from rural Java, and working class) and experiences.

Domestic workers also know that short stories are considered "safe." Employment agencies (and sometimes, employers) check workers' luggage and confiscate any pamphlets or books published by NGOs or government agencies on labor rights because they are considered "dangerous."[16] Workers, however, are allowed to keep fiction books for their leisure or entertainment after work. By writing short stories, they can share their life stories, alert fellow workers of their plight and rights, and extend solidarity among themselves—freely. Thus, the short story becomes a strategic tool to resist surveillance and control over their lives. With their works of fiction, these workers are not only clearing a literary space in Indonesia, but empowering women of the working class.

MANAGING LIFE IN URBAN HONG KONG

As noted above, these published stories are mainly written by women who are working (or have worked) in Hong Kong as domestic helpers. Hong Kong as a "global city" may provide a situation for these migrant workers to write in spite of their work, but this alone is not a sine qua non for their deep involvement in literary production.[17] Their stories are inspired, formed, and result from their personal experiences working and living abroad. Their experiences

as a foreign worker must have been so overwhelming that they feel the need
to share it, yet, at the same time, their stories also show how they try to overcome the sociopolitical barriers they face and aspire for change.

The fact that their stories are written for fellow domestic workers to read
is crucial to their writing. The daily activity of a domestic worker is included
in their stories precisely because their readers can relate to it. For example, in
her short story "G/0,03,10,13,18," Sorrita describes the daily routine of Tanti,
who has been a domestic worker in Hong Kong for the last four years. From
early morning, Tanti washes her employer's car, prepares her employer's
children for school, cleans up the apartment, and does household chores,
including shopping at the market for daily meals. Such routines are common
for fellow domestic workers. Interestingly, the title of the short story indicates
the floors of the apartment building where Tanti works and lives, and where
she meets fellow domestic workers from other countries in the elevator of the
apartment building:

> Now inside the elevator there are three ladies [each from]: Indonesia, Thailand,
> and the Philippines. All came to Hong Kong to toil for their future. They have
> helped to strengthen the foreign exchange of their respective countries. Ting!
> The 10th floor. Tanti got off and casually said, "bye bye." Ting! The 13th floor.
> Anna got off uttering goodbye to Felly. Ting! This time Felly got off from the
> elevator when it reached the 18th floor, and she was just smiling in exhaustion at
> her increasingly dusk age. Yes, Tanti always passed by all those numbers every
> day during her 4 years at Visalia Garden [name of the apartment building].[18]

The story describes the diversity of people working in Hong Kong, a phenomenon that many first-time domestic workers may find strange compared
to their hometowns, which have strong traditional values and one dominant
cultural reference. The elevator is a microcosm of the whole of Hong Kong,
an arena where domestic workers of different nationalities meet and inter-
act despite having limited time to talk to each other. The story highlights
that understanding this cultural diversity and developing tolerance are key
for domestic workers to manage their life in Hong Kong and suggests that
domestic workers step out of their own cultural comfort zone by cultivating
friendships with people from different backgrounds and various nationalities.

Inspired by experiences of managing life in urban Hong Kong, the stories
often write an idealized female domestic worker-survivor as the main protagonist—a character who does not want to give up easily and is ready to face
obstacles in her life despite the challenges and prevailing conservative social
norms. It is as if, through their stories, both authors are in active discussion
with their readers about common issues they face as female foreigner workers. The stories alert fellow workers to life difficulties in the modern world,

but at the same time encourage them to make the most of whatever social opportunities Hong Kong offers as an urban city. In this regard, their stories might be seen as part of the *Bildung* narrative.[19]

What is obvious from their writings is that both Bo Niok and Sorrita do not confine themselves within the normal routines of their work, but instead, have the courage to explore different parts of life in Hong Kong. For them, Hong Kong is not only a geographical island where domestic workers can toil, but also a modern city where (rural) Indonesian young women can learn about various aspects of life and lifestyles that are often inaccessible to them in their home villages. The two encourage their readers to embrace adventures in urban Hong Kong, to gain thrilling experiences one can (only) have in the city, and to take any opportunity it offers, rather than just exchanging gossip with fellow domestic workers about their employers' habits or grouping around Victoria Park.

In her stories, Sorrita takes her readers on a journey to explore the many faces of Hong Kong by describing various parts of the city, especially its entertainment area around Wan Chai. In "Sepasang Penari Naga Kecil" (A Pair of Little Dragon Dancers), the main protagonist, Dhani, is a young domestic worker who likes to try "new things" in Hong Kong. Leaving behind her friends at Victoria Park, Dhani walks alone to the terra incognita area of Hong Kong that her friends dare not enter:

> Dhani was walking alone, tracing one after another the line of bars and pubs in the Wan Chai area. Her destination was none other than Laguna. For Dhani, Laguna held a lot of memories. All were sweet memories, although sometimes they tasted bitter, too. It was in Laguna that Dhani befriended some Caucasian [males]. Fortunately, all her Caucasian acquaintances were nice. They sometimes advised her not to slip into the dark ravine. That's the reason why she liked this place, although many people out there might not consider it as a decent place. Everything is actually dependent on who is involved, and whether she knew how to take care of her own self.[20]

Sorrita's conservative readers may not agree with her suggestion (through her character) to walk alone in the Wan Chai entertainment area, but she lures them in with the promise of "friendship with Caucasian [males]," something that can be taken literally as it is, but also serves as a symbol of experiencing something "foreign," "extraordinary," or "beyond the daily routine"—something a domestic worker can (only) experience in Hong Kong. For Sorrita, leaving behind the flock and daring to step into the terra incognita can open one's mind and lead to various life opportunities that probably have never even been thought of before. Sorrita also warns her readers that all is not always rosy in the adventure, as one should "know how to take care of her own self" so that she does "not to slip into the dark ravine."

For the more mature Bo Niok, Hong Kong offers different social opportunities for a domestic worker to benefit from. In "Nazar yang Tertunda" (A Late Vow), the female protagonist likes to spend her free time visiting various tourist locations that are far from the crowds of migrants at Victoria Park. Interestingly, she prefers to take classes as a means to develop her personal skills:

> I spent my subsequent holidays by going for a picnic in Aviary Pagoda and Stanley Beach. I also took a taekwondo class and some courses in City College so I had no more time to wander aimlessly.[21]

Bo Niok must have noticed how fellow Indonesian domestic workers are confronted with the choice of resisting or embracing the urban life of Hong Kong, and the different ways they spend their holiday time. Through the more comprehensive map of Hong Kong that her protagonist holds, readers realize that the city is not restricted to its entertainment districts: it also provides many modern facilities and opportunities for the people who live there, especially for domestic workers. She is redefining who workers are and what they can do. In her stories she reminds her readers that social resources (such as language training, college courses, and sport activities) are within the reach in urban Hong Kong, and available for workers to take advantage of. As a global capitalist city, Hong Kong exploits overseas workers for their cheap labor, but it also provides access to social and economic opportunities not available in their hometowns, to develop themselves as independent women. In *Geliat Sang Kung Yan*, readers see that the city offers resources to reach their dreams and goals, not only in term of income, but also in terms of personal development as human beings. In this way, readers are encouraged to accumulate skills that are considered useful and productive while they are in Hong Kong.

Bo Niok also describes the joy of writing experienced by her protagonist in "Istana Rumbia" (The Palace of Sago Palm Leaves), showing how writing is a worthwhile activity for her spare time:

> While working as a baby-sitter, she preferred to spend her free time writing. It was her diary that had always faithfully accompanied her when she missed her family and loved ones back home.[22]

This particular short story shows that although the free time they have is limited, domestic workers realize the need to write down their experiences, thoughts, and feelings.[23] For Bo Niok, writing offers a solace from her demanding work,[24] and she wants fellow workers to try writing diaries as a first step in developing one's writing skill, and to further develop their own style. Syifa Aulia, a former domestic worker who became a freelance writer, suggests that writing is "one of the best ways" for domestic workers to show their worth beyond the degrading public image so often projected about them.[25] In this way, readers are encouraged to start writing and become inspired to write their own personal experiences. In turn, fellow workers who read these stories are not passive subjects: they find guidance, inspiration, and a common voice to negotiate their own conditions in Hong Kong.

Far from implying that writing is the only, or main, activity that domestic workers should engage in during their free time, these stories acknowledge that writing cannot be isolated from the many other activities workers engage in during their everyday life.[26] In their writing, these workers are actively making choices about which issues they want to share with the public (while keeping other issues only for themselves), how to make subtle suggestions to their readers, and the best way to gain an audience for their stories. As authors, domestic workers make their own observations, develop opinions, and improve their awareness of self and society in general. In this context, writing, and the stories they create as a result of it, demystifies the public image of domestic workers as poor, weak, and illiterate.

ALIEN ROMANCE IN HONG KONG

As noted earlier, overseas workers are in constant interaction with many people from different backgrounds, and this interaction often helps them to locate their own place in society. Being abroad (in this case, urban-liberal Hong Kong) underscores the sense of freedom they have to develop a relationship free from the supervisory eyes of their family and no longer confined by the politics of *malu*. They are aware that they may (or can) only do this abroad. The venture that female domestic workers take in developing a relationship with men in urban Hong Kong resonates with what Anna Lowenhaupt Tsing describes as "alien romances" in her anthropological work on Borneo, in which Meratus women openly share their stories about having relationships with non-Meratus men that involve "a romance of mutual flirtation, not a female obedience."[27]

Similar to the constantly traveling Meratus women, overseas Indonesian domestic workers get a taste of personal autonomy, and many of them enjoy the socially relaxed atmosphere of Hong Kong, which exposes them to eye-opening experiences, (unexpected) brief encounters with various kinds of people, and numerous social opportunities. Both Tarini Sorrita and Maria Bo Niok explore this issue in their stories. They write about Indonesian female protagonists who form various relationships with males of different nationalities in the island city.

The stories illustrate how female workers are not just passively waiting for romance. They decide what kind of relationship they want to have and choose the men (including, in some cases, their employer) to be the subjects of their affection, fantasies, and sexual relationships. Importantly, they are not shy (*malu*) about this. In her short story "Hamil" (Pregnant),[28] Sorrita describes how Sasa, a young domestic worker, fantasizes of having a romance with her Caucasian Canadian employer whom she finds "good looking" (*cakep*):

> Undoubtedly, honestly speaking, Sasa's employer was indeed handsome. And more, he being a pilot was irresistible. And he was still single. His name was Michael. He was from Canada. Sasa met him only during dinnertime. It's because he always went working early in the morning. And so, it would be impossible for Sasa to fall in love with her employer. Being fond of him, however, was acceptable.[29]

The story describes how Sasa is lucky that her employer was kind-hearted and not demanding, and that her domestic obligation is mainly to prepare dinner for him. Thus, Sasa is grateful that she has ample time for herself. Although she finds him handsome and his occupation "irresistible" (*tidak kuat*), she is not sure if "*simpati*" (fondness/care) can be translated to love, thinking it is "impossible."[30] As the story unfolds, however, Michael not only likes Sasa's cooking, he falls in love with her. They accept each other and Sasa cannot believe that she finally has Michael as her boyfriend. The story ends with Sasa wondering if the relationship will continue to marriage.

In a similar vein, Karin Maulana, a domestic worker and author, tells the story of "Sasmitha," a domestic worker in Hong Kong who, within seven months of working in the city, marries her Chinese-Hongkonger employer:

> I was really taken aback by her appearance. She was completely different from the person I had known back at the training center. Her rather curly hair was now as straight as a plank, and she had white highlights in it. Her dress and shoes also made her look fancier. "I'm now a married lady," she suddenly explained as if she knew what I was thinking. "You mean that . . . " I answered, looking for confirmation of what she seemed to be saying. "My widowed employer has taken me as his wife, though I still have to take care of his mom. My status is not maid any longer. I'm a permanent resident of Hong Kong now. I can do whatever I want to," she explained eagerly.[31]

The two stories explore different stages of "alien romance." Sasa is beginning a relationship with her employer and wonders if it can continue (and survive) to a marriage. Meanwhile, Sasmitha's appearance and social position (legal status) has changed after she married her employer. Both protagonists, however, realize that their interclass relationships come with consequences. In the case of Sasa, she is expected to perform domestic work—both as a wife and a mother, not as a working woman. Meanwhile, Sasmitha fully understands that she "still ha[s] to take care of his mother" and as a wife, her care work is unpaid labor. Both stories can be read as expressions of workers' desire to escape from oppressing realities, craft an upward social mobility, and seek refuge in the "foreign"—no matter how flimsy and elusive it can be. The romantic relationship they have with their respective employers may change their financial and social status, but it comes with other consequences to their freedom to work and generate income from their labor.

Interclass romantic relationships also include relationships with someone outside the working sphere, or in the case of Rika, the protagonist of one of Sorrita's short stories, a stranger. In "Memory of Dragon Boat Festival," Sorrita describes how Rika, a domestic worker, meets James, a Scot, in a Wan Chai area club, and proceeds to go out to dinner with him:

> She felt a little embarrassed walking with him, as he was much older than she was. There were twenty-six years between them. . . . She found him nice; he treated her better than any other Caucasian guy she had been with. . . . Days follow days, one full moon follows another. And today is the Dragon Boat Festival day again. In other words, it's been a year since the start of this love story between two persons from different worlds. Their love story is all about delight and bliss; they have never argued. There is only love and affection between them. Perhaps this is because he manages to keep up with her.[32]

Rika's first rendezvous with James is unexpected, although it is in a club in Wan Chai area where domestic workers (like Rika) go for night entertainment and to meet foreign males (most often, Caucasians). Although readers are informed that Rika went to the club just to dance (not looking for a date or partner), they are not told what James thinks of Rika and why he wants to date her. Nonetheless, she is willing to give it a try and later finds that James is a kind man "not like any other Caucasian males" (whom Rika might have dated before). Despite their age gap, the relationship works well. Interestingly, when the relationship continues for almost one year, she sees it as a sign from God and hence, she prays for it to last eternally. The fact that James is not a Muslim is not an issue for Rika. Her concern is more to maintain her relationship with James, a relationship she sees as between "two persons from different worlds" finding a common ground. The story demonstrates how domestic workers are not afraid to explore unchartered territories in seeking romance during their time abroad, pursuing relationships across racial, national, religious, and class differences.

These stories underscore a common perception shared among domestic workers that having an interclass relationship may eventually lead to social mobility and financial stability. This element is crucial, as these workers are coming to Hong Kong first and foremost to better their lives, not to find a romantic relationship. Interclass relationships are seen as a fast and legitimate (if not the only) track for domestic workers to taste success and moreover, to show off their "success" to fellow migrants. As there is no feeling of inadequacy or inferiority portrayed in these protagonists, the stories inform us that interclass relationship for migrant workers is not based on a "Cinderella complex." Instead, they show that migrant workers have the self-esteem and boldness to develop a romantic relationship outside of their class (even by marrying their employer). The goal is to have a successful life as a migrant. Overseas domestic workers as authors realize that interclass relationships, no matter how elusive (or in their own word, impossible), can be a path to instant success. They do not rule out an interclass relationship—even as a flimsy possibility—as a way for migrants to reach success in Hong Kong.

Interclass relationships are not the only kind of alien romance that Indonesian domestic workers form during their stays in Hong Kong. In their stories, both Sorrita and Bo Niok describe relationships between domestic workers and working-class men of different nationalities. These relationships, involving either mutual romance or "contract boyfriends," are often developed by mutual consent, despite the authorities not expecting them to take place.[33]

In *Jhony kerbau India* (*Jhony, the Indian water buffalo*), Bo Niok describes how the widow Markonah easily falls into the amorous trap of the playboy Jhony, an Indian truck driver who she meets in front of her employer's apartment building:

> They had met when she was taking her employer's daughter to school. A truck had been parked right in front of the apartment's main gate. The driver had been observing her walking to school with the little girl. After she returned from the school, Jhony, who was the truck driver, approached her and gave her a rolled-up piece of paper with his mobile number on it. Markonah was a widow and not young anymore, so she was delighted to find his number on the piece of paper. She phoned him as soon as she got back to the apartment. Jhony was round, with a beer belly, and his skin was as dark as that of a water buffalo. He was Markonah's first lover after six months in Hong Kong. She wasn't going to waste her time with him.[34]

After that day, Markonah continues to meet Jhony. But after she becomes pregnant, he abandons her. Brokenhearted, Markonah decides to terminate her unplanned pregnancy (readers are not told how she could do so in Hong Kong) and finds solace with her female friend who supports her. While Markonah does not have a successful alien romance like Sasa, Sasmitha, and Rika do, she does have her time "enjoying" a foreign man.

These stories reflect the general contour of the lives of young and single females who, in their search for a place in the society, take the opportunity to seek out romance regardless of how fragile the relationships could become. Workers often develop relationships as a means to reach for their dreams, as it is something they have little chance to experience in Indonesia. In their short stories, Sorrita and Bo Niok encourage their readers (fellow domestic workers) to keep alive their common dream of "meeting a kind and under-standing man," as they are aware that their readers also often fantasize about "extraordinary" possibilities in their potential relationships. Thus, stories of alien romance illustrate how domestic workers as authors suggest putting aside *malu* as the main cultural reference in their life and work in Hong Kong.

The fact that employment contracts for domestic helpers are mostly fixed for two years, however, underscores the limitations of alien romances in Hong Kong. In her short story, "Tenda Putih dan Kutang Victoria" (White Tent and Brassiere at Victoria Park), Sorrita describes a fellow worker, Parti, who is well known within the community even before departing to Hong Kong as "the daringly sexy young lady" (*gadis seksi yang sangat berani*). Parti's employment contract is terminated, according to rumors, due to her "adventurous behaviour" with various men during her days off.

Such characters illustrate how domestic workers are willing to take social and economic risks in their search for romance in Hong Kong, romances based on fantasies, mutual flirtation, and shaped, and often generated, by libidinal impulses.[35] As suggested in their stories, sexual desire or physical attraction is in fact a complex interaction between workers' biological urges, cultural and personal circumstances, and their experiences of living and working in urban Hong Kong. It cannot be confined within the politics of *malu* and without any personal hesitation, domestic workers as authors are breaking cultural taboos in their search for pleasure and romance, which is often considered a male privilege.

These stories depict domestic workers not as weak, helpless, and self-sacrificing, but as risk-taking and open-minded females; they are workers who have developed personal attachments to their work and lives abroad and as independent women they are not afraid to seek leisure and romance. In reality, workers may fail in their attempts at romance, but these stories show how the protagonist never gives up in her efforts to be free and inde-pendent, a lesson that readers can find as encouragement. It is a process of personal struggle to strengthen their personality as an individual. In this way, these stories can be read as a social document of workers' collective idealization of becoming independent, and as proof of their ongoing struggle to reach it.

Thus, these stories reveal the negotiations and choices that workers make in their own way within a short period (as long as their employment contract allows) to gain new experience(s), different sensation(s), and personal advantage(s) from alien romance with foreign men in Hong Kong. From this reading of their stories about seeking romance in Hong Kong, we see an effort by the overseas workers to construct an identity of their own as adventurous and liberated women as characterized by the protagonists of the stories.

SAME-SEX RELATIONSHIPS: TOLERANCE AND SANCTUARY

The alien romance that Indonesian domestic workers experience in Hong Kong is one of "mutual flirtation, not a female obedience."[36] While its basic assumption is a heterosexual relationship, it does not reject the possibility that a similar romance can be found in same-sex relationships. Such relationships among Indonesian domestic workers, unlike among their Filipina sisters, are rarely reported in local media in Hong Kong and are therefore often not registered in the public mind.[37] Homosexuality is not illegal in Hong Kong or in Indonesia (although it remains a sensitive topic in both societies).[38] The issue here is not about literary representation of same-sex relationships, but how domestic workers as authors understand them. In their stories, both Sorrita and Bo Niok address the prevalence of female same-sex relationships among Indonesian domestic workers and offer some interesting insights.

In "Di Balik Pohon" (Behind the Trees), Bo Niok describes how an Indonesian domestic worker notices the public display of affection between two females (we are to assume they are fellow domestic workers) "behind the trees" on the beach near the Tuen Mun pier. Interestingly, she relates this encounter to another she witnessed in the employment agency's dorm in Indonesia, where migrant workers share a large room and have a communal bath every day:

> As I was putting my clothes on, I noticed a couple of ladies, who are about 35-years-old, were applying soap on each other's bodies very tenderly. Obviously, they were enjoying how they caressed each other. . . . Both of them, as I observed, always finished bathing last . . . in my own opinion, they are both adults and thus, they should have understood any consequences of their actions.[39]

With limited space and lack of privacy during their pre-departure stay at the agency's shelter, some workers are not hesitant to show their affection during the bathing time, the only time they can be naked (and see others naked, too). They must have known that what they were doing in the communal bathroom can be seen by others and transgresses the dominant heteronormative view in Indonesian society. Other workers in the shelter, as described by Bo Niok in the story, do not seem to mind: they tolerate the public display of affection from same-sex couples, and others' sexual orientation (and behaviour) is not a concern for them. After all, their primary concern is getting a job offer as soon as possible to shorten their stay in the shelter and leave for Hong Kong to work.

This passive tolerance of same-sex relationships among domestic workers continues during their stay in Hong Kong. In "Diskotik" (Disco club), Sorrita describes the situation inside Makati, a Wan Chai club:

> The bar was crowded with people of various behaviors and styles. There was one man accompanied by two ladies. There was also one lady holding hands with two men. There were also some loners like Rini, and a same-sex couple who was drunk in love and having fun, but the overall atmosphere of the disco club was fun as everyone minds their own business.[40]

Far from being judgmental, readers see that Rini, as a heterosexual female domestic worker, tolerates same-sex relationships since "everyone minds their own business." Even when these domestic workers see some of their fellow workers in a same-sex relationship,[41] they do not judge it because, as Bo Niok rightly notes, "they are both [consenting] adults."

Interestingly, Sim and Wee, based on their interviews with Indonesian domestic workers in Hong Kong, argue that same-sex relationships among workers are indicative "of women's emotional and physical needs during migration and as a defense against male predation."[42] In this line of argument, same-sex relationships are seen as a sanctuary that provides protection and support from the isolation, boredom, fear, and loneliness that these workers have to bear in their work and life in Hong Kong.[43] They are an unintended result of the hostile conditions that workers have to face in an unfriendly society that alienates them.[44]

Sim's argument is instructive to understand the hardships that domestic workers have to face, and how they may turn to same-sex relationships in search of emotional support and solidarity. However, the episode that Bo Niok describes takes place in Indonesia, not in Hong Kong.[45] As such, it requires a more comprehensive analysis of same-sex relationships among domestic workers. Both Bo Niok and Sorrita point to an underlying assumption shared among the workers that same-sex relationships are a mere temporary and transitional symptom that will disappear once the worker returns to her home village and once more becomes close to her family and resumes her "normal" life.[46] This assumption does not necessarily help explain same-sex behaviour but rather provides a rationale for the workers to (passively) tolerate such relationships.

Although each story treats this delicate topic quite differently, together they encourage fellow domestic workers to embrace what they witness and experience (in this case, same-sex relationships) as a way to enrich their own understanding of the world they live in. Same-sex relationships are a part of workers' lives in urban Hong Kong. Fellow workers as readers would find the stories as something they can identify with and refer to, in their efforts to understand their life-changing experiences in Hong Kong. Free from the politics of *malu*, women are no longer expected to suppress their desires and sexuality, including for same-sex relationships. Thus, these stories of same-sex relationships, just like stories of alien romance, are part of the workers' negotiation with the society in general and their yet-to-be-discovered selves. Domestic workers inevitably encounter people from various walks of life and different cultural backgrounds, including people of diverse sexualities. These stories indicate how they tolerate same-sex relationships, based on their own terms.

MOONLIGHTING AS SEX WORKERS

Not all migrant workers "succeed" in their work abroad in the ways they want to. Most endure hardships at work; others have to face deportation after their contracts are terminated without cause. Despite many obstacles, and although many others before them also failed to reach success, they continue to negotiate their status and public image as migrant workers.

None of these negotiation efforts are as difficult and problematic as sex work.[47] Those who do sex work have limited resources and means to defend themselves when they enter (or are forced to enter) the sex industry (either due to facing financial troubles or having fallen victim to human trafficking). At the same time, their work in the sex industry strengthens the public perception of domestic workers as loose women—a perception that degrades women's status in the society and is male-biased. Their efforts to change this public perception and gain acceptance in the society (both in Hong Kong and in Indonesia) are part of a long and ongoing struggle of women to decriminalize sex work and emancipate female sex workers by securing their welfare.[48]

It should be noted that no story portrays a domestic worker moonlighting as a sex worker in Sorrita's (2006a) or Bo Niok's (2007b) anthologies. There are, however, a number of allusions in their stories that deal with the issue. In

Sorrita's "Diskotik" (Disco club), for example, Rini, an Indonesian domestic worker, visits a Wan Chai club for the first time and describes the customers there:

> Half of the women in Makati are Indonesian domestic workers, and another half are from the Philippines. About 10% of them are getting their income from that place. As for the males, 50% are Caucasians and 30% are Chinese. The rest is still 20%, right? Well, it's like the *es campur* (mixed fruits ice dessert) from the Malang bistro.[49]

Readers may find it strange that despite it being her first visit, Rini is able to estimate (and suggest to the readers) that 10 percent of the women are "getting their income from that place," meaning, working as sex workers to find clients in the club. Whether this estimate is correct or just a guess, it seems that Sorrita wants to inform her readers (in particular, fellow Indonesian domestic workers who come to Hong Kong for the very first time) that disco clubs like Makati, contrary to long-standing beliefs in Indonesia, are not "bad" or "dangerous" for women (including domestic workers) to visit. By stating in her story that "only" 10 percent of the women in Makati (and disco clubs, in general) are sex workers, Sorrita wants to convince her readers that such clubs as a nightlife establishment are safe enough for female domestic workers to visit and have fun, as Rini did in her first visit to Makati.

Sorrita does not hide the fact that some Indonesian domestic workers moonlight as sex workers in Hong Kong, as it is openly acknowledged, including by domestic workers themselves. The problem is, this fact is often taken out of context to form a public perception and stereotype of domestic workers as loose women. Ironically, this perception is shared among domestic workers themselves (either intentionally or not). In "Kaos silk biru San Fransisco" (The San Francisco Blue Silk T-Shirt), Sorrita describes Rika as a domestic worker who likes to dance and thus, often visits Laguna, a disco club in Wan Chai. Rika is "different, unlike other women who go there." Sorrita wants to distinguish Rika as a "good" woman (who just wants to dance and do nothing else) from "bad" women who perform sex work. She reminds her readers (fellow domestic workers) that sex workers are "different" from them, the "good" domestic workers.

Sorrita's emphasis on being "different" implies an "Other"-ing of sex workers.[50] She reminds her readers, who may want to visit a disco club, of the need to differentiate themselves from sex workers, for their own sake. They should not associate themselves (or be associated) with the sex workers, and surely, they would not want (foreign) males to assume they are a sex worker, as it could ruin their chance for a genuine "alien romance." Here lies the irony: while the short story suggests to its readers (domestic workers) that they need to leave behind their *malu* behavior in order to experience different and new things in Hong Kong, including stepping into the disco clubs of Wan Chai in their search for "alien romance" with foreign males, they need to be "different" from the sex workers by keeping themselves composed as "good" women in their appearances and habits and, not grouping with the sex workers.

Bo Niok does not discuss the issue of sex workers in her anthology *Geliat Sang Kung Yan* (2007b). It seems she realizes this gap and thus, writes one story focusing on this issue in her subsequent anthology. "Cinta Murah Bukit Merah" (Cheap love in Bukit Merah) tells the stories of two "alien romances" (Bo Niok 2011b). Ovi is brokenhearted when Vijay, her (Indian) boyfriend, leaves her after finding out she is pregnant. Meanwhile, Sulis has two regular "contract boyfriends" at the same time, a Chinese man and a Malay man:

> Sulis said she didn't care about their physical features. It was not the way they looked or their bodies that she loved. What she liked was that each man paid her one hundred Singapore dollars for each date. . . . "Our monthly wages as maids in Singapore are not enough to allow us to lead a real life. That's why I need to do this. But I don't go with just anyone. I have regular partners, although I have two of them right now at the same time. One hundred dollars is not a small sum of money. And that's just for one date," she explained enthusiastically.[51]

The story informs us that, for many domestic workers who moonlight as sex workers abroad (both in Singapore and Hong Kong), the sex industry offers easy money that can solve their financial troubles (either to maintain their familial obligation as a "good" daughter and woman by sending extra income home, or to sustain their lifestyle in the foreign land). It is obvious that Bo Niok shares this classic belief that economic motive is the (main) reason for many domestic workers to moonlight as sex workers.

In a similar vein, in "Kupu-kupu Puncak Beton" (Butterfly of Concrete Peaks),[52] Nessa Kartika tells the story of Novi, a domestic worker in Singapore, who, in her search of alien romance, meets Rana, a Bangladeshi man, in the market. After she is unexpectedly treated as a sex worker on their first rendezvous, Novi ends up moonlighting as a sex worker, but, the story informs us, ultimately, she does not regret it:

> If only she [Novi] could rewind time, she wouldn't have been so naïve as to have fallen so easily into the world of a butterfly. But it was done now. . . . Novi was smart now and she got what she wanted. She would refuse to meet if she wouldn't get anything from the guy. She would ask for money, for all sorts of things. Sometimes she would just ask for a top-up for her mobile phone in exchange for satisfying a guy's lust. Today was just another day in the usual

run of things. She wasn't the only migrant worker who had taken on this type of side job. She had no regrets.[53]

Novi's story is, indeed, a tragic one. While she understands that she cannot turn back time and change her past, she still considers sex work as a way to make extra income. On the other hand, this story may be read as a cautionary tale to readers (fellow domestic workers) in search of alien romance to be cautious and selective, and not to trust men easily. They can be genuine in their search for alien romance, but they need to remain on guard against the risks of being ill-treated by men, especially those who just want to take advantage of them. If not, they could end up like Novi and will not be able to escape from the "cycle of the butterfly."

Although Nessa Kartika may have a good intention in sharing this cautionary voice to her readers, she, like Bo Niok, does not question the classic belief among domestic workers that sex work is easy money.[54] One domestic worker in Hong Kong who happened to know Seneng Mujiasih and Sumarti Ningsih explained to the media that economic motive was the reason the two women performed sex work.[55] Many domestic workers, indeed, hold similar belief that their fellow sisters enter the sex industry as an easy way to supplement their income.[56] Migrant stories take this belief as a theme and in turn, help distribute it among their readers and thus, may have strengthened it. As such, their stories reflect migrants' shared perception of sex work, regardless of how inaccurate it can be.

When we consider the life circumstances of Seneng Mujiasih and Sumarti Ningsih, we know that both were living a precarious life in Hong Kong. Their lives as sex workers were far from being glamorous and easy.[57] The fact that both of them were breadwinners of their respective families (thus, they needed to send money home regularly) put more pressure on them to earn extra income. Many sex workers are trapped in a culture of silence due to discrimination and (mis)perceptions of their work, even by fellow domestic workers. While "good" domestic workers can congregate in a number of public spaces in Hong Kong (such as in Victoria Park), sex workers have very limited options to make friends in public spaces outside their work sites (mainly, the disco clubs in the Wan Chai area). Often considered and treated differently by their fellow working-class sisters, sex workers find it difficult to find friends among fellow domestic workers, and this may create further isolation in their life and work in Hong Kong.

Sorrita, Bo Niok, and Kartika have shared their stories among fellow domestic workers to inform and alert them about the many facets of modern life abroad, including sex work. They share their experiences and thoughts about life and work abroad, including raising cautionary voices about the predatory tendencies of men to treat domestic workers as sex objects.

However, they also share the common (mis)perception of sex work (especially by domestic workers moonlighting as sex workers) that fails to separate the economic motive as the entry point to sex work and the material conditions that these women have to face in their daily lives (either as a single mother, the sole breadwinner, or a victim of human trafficking) that force them to engage in that activity as a viable option to maintain life.[58] Overseas domestic workers may take practical yet important lessons from the stories to try new experiences beyond the boundaries of *malu* as their cultural norm and to guard against a man's bad intentions. The stories fail, however to liberate readers from common (mis)perceptions of sex work. We begin to understand that the difficulties and problematic nature of sex work among overseas domestic workers will persist unless they are ready to free themselves from common (mis)perceptions, treat and see sex workers as equal sisters, and join hands to liberate the profession together.

OVERSEAS WORKERS AS ADVENTUROUS AND LIBERATED WOMEN

Tarini Sorrita's *Penari Naga Kecil* and Maria Bo Niok's *Geliat Sang Kung Yan* provide insights on the real working life that female domestic workers have to face and the opportunities they often encounter in urban Hong Kong. The stories illustrate how overseas Indonesian domestic workers, through writing, voice collective interests as workers, resist cultural-economic domination by their employers, and take advantage of their life experiences while being in the urban capitalist city of Hong Kong. Their stories are a part of the struggle by working people "whose voices belong and deserve to be heard in public spaces that reach far beyond their household workplaces."[59] The journey they take requires personal courage and in turn brings about a mental leap in their understanding of self and status. Their stories of managing their lives independently, looking for entertainment and alien romance, and exploring their sexual desires demonstrate how these domestic workers are starting to seize their own liberation, and in the process, enjoy life beyond the cultural standard of *malu* and being a "good" daughter and woman. In this way, their writings compel the public to reconsider commonly held perceptions of their life and work abroad.

While their writings may not become a key reading within Indonesia's national literature, they are important in inspiring women of the working class. They are a product of reflection on the nature of migration for work and a courageous effort to formulate words to express their own voice, demonstrating an assertion against the powers that regulate them. The writings of Sorrita and Bo Niok have inspired fellow overseas workers to craft their own path in seeking possibilities and to overcome problems they face in life and work. Rather than a "submissive reading,"[60] fellow domestic workers seek their own lessons in the stories to liberate themselves from the normality of their life and work. The fact that domestic workers are now capable of speaking for and taking care of themselves shows the agency that female domestic workers have developed: each of them is a capable, self-reliant, and articulate individual with strong determinations in life.[61] Their writings, especially their works of fiction, are important in understanding the life and labor of migrant domestic workers in Hong Kong, from their own perspectives. They are part of workers' collective efforts to actively define the world they live in and to pursue self-autonomy. In that way, their written expressions not only offer a clear window to the real world of overseas domestic workers as they experience and understand it, but also serve as a narrative for a change.

Nonetheless, we also need to remember that the literary writings of these overseas Indonesian domestic workers are in fact a by-product of the globalization they are experiencing. Their existence as overseas domestic workers is a result of the economic integration of our contemporary world, especially in East Asia. In that sense, governmental regulation of these overseas workers and their efforts to claim autonomy remains entrenched in structures of social, political, and "bio" power created by global capitalism. Cheah reminds us that "one cannot transcend this field of instrumentality because humanity itself is produced by technologies of biopower."[62] Their writings may empower fellow workers to take advantage of globalization, to ease the negative impacts of the appropriation of their labor by the capitalist system, and to reduce the burdens of the state's bureaucratic power, but whether these writings provide alternatives beyond existing economic and social limitations is not clear. We may consider these short stories as their strategic instrument, as I suggest in this chapter, and as a "weapon of the weak" that worked well during the decade of 2005–2016, before social media became the primary means of communication among domestic workers. Stories penned in the future by overseas workers may use means other than writing stories that they consider more effective in reaching their objective of change, and, ultimately, freedom.

NOTES

1. Seneng Mujiasih was also known as Jesse Lorena Ruri. For newspaper reports on the case, see "Hong Kong Murders: Family Mourns Death of Sumarti Ningsih," *BBC*, November 4, 2014; "Jesse Lorena yang Dibunuh di Hong Kong Disebut WNI asal Sulawesi Tenggara," *Kompas*, November 4, 2014; "Indonesian women killed in Hong Kong are Forgotten at Home," *Associated Press*, November 2, 2016.

2. In his work on the social interactions of people living in the apartment blocks of Chungking Mansions, Matthews (2011: 84) records an encounter with three Indonesian female domestic helpers one Sunday morning. They were waiting together for their respective "contract boyfriends," who were Saudi Arabian, Pakistani, and Indian. While waiting, the women chatted about their boyfriends and were, apparently, happy to share their stories to Matthews, a stranger they had just met. For Matthews, the encounter illustrated the fluid interactions across ethnic and national boundaries among the people who are living in (and visiting) the Chungking mansions. Matthews talked with many people, including traders, owners and managers, temporary workers, asylum seekers, sex workers, heroin addicts, and tourists.

3. See Loveband (2006); Williams (2007).

4. See Suryomenggolo (2019) for some of these short stories in English.

5. See Young (1994).

6. *Kung yan/ Gu yong* (in Cantonese, domestic worker). It is important to note that their work is not limited to manual labor and often includes caring for the elderly and children. This element of work is also reflected in their short stories. For example, Maria Bo Niok's short story "A, Ne, Ge!" narrates the story of Rosidah, a domestic worker/caregiver to a paralyzed fifty-six year old woman.

7. In her anthology *Penari Naga Kecil*, Tarini Sorrita explicitly mentions two previous works by fellow domestic workers: Rini Widyawati's *Catatan Harian Seorang Pramuwisma (Journal of a Domestic Helper)* in "Buku" [Books], and the anthology *Hongkong, Namaku Peri Cinta (Hongkong, My Name is Love Fairy)* in "Kaos Silk Biru San Fransisco" (Blue silk t-shirt of San Francisco), integrating them in her short stories when the protagonists are described as having a hard time distributing books among fellow workers in Hong Kong. Maria Bo Niok is also aware of other works. She was actively involved in organizing the launch and discussion events of *Hongkong, Namaku Peri Cinta* in Wonosobo (her hometown) on October 15, 2005, and Tarini Sorrita's *Penari Naga Kecil* in Yogyakarta on February 12, 2006, in her effort to promote domestic worker narratives among the literary critics. See Syifa Aulia (2007); Bayu Insani (2010). On Rini Widyawati's *Catatan Harian Seorang Pramuwisma*, see chapter 5.

8. Domestic workers form their own writing groups where they meet regularly (monthly/weekly basis). Support groups and NGOs in Hong Kong have played a role in organizing these domestic workers, and some have provided these workers with support to develop their writing skills. See Wee and Sim (2003) and Asato (2004).

9. Their works of fiction are not limited to issues of life and work as overseas domestic workers, and the characters are not only domestic workers. For example, Sorrita's short story "Adegan" (The Scene) is about homosexuality in Hong Kong (Sorrita 2006); Mell (2014) tells the story of Ella Tan, a daughter of mixed marriage, who is adjusting to her new life in Taiwan as a university student; Bo Niok (2011a) tells the story of a family separated due to the 1965 political situation in Indonesia.

10. One of Bo Niok's children, Nessa Kartika, is a former overseas domestic worker in Hong Kong and Singapore. Like Bo Niok, she writes short stories. See Nessa Kartika (2010, 2011).

11. Wonosobo regency has the highest percentage of the poor in Central Java province (21 percent in 2015 compared to the average rate of 13 percent). It also has the highest index of depth of poverty (or poverty gap), which was measured as 4.02 in 2016. As such, many young females from Wonosobo's poor working families find employment abroad as domestic workers.

12. Bo Niok does not hide the fact that her divorce played a part in her decision to work abroad.

13. For domestic workers' writing experiences, see Bayu Insani (2010), Bayu Insani and Ida Raihan (2010) and Dhieny Megawati et al. (2012). One worker, Pandan Arum (nom de plume of Nyami Kaswadi) (in Dhieny et al. 2012: 13) notes:

> Writing has become a powerful therapy. Since I have some of my writings published, my friends have become my informants. They would tell me anything they find interesting for me to write. If it is published, they would be happy about it. They also have become avid readers as they feel my happiness.

14. Exceptions do exist. For example, see "Di Bawah Purnama Aku Berdoa" (Under the Full Moon I Pray), a television soap opera aired in March 1997 and directed by Dimas Haring, on the working life of a domestic worker in Saudi Arabia, and "Minggu Pagi di Victoria Park" (Monday Morning at Victoria Park), a movie directed by Lola Amaria, on the life of overseas Indonesian workers in Hong Kong. The opening part of the soap opera presents a quote from the New Order's Minister of Manpower, Abdul Latief. The movie, meanwhile, is a step forward by middle-class cinema artists attempting to raise the situation of migrant workers to the Indonesian public. Both the soap opera and the movie, however, rely on common stereotypes of migrants' lives and work. For a background of the soap opera, see *Kompas*, March 7, 1997, and of the movie, see *Majalah Tempo* 42/38 (December 7, 2009): 69–76.

15. Upper- and middle-class writers are experimenting with writing about "sensitive" social issues such as gender and female sexuality to claim personal liberation.

16. See Rini Widyawati (2005: 112–113) and Lestari (2010). See also chapter 5.

17. Hong Kong may provide an environment for these workers to organize and defend their interests as workers and also to pursue "meaningful" activities on their days off, but this alone is not the main impetus for their activism. Hsia (2009: 129) notes that "(n)o matter how liberal the context of reception, however, conditions for migrants would not have changed without pressure from a strong social movement."

18. Sorrita (2006a: 14).

19. Cheah (2007: 105) notes that

> It is suggested that migrants will undergo a form of *Bildung* overseas. They will learn new skills and gain work experience and return to impart this training, thereby enhancing the technological and knowledge resources of the nation and facilitating its development. Hence, any attempt to reaffirm the humanity of these FDWs necessarily relies on the same technologies.

20. Sorrita (2006a: 76).

21. Bo Niok (2007b: 183).

22. Bo Niok (2007b: 29).

23. In her other novel, *Ranting Sakura* (Sakura twig) (2007: 92), Bo Niok describes Amei, the female protagonist, as a domestic worker who prefers to write down her joys and sorrows in her diaries: "It was only in her diary where she could express herself. In her diary, she also wrote poems when inspiration came."

24. In a newspaper article on Bo Niok's writing, Tanesia (2006) notes that

[b]eing away from her family often made Maria feel [*sic*!] sad, bored, and lonely . . . . To help relieve her stress, she would write what she felt on pieces of paper or on the backs of old calendars. It did help. But most of the time she threw away what she wrote.

25. In the words of Aulia (2007): "my friends and I tried to rise beyond the fact that our profession was considered beneath most people, and writing was one of the best ways for us to do so."

26. Sorrita (2006a: 57) notes how some domestic helpers are active in musical bands.

27. Tsing (1996: 309).

28. A version of this story is published in a different anthology, *Nyanyian Imigran*, see Sorrita (2006b). Throughout this chapter, I use the version in Sorrita's own anthology (Sorrita 2006a).

29. Sorrita (2006a: 40).

30. "Love Is Not Impossible" by Nessa Kartika (2011) tells the love story between Evin, an Indonesian working as a care giver of an ailing Chinese Singaporean male, and her employer's son, Dave. Evin first saw her relationship with Dave as an "impossible" one, but after witnessing Dave's persistent effort, she changes her mind, and hence, the story concludes, as the title suggests, that interclass/ interracial "love is not impossible."

31. Maulana (2011: 147).

32. Sorrita (2006a: 37–38).

33. Hong Kong uses race and gender segregation when authorizing work visas in order to indirectly regulate workers' sex lives. This practice assumes that migrant workers, individually and collectively, will remain confined within their particular nationality. Yet migrant workers, despite differences in their skin colors, nationalities, and religions, are forming intimate relationships as they like and see fit to fulfill their desires for alien romance, either for a short term or a long one.

34. Bo Niok (2007b: 123–124).

35. This is not to say that these workers are simply "promiscuous and predatory females." See the discussion on this issue in Yeoh and Huang (2000).

36. Tsing (1996: 309).

37. Constable (1997: 552) notes that "In early 1996 employers became increasingly concerned about lesbianism when a television news documentary quoted a member of a domestic workers union who estimated that a quarter of all Filipina domestic workers were lesbians."

38. Same-sex relationships and the discourse around them still instigate public controversy in Indonesia. In recent years there have been a number of raids (conducted by the police and intolerance/violent groups) against some LGBT events.

While homosexuality is not illegal, criminal persecutions target homosexuals for petty crimes.

39. Boo Niok (2007b: 176–177).

40. Sorrita (2006a: 29–30).

41. Same-sex relationships between Indonesian workers and workers of other nationalities are very rare. As far I know, there is no written report or short story that discusses same-sex relationship between an Indonesian worker and a person of a different nationality; yet rumors of international same-sex relationships do exist.

42. Sim and Wee (2009: 179).

43. For alienation among Filipina domestic workers, see Lindio-McGovern (2004).

44. See also Susana Nisa's short story (2016) that narrates the relationship between Kie and Regha.

45. See also Juwanna's short story (2010) that narrates a story of Anna Ayatul Nisa, known as Arda, who claims to have been a "genuine lesbian" ever since she was small (in Indonesia) and "has never fallen in love with a man."

46. See also Ida Raihan's short story (2010) that narrates the story of Sita, who intends to resume her "normal" life upon going back to her home village.

47. It is important to note that there are various kinds of workers in the sex industry: current domestic workers who moonlight as sex workers, former domestic workers who turn to the sex industry, undocumented workers who work full time or part time in the industry, and so on. The cases of Seneng Mujiasih and Sumarti Ningsih show this "flexibility" of the sex industry. This chapter uses the blanket term "sex workers" to cover this mixture.

48. Various country-based studies have shown that criminalization of sex work does not necessarily lead to its eradication. Promoting gender equality and protection against discrimination and violence (including, domestic violence) form one of the basic elements to guarantee freedom for sex workers in life and at work. See Jeffrey (2002); Grant (2014).

49. Sorrita (2006a: 27).

50. Whether this emphasis on being "different" indicates an envy of sex workers, who are seen as more liberal or have uninhibited outlook on sex (and alien romance), needs further research.

51. Bo Niok (2011b: 16–17).

52. "Kupu-kupu" (butterfly) is a euphemism for sex worker.

53. Kartika (2011: 65–66).

54. A number of ethnographic studies note that many sex workers dispute the claim that sex work is easy money.

55. "Lydia [not her real name] knew both Sumarti and Seneng . . . . Lydia says Sumarti and Seneng were friends with another Indonesian illegal worker, who moonlighted as a sex worker in the city. 'Maybe the two girls saw the life that their friends who worked in the bars had, lots of money and fashionable clothes. It was a temptation for them, a life too hard to resist.'" *BBC*, November 23, 2014.

56. It is not difficult to find overseas domestic workers who are willing to "testify" that sex work offers better cash than their monthly income as a domestic worker,

however it is important to note that domestic workers do not see sex work as their primary job, nor do they see it as the primary reason to work abroad.

57. Whether domestic workers see sex work in Hong Kong rather than returning to their hometowns (with the limited options they encounter there and wish to escape from), as a better means of upward social mobility is a theme that needs further research. It is beyond the scope of this chapter.

58. One short story by Mega Bintang (2012) describes being a single mother.

59. Constable (2009: 161).

60. See Najmabadi (2004).

61. It is interesting to note that upon her return to Indonesia, Yulia Jafar Purwanto, a former domestic worker in Hong Kong, developed her career as scriptwriter for television dramas. Many of her scripts tell stories of life and romance, but not of domestic workers.

62. Cheah (2007: 112).

Conclusion

A range of social and political conditions precipitated the rise of female working-class writings during the last forty years of Indonesia's industrialization and twenty years of political change. The 1973 policy of compulsory primary schooling unlocked the gates of education for the working class, especially its women. The labor market under the New International Division of Labor accelerated the process: today, women workers can read and write. Literacy may have taken working women away from the oral tradition of their parents, but it has also allowed them to write more than a few passing lines on paper. Writing connects them to fellow workers *and* to a much broader audience, one that they could not have previously accessed. It is within the changing "literacy landscape" of Indonesia's economic development that workers have appropriated writing and used it not only to express themselves but also to advance their collective interests. This was especially prominent during the last decade of the New Order regime, which silenced dissenting voices and suppressed worker protests, leaving workers with few options or channels of expression. Writing allowed workers to evade the state's censorship and surveillance and to convey their experiences, thoughts, and dreams to others. Since 1998, with the freedom of expression guaranteed, more women workers have begun to write. In writing, they show their collective agency to shatter the politics of *malu*, challenge the factory regime, demand equality and fair treatment, change work conditions, and resist the state's suppression.

Based on the discussions in previous chapters, this final chapter offers four concluding remarks to highlight the significance of female working-class writings in the context of the political economy of development and cultural changes in modern Indonesia. First, it considers the literary forms of their writings given the limited time and facility they have to narrate their stories, which demand creativity to transmit their messages. Second, it considers their writings collectively as an important literary breakthrough that transcends the oral tradition of the working class. Third, it discusses the extent and limits of these authors' representation of working-class experience of life and work. Finally, it views their writings as a contribution to a female-specific, if not feminist, activism among the working class in the Global South.

LITERARY INNOVATION

As we can see by the works discussed in this book, women workers choose to write their narratives in various forms, including defense speeches, personal notes, magazine articles, protest essays, journals, diaries, and works of fiction. They do this to suit their specific purposes, and the forms they choose depend on the circumstances they are facing when they write as well as consideration for the limited time of their intended readers (fellow women workers).

These literary forms also reflect the general sociopolitical situation at the time of their writing. Under the suppression of the New Order regime, for instance, women workers used alternative channels of expression to avoid censorship. In the absence of a free press or freedom in the publishing industry, a defense speech was a suitable form that allowed some women workers to reach a larger audience. The defense speech of Ida Irianti, for example, survived the state's censorship and became available to the public as a court document, reaching more readers than she could have imagined. Later, in the 1990s, women workers often wrote short memoirs as a personal record of their work experiences. In that context, Meppy's memoir is an important example, as it includes her experiences of violence during an arbitrary detention by the military.

With the collapse of the New Order regime, workers have gained access to a plethora of media outlets through which they can share their experiences and thoughts. A free press is now legally guaranteed. Workers, like many other social groups, take advantage of this to advance their interests. Women workers also use the free press to defend their rights as women, and educate the public. Similar to the worker-writers of the Dabindu collective in Sri Lanka,[1] Indonesian women workers write in various narrative forms on issues that matter most to them as women, including sexual harassment in the workplace and reproductive rights. Their articles and essays on these issues are literary interruptions; they are an important testimony of specific demands that have long been ignored within the male-dominated labor movement and convey the urgent need to ensure the fundamental rights of women in the workplace and in life in general.

Meanwhile, writing journals, diaries, and fiction has been the most common form adopted by Indonesian domestic workers abroad. Their working conditions as live-in maids and caregivers leave them with more limited private time and space compared to their sisters working in factories. Writing in this form creates a safe and private space in which they can strategically avoid employer surveillance. Like the "slum romances" written by female Korean factory workers,[2] short stories allow Indonesian women workers to blur the lines between their inhuman working conditions and personal fantasies of freedom, and to attract the attention of their target readers with entertainment value.

Adoption of these various forms can be seen as literary innovation in itself. Women workers write based on their own life and work experiences despite limited time, space, and adequate facilities. Like their working-class sisters elsewhere, Indonesian working-class women do not assert their individuality in their writings, as upper-and middle-class writers do, and they write without any pretension of gaining fame.[3] Instead, they write as a personal outlet and as a means to overcome trauma; they write to connect, empathize, and warn their fellow workers. They write for and on behalf of those of their class who do not have (and are denied) the same opportunity and facilities to write.

A LITERARY CONSTRUCT

As noted in the Introduction, working-class writings are penned by active workers who earn their living from manual work. The female worker-writers discussed in this book write based on their work experiences and life stories. Like their sisters elsewhere, many of them began to write only after they saw and/or experienced problems in the workplace.[4] They use writing as a means to solve these problems—problems that not only affect them personally, but also the working class as a whole. They do not write as leisure, nor, certainly, as a vocation.[5] Instead, by making their problems in the workplace the theme (and often, the central theme) of their writings, they inform—and warn—readers (fellow workers) and open a channel through which to share how to deal with workplace conditions.

Women workers have shown that although they are new readers, they are committed authors. Their works describe different social and temporal contexts and the magnitude of challenges they have to face. What unites them is a common search to voice and advance their interests as women workers. This, in a broad sense, is a common theme in the working-class struggle. Ironically, however, it is their writings that set them apart from the general working class. Women worker-writers have gained literacy, like the rest of the working class, as a result of the demand of global capital for cheap labor and the state's policy of compulsory primary education. While schooling under the authoritarian regime may have reproduced existing social structures and promoted discipline and morality, these women's writings are, for the most part, untethered from the cultural hegemony of the elites. Unlike the rest of the working class, however, they use literacy, instead of depending solely on the oral tradition of their class, in order to cope with the changing economic and political landscape, voice their experiences in life and at work, and share their stories among fellow workers. Their written stories may have departed and take elements from the working-class oral tradition, but they are constructing a literary space of their own.

As members of the working class, these writers have consciously moved away from the oral tradition. They see its limits to address the problems they face and thus, turn to writing. Their introduction to literacy/writing may be new, but they realize its effectiveness to voice and share their stories to a wider audience and they therefore construct a writing style that suits their purposes. It includes phrases and styles that mimic spoken expressions; these are elements that show traces of the oral tradition, a tradition that remains important in many parts of the Global South.[6]

The entry of working-class women into the reading public has allowed them to express themselves on paper and advance their collective interests. They can now read and write as they please and take advantage of writing to advance their interests. Although this creates the illusion of equality in the "republic of letters," unlike upper-and middle-class women authors who have established a space of their own, women workers do not have a similar amount of support, facilities, attention, and personal social connections to write and spread their truth. Moreover, Indonesian upper- and middle-class women, due to the status of their own class and the different agendas they have, often ignore or misread writings of their working-class sisters. Working-class women's writings are often considered less significant within the nation's literary circles.

Beyond the commonly accepted "aesthetic standards," working-class women's writings are an important literary intervention to understand the changing social and political landscape of the nation. Working-class female authors share similar experiences of injustices with others who are sidelined and silenced. Their writings draw a stark contrast with the dominant discourse of Indonesia's rising prosperity due to economic "development" since the 1970s. Until the late 1980s, these authors were often confined to express themselves within the boundaries of working-class oral tradition or through alternative channels to avoid the state's authoritarian suppression of dissent. Since then, however, women workers have used various written forms to articulate their daily realities and reach out to fellow women workers beyond their immediate surroundings, especially those who have similar experiences of gender discrimination, violence, and injustice. Their writings are meant primarily as a means to communicate among themselves beyond the limitations of oral tradition. As such, they create a broader sense of the collective, which is based on gender and class. By voicing their concerns and sharing their hopes with fellow workers, these authors conscientize, and in some cases begin to organize, female workers previously unreached by the traditional labor movement in Indonesia.

Along the path of Indonesia's industrialization and despite unfavorable social and political conditions of the last forty years, women workers have been actively writing about their work experience and life stories in various forms. Writing provides them with a new space to defend and advance their common interests as women workers beyond the limits of oral tradition, becoming a form of fearless speech. Thus, their writings should be included in the corpus of Indonesian women's writings and treated as an inseparable part of women's stories in modern Indonesia.

It has been noted in studies of other countries that workers, as they write, have the desire to improve their personal selves and skills.[7] When they write, they may unconsciously create a distance and differentiate themselves from other fellow workers. The urge to make sense of the social and political situations that shape their life and experiences forces them to step out of the crowd for a moment. Writing gives them a sense of self-confidence and freedom (no matter how limited and elusive it is), that is, the required condition to improve their personal selves as authors. Yet, writing also brings them a feeling of social isolation. Such feelings of detachment and isolation when they write may prove to be unbearable and force them to return to the oral tradition. The benefits of writing may not be worth the costs or trouble of being separated from the oral tradition of their class. Hence, for many working-class authors, their writings are a first and last attempt to put words on paper. As such, writings by Indonesian working-class women, as a literary construct, are temporal: they are useful when worker-writers have the need to share their stories to a wider audience and only until they decide to return to oral tradition. In recent years, many workers have found social media useful (and practical) as a means to reach out to fellow workers within the workplace and beyond, including to call for and participate in international solidarity. Nonetheless, writings remain solid proof of their strategic involvement, participation, and intervention in defending their rights and claiming the public sphere.

REPRESENTATION OF THE WORKING CLASS

The writings of Indonesian female workers reflect two important realities. First, despite the post-1998 democratization of Indonesia, women workers remain subjected to and incorporated into the logics of global commodity chains. The process of integrating Indonesian women workers into the global labor market has advanced at a steady pace since the late 1970s and with it, labor conditions in Indonesia, like other low-income and lower-middle-income countries in the Global South, have changed. Economically, due to the accumulating pressure of foreign capital and the adoption of advanced production technologies, workers are treated as commodities and the flexibilization of labor has become the norm. Politically, due to the reforms of 1998 and the subsequent democratization, workers' basic rights have become legally guaranteed; workers can now establish and join any union organization as they wish. Women workers have experienced all of these changes. Thus, their writings collectively narrate the process of Indonesia's economic and political developments during the last forty years from their perspectives and highlight the emergence of working-class selves in industrializing Indonesia.

Second, their writings demonstrate that women workers struggle to achieve fair treatment and better working conditions, and to gain a sense of freedom—no matter how limited or temporary. Women worker-writers do not merely accept their working conditions. Many of these authors are also union activists and/or are actively involved in the movement for change, underscoring the urgency of their writings. For them, writing alone is not enough; further action is just as important. Although their writings primarily function as a more effective way to communicate among themselves beyond the limits of oral tradition, they also inspire other readers to join in their struggle. Women workers as readers find the writings of fellow workers a mine of experiences and a source of personal inspiration to be courageous (*berani*). Thus, these writings reflect a sociotextual conversation between authors and readers in their collective struggle as workers to change their workplace conditions.

Long working hours, onerous demands from the family, and the social chains of *malu* discourage many women workers from writing. Women working in certain physically demanding sectors, such as on plantations and in the mining industry, have even less opportunity and facilities than those working in the manufacturing sector and domestic work abroad. Yet, like their Korean sisters during the capitalist expansion of the postwar period,[8] Indonesian women workers write their stories during the country's expansion of labor-intensive industrialization. They do so by dedicating some of their already limited time to writing, and many also train themselves in writing. It is this quality that distinguishes them as authors: they write not due to a certain income level or social connections, but as a way to break the politics of *malu*, to stand up against injustices, and to defend their rights and interests as women workers.

Nonetheless, the issue of representation remains. The majority of female workers do not have (and are denied) the opportunity and facilities to write their stories; they remain subaltern and as such, we have no access to hear or read their stories.[9] The writings that are available to us (and discussed in this book) are but a small fraction; they cannot be read and compared alongside the numerous untold, and unwritten, stories of women workers. It is therefore important to note that these texts are available to us due to their "survivability." Indeed, the issue of representation is intertwined with how certain texts are written, published, and can "survive" the challenges of time and social conditions.

Writings by working-class women are not as numerous as those of their male counterparts or their upper- and middle-class sisters. Their scarcity reflects the unequal status of working-class women as well as their exclusion from literary (re)production, distribution, and preservation. Acknowledging this reality, progressive feminist scholarship in the West has turned its attention to unconventional sources (such as personal letters, diaries, and court documents) to (re)write women's history and bring women's experiences and perspectives front and center.[10] In Southeast Asia, however, such unconventional sources are also scarce and understandably, it is more difficult, although not impossible, to (re) construct the experiences of working women.[11]

In this context, writings by Indonesian female workers offer an alternative archive of the working-class struggle from the Southeast Asian region and beyond. Despite being fragmented and limited, they speak for all female workers who could not break the social chains of oppression, do not have (and are denied) the opportunity and facilities to write, and whose writings are neither published nor registered in the nation's discourse. Their writings highlight the range of styles, rhetorics, and articulation used by working women from the Global South—a range based on an industrialization and political realities different than those in the West. Irrespective of nationality or society, women workers everywhere face cultural and financial barriers due to patriarchy and the capitalist mode of production. Women workers in the Global South, however, toil further upstream in the global production system and, undeniably, are at the bottom of the world's economic ladder and as such, face extra barriers in representing themselves.[12] The representation of the working class presented in the writings of Indonesian women workers discussed in this book is an initial contribution to the ongoing feminist project of discovering and reappraising the works of all working-class female writers from various cultural contexts. They enrich our discussion of women's agency and modes of resistance in (re) creating social and political imaginaries based on their particular experiences.

FEMALE ACTIVISM FROM THE GLOBAL SOUTH

While the primary concerns of Indonesian women workers are challenging the gendered construction of *malu* and defending their workplace rights are unique to the specific context they face, their efforts to organize fellow women workers and seek justice have some parallels with the activism of women workers elsewhere. The overarching thing they share is a hope for gender equality among workers. Women workers are no longer afraid to advocate for their own interests and develop their own identities. They see and experience a set of workplace challenges that are different from male workers (even in the same workplace), and they approach these problems differently. Against the odds, this has empowered women: they become leaders, pioneers, and militant workers. Beyond the workplace, their activism engages with the social environment, gradually becoming a politically relevant movement—a direction they may not have initially imagined.

The power of workers to organize, however, is unfortunately under constant threat. Workers of the Global South are constrained by the "capitalist discipline" of globalization. Conditions such as the changing nature of production, the rise of precarious work in the labor market, the increase in unemployment and social inequality, and government labor policies unfavorable to their cause are not within their current capacities to change. They have to strengthen their organizations by, among other things, taking note of previous strategies used by their brothers and sisters on the other side of the global production chain and contextualizing them to their local situation. International solidarity enables workers of the Global South to connect and build alliances; their organizations, though, need to explore new forms of organizing beyond the heretofore repertoire of labor to tackle neoliberal development. Unfortunately, women workers are often excluded from these efforts, although being a majority in certain industrial sectors and despite the increase in women's labor force participation across the Global South since the 1970s.

Feminization of the labor market has, indeed, enabled women workers to have the benefit of paid employment, contribute to family's income, shape their social identities, and experience a relative freedom in the public sphere. But women workers recognize that the labor market fails to provide a favorable, equal, and safe environment to them. The writings of Indonesian women workers expose these issues and the lack of support for female workers, providing a window to the bigger landscape of experiences shared by all women workers of the Global South. While work and workplace issues are certainly central to these working-class writings, gender also unquestionably plays a defining and significant role. Due to their gender, women workers experience wage discrimination, job insecurity, various kinds of harassment and violence, and unfair treatment in the workplace, often on a regular basis. Such an experience is a message that their labor is less valuable and meaningful than men's labor. Despite social and political limitations, women workers stand up, confront matters on their own, and find solutions together with fellow women workers to challenge gender discriminations, question women's gendered roles, and demand equal and fair treatment for all in the workplace.

Their writings are a testament to their collective efforts to resist globalizing and capitalist market forces that disadvantage them. Women workers may not have the erudite vocabularies of a well-developed feminist idea, but their activism articulates the common call for gender equality and therefore represents a burgeoning working-class feminism in the Global South.

NOTES

1. Parera (2014: 90) notes that "the *Dabindu* periodicals encompass a vast heterogeneity of narrative forms."

2. On Korean "slum romances," Barraclough (2009: 111) notes,

The authors make explicit the connections between the conditions of literary production, the emancipatory role literature can play both personally and socially, the joys of writing, and the haggard schedule a working woman must obey if she wants to publish anything.

3. On French working-class autobiographies, Traugott (1993: 28) notes that

they implicitly claim to be just like others of their class—an interesting inversion of the practice in the autobiographies of members of the elite, where the value of the narrative is established by the distinctiveness of the author's role as a key actor in the events recounted.

4. In contemporary China, female migrant workers started to write after working in the cities as members of a new urban precariat. For example, Fan Yusu, whose autobiography, *I Am Fan Yusu* (我是范雨素) (2017) has been widely read online.

5. None of the authors discussed in this book make a living from their literary works.

6. On working-class activism in Botswana, Werbner (2014: 65) notes "Despite being relatively uneducated, women as well as men spoke forcefully, one by one, with authority and at length, without notes."

7. See Kirk (2003), Rancière (1981), and Vincent (1981).

8. Barraclough (2012: 60) notes,

In South Korea the working-class autobiography came to fruition in the 1970s and early 1980s, as working-class people began to address their society, and attempt to change it, through literature. In the early 1980s, three proletarian women published autobiographies to tell their readers "a little more about the world."

9. See Spivak (1988) and Jacka (1998).

10. See Blanchard and Niget (2016), Boos (2003), and Canning (1996).

11. An exception to this is Trân's (2013: 33) description of Vietnam's labor resistance, which includes "popular poems expressing workers' sentiment and determination to protect their fellow women workers who were beaten by the bosses."

12. On the situation in Bangladesh, Rahman and Langford (2012: 100) note that "the majority of the female labor force presented themselves as uninformed about their basic rights and intimidated by authority figures."

Bibliography

Adepunk, Kristina, Tanti Mega, and Tarini Sorrita. 2008. *5 Kelopak Mata Bauhinia.* s.l.: Komunitas Cantrik and Forum Budaya Buruh Migran Indonesia.

Aeniah. 1998. Surat. *Rantau* XI: 21.

Agger, Inger, and Søren Buus Jensen. 1996. *Trauma and Healing Under State Terrorism.* London: Zed Books.

Agrawal, Nisha. 1995. Indonesia Labor Market Policies and International Competitiveness. World Bank Policy Research Working Paper 1515.

Akhmadi, Heri. 1979. *Mendobrak Belenggu Penindasan Rakyat Indonesia:* Pembelaan *di depan Pengadilan Mahasiswa Indonesia, dibacakan pada tanggal 7, 8, 9 Juni 1979 pada sidang Pengadilan Mahasiswa Indonesia di Bandung.* Bandung: LBH and KPM-DM-ITB.

Aleida, Martin. 2017. Surat Tapol kepada TKW, Cucunya. *Kompas*, May 21.

Aleksic, Kassia. 2017. Portrait d'une ouvrière devenue lesbienne et dirigeante syndicale en Indonésie. *Chimères* 92 (2): 23–35.

Altman, Janet Gurkin. 1982. *Epistolarity: Approaches to a Form.* Columbus: Ohio State University Press.

Amengual, Matthew, and Laura Chirot. 2016. Reinforcing the State: Transnational and State Labor Regulation in Indonesia. *ILR Review* 69 (5): 1056–1080.

Amnesty International. 2013. *Exploited for Profit, Failed by Governments: Indonesian Migrant Domestic Workers Trafficked to Hong Kong.* London: Amnesty International.

Ampi. 2011. Bangga sebagai buruh yang berjuang. *Suara Buruh* V (August): 11.

Anderson, Benedict. 1990. A Time of Darkness and a Time of Light: Transposition in Early Indonesian Nationalist Thought. In *Language and Power: Exploring Political Cultures in Indonesia*, 241–270. Ithaca: Cornell University Press.

Andrika, Astika, and Rizal Assalam. 2020. *Offshoring the Risks: Gendered Occupational Hazards in Malaysian and Indonesian Electronics Factories.* Hong Kong: Asia Monitor Reseource Centre.

Aron, Paul. 2006 (1995). *La littérature prolétarienne en Belgique francophone depuis 1990.* Loverval: Labor.

Arotçarena, Guillaume. 2015. *Priest in Geylang: The Untold Story of the Geylang Catholic Centre.* Singapore: Ethos Books.

Asato, Wako. 2004. Negotiating Spaces in the Labor Market: Foreign and Local Domestic Workers in Hong Kong. *Asian and Pacific Migration Journal* 13 (2): 255–274.

Aspinall, Edward. 2005. *Opposing Suharto: Compromise, Resistance, and Regime Change in Indonesia.* Stanford: Stanford University Press.

Atlyserita. 2013. FBLP PT. Asian Collection tak menyerah merebut hak. *Suara Buruh* (October): 3–4.

Atmoko, N. H. 2011. *Banjir Darah di Kamp Konsentrasi: Catatan Harian Aktivis PNI dalam Penjara G30S.* Yogyakarta: Galang Press.

Aulia, Syifa. 2007. Maids Turn Writers in HK. *Brunei Times,* October 12.

Avonius, Leena. 2008. From Marsinah to Munir: Grounding Human Rights in Indonesia. In *Human Rights in Asia: A Reassessment of the Asian Value Debate,* edited by Leena Avonius and Damien Kingsbury, 99–120. New York: Palgrave Macmillan.

Ba'asyir, Abu Bakar. 2006. *Catatan dari Penjara: Untuk Mengamalkan dan Menegakkan Dinul Islam.* Depok: Mushaf.

Bakker, Laurens. 2016. Organized Violence and the State: Evolving Vigilantism in Indonesia. *Bijdragen tot de Taal-,Land- en Volkenkunde* 172 (2–3): 249–277.

Barraclough, Ruth. 2009. Slum Romance in Korean Factory Girl Literature. In *Gender and Labour in Korea and Japan: Sexing Class,* edited by Ruth Barraclough and Elyssa Faison, 60–77. London and New York: Routledge.

———. 2012. *Factory Girl Literature: Sexuality, Violence, and Representation in Industrializing Korea.* Berkeley: University of California Press.

Beekman, E. M. 1988. *Fugitive Dreams: An Anthology of Dutch Colonial Literature.* Amherst: The University of Massachusetts Press.

Benjamin, Dwyne. 1996. Women and the Labour Market in Indonesia During the 1980s. In *Women and Industrialization in Asia,* edited by Susan Horton, 81–133. London: Routledge.

Besari, Siti. 1947. Kami menoentoet. *Kereta Api* 42–43: 12–13.

Beverley, John. 1992. The Margin at the Center: On *Testimonio* (Testimonial Narrative). In *De/colonizing the Subject: The Politics of Gender in Women's Autobiography,* edited by Sidonie Smith and Julia Watson, 91–114. Minneapolis: University of Minnesota Press.

Bintang, Mega. 2012. Matahariku. In *Miracle of Life: Sandiwara Upik Abu,* edited by Dhieny Megawati, Indira Margareta, Yuli Duryat and W. Ita, 47–53. Yogyakarta: Diandra Creative.

Blackburn, Susan. 2004. *Women and the State in Modern Indonesia.* Cambridge: Cambridge University Press.

Blanchard, Véronique, and David Niget. 2016. *Mauvaises filles: incorrigibles et rebelles.* Paris: Textuel.

Blofield, Merike. 2012. *Care Work and Class: Domestic Workers' Struggle for Equal Rights in Latin America.* Pennsylvania: Pennsylvania State University Press.

Bodden, Michael. 1997. Workers' Theatre and Theatre About Workers in 1990s Indonesia. *RIMA: Review of Indonesian and Malaysian Affairs* 31 (1): 37–78.

Bo Niok, Maria. 2007a. *Ranting Sakura*. Yogyakarta: P_Idea.

_____. 2007b. *Geliat Sang Kung yan*. Yogyakarta: Gama Media.

_____. 2008a. *Sumi: Jejak Cinta Perempuan Gila*. Yogyakarta: Arti Bumi Intaran.

_____. 2008b. Keinginan Perempuan. *Pikiran Rakyat*, February 9.

_____. 2009. *Mukenah dan Sajadah untuk Soya*. Yogyakarta: Garailmu.

_____. 2011a. Jejak Bakiak Cinta. In *Sebuah Nama yang Terlupa*, edited by Nessa Kartika and Maria Bo Niok, 1–10. Yogyakarta: leutikaprio.

_____. 2011b. Cinta Merah Bukit Merah. In *Sebuah Nama yang Terlupa*, edited by Nessa Kartika and Maria Bo Niok, 11–18. Yogyakarta: leutikaprio.

Boos, Florence. 2003. The "Queen" of the "Far-Famed Penny Post": "The Factory Girl Poet" and Her Audience. *Women's Writing* 10 (3): 503–526.

Bowen-Struyk, Heather, and Norma Field (Eds.). 2015. *For Dignity, Justice, and Revolution: An Anthology of Japanese Proletarian Literature*. Chicago: The University of Chicago Press.

Breman, Jan. 2010. *Outcast Labour in Asia: Circulation and Informalization of the Workforce at the Bottom of the Economy*. New Delhi: Oxford University Press.

Britwum, Akua, Karen Douglas, and Sue Ledwith. 2012. Women, Gender and Power in Trade Unions. In *Labour in the Global South: Challenges and Alternatives for Workers*, edited by Sarah Mosoetsa and Michelle Williams, 41–64. Geneva: International Labour Office.

Brown, David, and Ian Wilson. 2007. Ethnicized Violence in Indonesia: The Betawi Brotherhood Forum in Jakarta. Working Paper No. 145. Perth: Murdoch University.

Cahyono, Kahar. 2011. *Memoar Gerakan Buruh Tangerang: Jejak langkah Sang Aktivis*. Yogyakarta: leutikaprio.

Cameron, Lisa, D. C. Suarez, and W. Rowell. 2019. Female Labour Force Participation in Indonesia: Why Has It Stalled? *Bulletin of Indonesian Economic Studies* 55 (2): 157–192.

Camposano, Clement. 2018. Facebook and the Intricacies of Migrant Self-Making Among Ilonggo OFWs in South Korea. *Philippine Studies: Historical and Ethnographic Viewpoints* 66 (1): 19–47.

Canning, Kathleen. 1996. *Languages of Labor and Gender: Female Factory Work in Germany, 1850–1914*. Ithaca: Cornell University Press.

Caraway, Teri. 2007. *Assembling Women: The Feminization of Global Manufacturing*. Ithaca: Cornell University Press.

Chandra, Siddharth. 2002. The Role of Female Industrial Labor in the Late Colonial Netherlands Indies. *Indonesia* 74: 103–135.

Cheah, Pheng. 2007. Biopower and the New International Division of Reproductive Labor. *Boundary 2* 34 (1): 90–113.

———. 2010. Necessary Strangers: Law's Hospitality in the Age of Global Migration. In *Law and the Stranger*, edited by A. Sarat, L. Douglas, and M. Umphrey, 21–63. Palo Alto: Stanford University Press.

Chun, Soonok. 2003. *They Are Not Machines: Korean Women Workers and Their Fight for Democratic Trade Unionism in the 1970s*. Aldershot: Ashgate.

Constable, Nicole. 1997. Sexuality and Discipline among Filipina Domestic Workers in Hong Kong. *American Ethnologist* 24 (3): 539–558.

_____. 2009. Migrant Workers and the Many States of Protest in Hong Kong. *Critical Asian Studies* 41 (1): 143–164.

Coppel, Charles. 1983. *Indonesian Chinese in Crisis*. Kuala Lumpur: Oxford University Press.

Dalijo, Ally. 2010. *Karat Luka*. Hong Kong: Teater Angin Publisher.

De Guzman, Odine. 2008. Testimonial Narratives: Memory and Self-representation in Letters by Women Migrant Workers. In *Philippines Studies: Have We Gone Beyond St. Louis?*, edited by P. Patajo-Legasto, 600–619. Quezon City: University of The Philippines Press.

_____. 2011. Narrating Migration, Reading A Political Itinerary: Connie Bragas-Regalado, Overseas Filipino Worker. In *Traveling Nation-Makers: Transnational Flows and Movement in the Making of Modern Southeast Asia*, edited by Caroline S. Hau and Kasian Tejapira, 248–280. Singapore and Kyoto: NUS Press and Kyoto University Press.

Devasahayam, Theresa. 2016. "A Place to Call Home": The Catholic Church and Female Foreign Domestic Workers in Singapore. In *Women Migrant Workers: Ethical, Political and Legal Problems*, edited by Zahra Meghani, 179–196. New York: Routledge.

Deyo, Frederic. 1987. State and Labour: Modes of Political Exclusion in East Asian Development. In *The Political Economy of the New Asian Industrialism*, edited by Frederick Deyo, 182–202. Ithaca: Cornell University Press.

Dhanani, Shafiq, and Iyanatul Islam. 2004. *Indonesian Wage Structure and Trends, 1976–2000*. Geneva: ILO.

Eldridge, Philip. 1995. *Non-Governmental Organizations and Democratic Participation in Indonesia*. Kuala Lumpur: Oxford University Press.

Elliot, Jan. 1997. Equality? The Influence of Legislation and Notions of Gender on the Position of Women Wage Workers in the Economy: Indonesia 1950–1958. In *Women Creating Indonesia: The First Fifty Years*, edited by J. G. Taylor, 122–155. Clayton: Centre for Southeast Asian Studies, Monash University.

Farid, Hilmar. 1997. Covering Strikes: Indonesian Workers and "Their" Media. In *State and Labour in New Order Indonesia*, edited by Rob Lambert, 123–145. Perth: University of Western Australia Press and Asia Research Centre, Murdoch University.

Faue, Elizabeth. 2002. *Writing the Wrongs: Eva Valesh and the Rise of Labor Journalism*. Ithaca: Cornell University Press.

Foley, Barbara. 1993. *Radical Representations: Politics and Form in U.S. Proletarian Fiction, 1929–1941*. Durham: Duke University Press.

Ford, Michele. 2008. Indonesia: Separate Organizing Within Unions. In *Women and Labour Organizing in Asia: Diversity, Autonomy and Activism*, edited by Kaye Broadbent and Michele Ford, 15–33. London and New York: Routledge.

Gallaway, Julie, and Alexandra Bernasek. 2004. Literacy and Women's Empowerment in Indonesia: Implications for Policy. *Journal of Economic Issues* 38 (2): 519–525.

Garland, Carolina. 2005. Trauma and the Possibility of Recovery. In *Introducing Psychoanalysis: Essential Themes and Topics*, edited by Susan Budd and Richard Rusbidger, 246–262. London: Routledge.

Geertz, Clifford. 1973. Person, Time and Conduct in Bali. In *The Interpretation of Culture*, 360–411. New York: Basic Books.

Geneste, Philippe. 1992. *Visages de la littérature prolétarienne contemporaine.* Mauléon: Acratie.

Goodridge, John, and Bridget Keegan (Eds.). 2017. *A History of British Working-Class Literature*. Cambridge: Cambridge University Press.

Grant, Melissa Gira. 2014. *Playing the Whore: The Work of Sex Work*. London: Verso.

Hadiz, Vedi. 1997. *Workers and the State in New Order Indonesia.* London: Routledge.

Hancock, Peter. 2006. Violence, Women, Work and Empowerment: Narratives from Factory Women in Sri Lanka's Export Processing Zones. *Gender, Technology and Development* 10 (2): 211–228.

Handayani, Sih. 1995. Sumarni: Buruh Pabrik Utama Tex. In *Lika-liku Kehidupan Buruh Perempuan*, edited by Masri Singarimbun and Sjafri Siarin, 256–282. Yogyakarta: Pustaka Pelajar and Yayasan Annisa Swasti

Hart, Monica Smith. 2015. The Factory Exile: Ellen Johnston's *Autobiography, Poems and Songs. Victorian Poetry* 53 (1): 77–99.

Hartati. 1955a. Lamunan dan Impian Pegawai Negeri. *Madjalah Merdeka* VIII (7) (February 12): 16–17.

_____. 1955b. Apa Memelihara Babu atau Pelajan itu Perlu? *Madjalah Merdeka* VIII (30) (July 23): 8–9.

Harvey, David. 1989. *The Conditions of Postmodernity: An Enquiry into the Origins of Cultural Change*. Oxford: Basil Blackwell.

Haspels, Nelien, Zaitun Mohamed Kasim, Constrance Thomas, and Deidre McCann. 2001. *Action Against Sexual Harassment at Work in Asia and the Pacific*. Bangkok: International Labour Office.

Hau, Caroline. 2004. *On the Subject of the Nation: Filipino Writings from the Margins, 1981–2004*. Quezon City: Ateneo de Manila University Press.

Herod, Andrew. 2001. *Labor Geographies: Workers and the Landscapes of Capitalism*. New York: The Guilford Press.

Hess, Michael. 1997. Understanding Indonesian Industrial Relations in the 1990s. *Journal of Industrial Relations* 39 (1): 33–51.

Heyzer, Noeleen. 1986. *Working Women in South-East Asia: Development, Subordination and Emancipation*. Milton Keynes: Open University Press.

Hill, Hal. 2000. *The Indonesian Economy* (2nd Ed.). Cambridge: Cambridge University Press.

Hindley, Donald. 1964. *The Communist Party of Indonesia, 1951–1963*. Berkeley and Los Angeles: University of California Press.

Hirai, Kyonosuke. 2008. The Romantic Ethic and the Notion of Modern Society: Imagining Communities among Northern Thai Factory Women. In *Imagining Communities in Thailand: Ethnographic Approaches*, edited by Shigeharu Tanabe, 135–159. Chiang Mai: Mekong Press.

Hirano, Keiko. 2017. 「技能化」の含意——インドネシアの移住・家事労働者と C189 (The Implication of the Shift to Skilled Workers in Indonesia's Labor Export Policy: Migrant and Domestic Workers in Indonesia and C189). 「北海道教育大学紀要（人文科学・社会科学編)」68 (1): 53–61.

Hoskins, Janet. 1998. *Biographical Objects: How Things Tell the Stories of Peoples' Lives*. London: Routledge.

Hossine, Md. Mukul. 2016. *Me Migrant*. Singapore: Ethos Books.

Hsia, Hsiao-Chuan. 2009. The Making of a Transnational Grassroot Migrant Movement. *Critical Asian Studies* 41 (1): 113–141.

Hsiao, Michael Hsin-Huang. 1996. Changing Literary Images of Taiwan's Working Class. In *Putting Class in Its Place: Worker Identities in East Asia*, edited by Elizabeth Perry, 103–126. Berkeley: Institute of East Asian Studies, University of California.

Hugo, Graeme. 2006. Women, Work and International Migration in Southeast Asia: Trends, Patterns and Policy. In *Mobility, Labour Migration and Border Controls in Asia*, edited by Amarjit Kaur and Ian Metcalfe, 73–113. Basingstoke: Palgrave Macmillan.

Hutabarat, Tua Hasiholan. 2006. *Realitas Upah Buruh Industri*. Medan: Kelompok Pelita Sejahtera, with the support of n(o)vib.

Idrus, Nurul Ilmi. 2008. Makkunrai Passimokolo': Bugis Migrant Women Workers in Malaysia. In *Women and Work in Indonesia*, edited by Michele Ford and Lyn Parker, 155–172. London and New York: Routledge.

INDOC (Indonesian Documentation and Information Centre). 1981. *Indonesian Workers and Their Rights to Organise*. Leiden: INDOC.

_____. 1983. *Indonesian Workers and Their Rights to Organise. Update: Increasing Militarisation of Labour Relations*. Leiden: INDOC.

Indraswari, and Juni Thamrin. 1994. *Potret Kerja Buruh Perempuan: Tinjauan pada Agroindustri Tembakau Ekspor di Jember*. Bandung: Akatiga.

Insani, Bayu. 2010. Para TKW dan Kegemaran Membaca Buku [Overseas Workers and Their Fondness for Book Reading]. *Jawa Pos*, February 14.

International Labour Organisation (ILO). 1996. *Equality in Employment and Occupation: Special Survey on Equality in Employment and Occupation in respect of Convention No. 111*. Geneva: ILO.

_____. 2000. *Decent Work for Women: An ILO Proposal to Accelerate the Implementation of the Beijing Platform for Action*. Geneva: ILO.

Iqbal, Said. 2014. *Gagasan Besar Serikat Buruh*. Yogyakarta: leutikaprio.

Irianti, Ida. 1988. Pembelaan, Kasus no. 608/Pid/S/88/PN.Jkt.Tim. (Photocopied Material).

Islam, Iyanatul, and Suahasil Nazara. 2000. *Minimum Wage and the Welfare of Indonesian Workers*. Jakarta: ILO.

Jacka, Tamara. 1998. Working Sisters Answer Back: Reflections on Subaltern Theory and Chinese History. *Positions: East Asia Cultures Critique* 1 (1): 103–130.

Jahja, Junus. 1988. *Catatan Seorang WNI: Kenangan, Renungan & Harapan*. Jakarta: Yayasan Tunas Bangsa.

Jeffrey, Leslie Ann. 2002. *Sex and Borders: Gender, National Identity, and Prostitution Policy in Thailand*. Chiang Mai: Silkworm Books.

Jeon, Je Seong. 2002. 수하르또 치하 인도네시아에서 노동계급의 "조직화 없는 저항" : 수라바야 제화공장 여성노동자의 투쟁과 좌절 ("Resistance Without Organization" in the Soeharto's Indonesia: A Woman Worker's Struggle and Despair in a Shoes Factory in Surabaya). *East Asian Studies* 43: 31–49.

———. 2008. Strategies for Union Consolidation in Indonesia: The Case of SPSI Maspion Unit 1, Sidoarjo, East Java. *Labour and Management in Development* 9.

Juliawan, Benny Hari. 2010. Extracting Labor from Its Owner: Private Employment Agencies and Labor Market Flexibility in Indonesia. *Critical Asian Studies* 42 (1): 25–52.

Jumiati, Sri. 2015. Bersama Serikat Buruh, Aku terbebas dari Belenggu Kekerasan Dalam Rumah Tangga. In *Buruh Menuliskan Perlawanannya*, edited by Bambang Dahana, Syarif Arifin, Abu Mufakhir, Dina Septi, Azhar Irfansyah and Alfian Al-Ayubby Pelu, 287–301. Bogor: Lembaga Informasi Perburuhan Sedane (LIPS) and Tanah Air Beta.

Juwanna. 2010. Kerudung Turki. In *Kumpulan Cerpen: Penjajah di Rumahku*, edited by Nanang Junaedi, 153–163. s.l.: FLP Hong Kong.

Juwita, Etik. 2006. Hatiku Kapalan. In *Nyanyian Imigran*, edited by Djodi Sambodo and Mega Vristian, 21–28. Malang: Dragon Family Publisher.

Kartika, Nessa. 2010. Love is Not Impossible. In *Be Strong Indonesia #tiga*, edited by Anonymous. s.l.: writers4Indonesia publisher.

———. 2011. Kupu-kupu Puncak Beton. In *Singa Bauhinia*, edited by Nessa Kartika and Karin Maulana, 59–69. Yogyakarta: leutikaprio.

Kartika, Titiek 2014. *Perempuan Lokal vs Tambang Pasir Besi Global*. Jakarta: Yayasan Pustaka Obor Indonesia.

Kartini, Raden Adjeng. 1921. *Letters of a Javanese Princess*. Translated by Agnes Louise Symmers. London: Duckworth &Co.

Kemp, Herman C. (Ed.). 2004. *Oral Traditions of Southeast Asia and Oceania: A Bibliography*. Jakarta: Yayasan Obor Indonesia and KITLV-Jakarta.

Kemp, Melody. 2001. Corporate Social Responsibility in Indonesia: Quixotic Dream or Confident Expectation? United Nations Research Institute for Social Development (UNRISD) Programme Paper on Technology, Business and Society, Number 6.

Killias, Olivia. 2018. *Follow the Maid: Domestic Workers Migration in and from Indonesia*. Copenhagen: NIAS Press.

Kim, Seung-kyung. 1997. *Class Struggle or Family Struggle? Lives of Women Factory Workers in South Korea*. Cambridge: Cambridge University Press.

Kirk, John. 2003. *Twentieth-Century Writing and the British Working Class*. Cardiff: University of Wales Press.

Kobayashi, Shigeo (小林茂夫). 1988. 「プロレタリア文学の作家たち」 (*Authors of the Proletarian Literature*). Tokyo: Shin-Nihon.

Koetsawang, Pim. 2001. *In Search of Sunlight: Burmese Migrant Workers in Thailand*. Bangkok: Orchid Press.

Komariyah, Siti. 2011a. Saatnya Perempuan Mengambil Peran Perubahan. *Koran Perdjoeangan* XXXIX (May): 10.

_____. 2011b. The Untouchables Sistem Outsourcing dan Kontrak. *Koran Perdjoeangan* IVX (*sic!* XL) (September): 11.

Kondo, Dorinne. 1990. *Crafting Selves: Power, Gender, and Discourses of Identity in a Japanese Workplace.* Chicago: University of Chicago Press.

Koo, Hagen. 2001. *Korean Workers: The Culture and Politics of Class Formation.* Ithaca: Cornell University Press.

Krisnawati, T., and F. Mardzoeki (Eds.). 1999. *Saat Kau Berpangku Tangan Korban-korban Terus Berjatuhan: Kumpulan Surat-surat Sopiah TKW asal Indonesia yang Tewas dalam Perjuangannya Melawan Praktek Penindasan Buruh Migran Perempuan di Beirut – Lebanon (Oktober 1998 – Januari 1999).* Bekasi: Lembaga Advokasi Buruh Migran Indonesia Perserikatan Solidaritas Perempuan.

Kühl, Bianca. 2002. Labour Standards in the Indonesian Apparel and Shoe Industry: How Codes of Conduct Help to Implement Workers' Rights. *Pacific News* 18: 4–7.

_____. 2006. Protecting Apparel Workers Through Transnational Network: The Case of Indonesia. Ph.D. Dissertation, University of Kassel.

Lahiri-Dutt, Kuntala. 2006. Globalization and Women's Work in the Mine Pits in East Kalimantan, Indonesia. In *Women Miners in Developing Countries: Pit Women and Others,* edited by Kuntala Lahiri-Duttt and Martha Macintyre, 349–369. Aldershot: Ashgate.

Lahiri-Dutt, Kuntala, and Kathryn Robinson. 2008. Bodies in Contest: Gender Difference and Equity in a Coal Mine. In *Women and Work in Indonesia,* edited by Michele Ford and Lyn Parker, 120–135. London and New York: Routledge.

Lauter, Paul. 2005. Under Construction: Working-Class Writing. In *New Working-Class Studies,* edited by John Russo and Sherry Lee Linkon, 63–77. Ithaca: ILR, Cornell University Press.

LBH Surabaya. 1993. Kronologi hilangnya tiga orang tokoh buruh: Imam Basuki, Damiati, Meppy Doryati Emping (Photocopied Material).

Lestari, Eni. 2010. Learning to Lead: Against the Odds, Indonesian Domestic Workers Have Achieved Real Change in Hong Kong. *Inside Indonesia* 100 (April–June).

Li, Tania Murray. 2017. The Price of Un/Freedom: Indonesia's Colonial and Contemporary Plantation Labor Regimes. *Comparative Studies in Society and History* 59 (2): 245–276.

Lindio-McGovern, Ligaya. 1997. *Filipino Peasant Women: Exploitation and Resistance.* Philadelphia: University of Pennsylvania Press.

_____. 2004. Alienation and Labor Export in the Context of Globalization: Filipino Migrant Domestic Workers in Taiwan and Hong Kong. *Critical Asian Studies* 36 (2): 217–238.

Lindquist, Johan. 2009. *The Anxieties of Mobility: Migration and Tourism in the Indonesian Borderlands.* Honolulu: University of Hawai'i Press.

Linggasari, Yohannie. 2015. Kisah Perjuangan Hidup Mantan Buruh Lesbian. *CNN Indonesia,* May 1. https://www.cnnindonesia.com/nasional/20150501100000-20-50470/kisah-perjuangan-hidup-mantan-buruh-lesbian.

Liszek, Slava. 1994. *Marie Guillot: de l'émancipation des femmes à celle du syndicalisme.* Paris: L'Harmattan.

Lo Bue, Maria C., and Jan Priebe. 2018. Revisiting the Socioeconomic Determinants of Exclusive Breastfeeding Practices: Evidence from Eastern Indonesia. *Oxford Development Studies* 46 (3): 398–410.

Locher-Scholten, Elsbeth. 2000. *Women and the Colonial State: Essays on Gender and Modernity in the Netherlands Indies 1900–1942.* Amsterdam: Amsterdam University Press.

Loveband, Anne. 2006. Positioning the Product: Indonesian Migrant Women Workers in Taiwan. In *Transnational Migration and Work in Asia*, edited by K. Hewison and K. Young, 75–89. London: Routledge.

Mageo, Jeannette. 1991. Inhibitions and Compensations: A Study of the Effects of Negative Sanctions in Three Pacific Cultures. *Pacific Studies* 14 (3): 1–40.

Maimunah, Margaret Aliyatul. 2008. Kesadaran tentang Perlindungan Kesehatan Reproduksi Kasus Buruh Perempuan di Kawasan Berikat Nusantara (KBN) Tanjung Priok. In *Bertahan Hidup di Desa atau Tahan Hidup di Kota: Balada Buruh Perempuan*, edited by Aris Arif Mundayat, Erni Agustini and Margaret Aliyatul Maimunah, 67–103. Jakarta: Women Research Institute.

Manning, Chris. 1994. What Has Happened to Wages in the New Order? *Bulletin of Indonesian Economic Studies* 30 (3): 73–114.

_____. 1998. *Indonesian Labour in Transition: An East Asian Success Story?* Cambridge: Cambridge University Press.

Marco Kartodikromo. 1922. *Persdelict dan soerat perlawanan (di persidangan oemoem Landraad Djokjakarta pada hari kemis 8 December 1921, dengan poetoesan vonnis tanggal 8 December 1921 no 989/1921).* Yogyakarta: Sri Pakoealaman.

Mather, Celia. 1983. Industrialization in the Tangerang Regency of West Java: Women Workers and the Islamic Patriarchy. *Bulletin of Concerned Asian Scholars* 15 (2): 2–17.

_____. 2004. *Contract/Agency Labour: A Threat to Our Social Standards.* Belgium: ICEM.

Matthews, Gordon. 2011. *Ghetto at the Center of the World: Chungking Mansion, Hong Kong.* Chicago: University of Chicago Press.

Maulana, Karin. 2011. Sasmitha. In *Singa Bauhinia*, edited by Nessa Kartika and Karin Maulana, 144–152. Yogyakarta: leutikaprio.

McNally, Vincent. 2012. Abduction/Kidnapping. In *Encyclopedia of Trauma: An Interdisciplinary Guide*, edited by Charles R. Figley, 1–2. Los Angeles: Sage.

Mell, Shaliha. 2014. *The Dream in Taipei City.* Surakarta: Indiva.

Menchú, Rigoberta, and Elisabeth Burgos-Debray. 1984. *I, Rigoberta Menchú: An Indian Woman in Guatemala.* Translated by Ann White. London: Verso.

Meppy, D. E. 1993. Tragedi yang Pahit: Penahanan di Korem 084 (Photocopied Material).

Mills, Mary Beth. 2005. From Nimble Fingers to Raised Fists: Women and Labor Activism in Globalizing Thailand. *Signs: Journal of Women in Culture and Society* 31 (1): 117–144.

Mizuno, Kosuke. 2020. 民主化と労使関係 ― インドネシアのムシャワラ
ー労使紛争処理と行動主義の源流 (*Democratization and Labor Relations in
Indonesia: Musyawarah, Labor Dispute Resolution and Activism*). Kyoto: Kyoto
University Press.

Moeljono, Djoko Sri. 2013. *Banten Seabad Setelah Multatuli: Catatan Seorang Tapol
12 Tahun Dalam Tahanan, Kerja Rodi dan Pembuangan*. Bandung: Ultimus.

Moon, Kyoung-Hee, and Kaye Broadbent, 2008. Korea: Women, Labour Activism
and Autonomous Organizing. In *Women and Labour Organizing in Asia: Diversity,
Autonomy and Activism*, edited by Kaye Broadbent and Michele Ford, 136–155.
London and New York: Routledge.

Mufakhir, Abu. 2012. Menjawab Opini *Tempo*: Soal Aksi Mogok Nasional Buruh
Bekasi. *Lembaran Buruh* 29 (May): 8–10.

Mutsaers, Lutgard. 2014. "Barat ketemu Timur": Cross-Cultural Encounters and
the Making of Early Kroncong History. In *Recollecting Resonances: Indonesian-
Dutch Musical Encounters*, edited by Bart Barendregt and Els Bogaerts, 259–279.
Leiden and Boston: Brill.

Najmabadi, Afsaneh. 2004. The Morning After: Travail of Sexuality and Love in
Modern Iran. *International Journal of Middle East Studies* 36: 367–385.

Nisa, Susana. 2016. Tuhan, Aku Pulang. In *Bacaan Selepas Kerja*, 378–382. Hong
Kong and Yogyakarta: Para Site and KUNCI Cultural Studies.

Ockey, James. 2004. *Making Democracy: Leadership, Class, Gender and Political
Participation in Thailand*. Honolulu: University of Hawai'i Press.

Ofreneo, Rene, and Isabelo Samonte. 2005. Empowering Filipino Migrant Workers:
Policy Issues and Challenges. International Migration Papers No. 64. Geneva: ILO.

Oishi, Nana. 2005. *Women in Motion: Globalization, State Politics, and Labor
Migration in Asia*. Stanford: Stanford University Press.

Okamoto,Masaaki.2015.暴力と適応の政治学―インドネシア民主化と地方政治
の安定(*The Politics of Violence and Adaptation : Indonesian Democratization and
Local Political Stability*). Kyoto: Kyoto University Press.

Osterreich, Shaianne. 2013. Precarious Work in Global Exports: The Case of
Indonesia. *Review of Political Economy* 25 (2): 273–293.

Pakpahan, Muchtar. 2002. *Rakyat Menggugat I: Sebuah Pleidoi*. Jakarta: Bumi
Intitama Sejahtera.

Pandjaitan, W. 1963. *Petundjuk tentang Masaalah Perburuhan*. Medan: Ikatan
Keluarga Pegawai Djawatan Pengawasan Perburuhan.

Park, Min-na. 2005. *Birth of Resistance: Stories of Eight Women Worker Activists*.
Translated by Sarah Eunkyung Chee. Seoul: Korea Democracy Foundation.

Parker, Lyn, I. Riyani, and B. Nolan. 2016. The Stigmatisation of Widows and
Divorcees (Janda) in Indonesia, and the Possibilities for Agency. *Indonesia and the
Malay World* 44 (128): 27–46.

Pearson, Ruth, and Gill Seyfang. 2002. "I'll Tell You What I Want…": Women
Workers and Codes of Conduct. In *Corporate Responsibility and Labour Rights:
Codes of Conduct in the Global Economy*, edited by Rhys Jenkins, Ruth Pearson
and Gill Seyfang, 43–60. London: Earthscan.

Peletz, Michael. 1996. *Reason and Passion: Representations of Gender in a Malay Society*. Berkeley: University of California Press.

Perera, Sonali. 2008. Rethinking Working-Class Literature: Feminism, Globalization, and Socialist Ethics. *Differences: A Journal of Feminist Cultural Studies* 19 (1): 1–31.

_____. 2014. *No Country: Working-Class Writing in the Age of Globalization*. New York: Columbia University Press.

Perrot, Michelle. 2012. *Mélancolie ouvrière*. Paris: Grasset.

Pierse, Michael (Ed.). 2018. *A History of Irish Working-Class Writing*. Cambridge: Cambridge University Press.

Pinches, Michael. 1991. The Working-Class Experience of Shame, Inequality, and People Power in Tatalon, Manila. In *From Marcos to Aquino: Local Perspectives on Political Transition in the Philippines*, edited by Benedict J. Kerkvliet and Resil B. Mojares, 166–186. Honolulu and Manila: University of Hawai'i Press and Ateneo de Manila University Press.

Piocos, Carlos III. 2016. On Being Moved: Affect and Politics in Narratives of Southeast Asian Migration. Ph.D. Dissertation, University of Hong Kong.

PKI. 1960. *Dokumen-dokumen Kongres Nasional VI Partai Komunis Indonesia (7–14 September 1959)*. Djakarta: Jajasan Pembaruan.

Poeze, Harry. 1986. *In het land van de overheerser I: Indonesiërs in Nederland (1600–1950)*. Dordrecht: Foris Publications.

Politakis, George. 2001. Night Work of Women in Industry: Standards and Sensibility. *International Labour Review* 140 (4): 403–428.

Pospos. P. 1950. *Aku dan Toba: Tjatatan dari Masa Kanak-kanak*. Djakarta: Balai Pustaka.

Poulaille, Henry. 1986 (1930). *La nouvelle âge littéraire*. Bassac: Plein Chant.

Praptinah. 1954. Kerdja Malam Wanita. *Tindjauan Masaalah Perburuhan* V (11): 13–14.

Praptini. 1951. Buruh Wanita dan Haknja. *Warta Sarbupri* II (10 Desember).

Premanathan, Sharanya, and Tshiung Han See. 2017. *Voices of the Displaced: Poems from the Malaysian Migrant Poetry Competition, 2015–2016*. Petaling Jaya: Gerakbudaya Enterprise.

Prihanani. 2009. Pengaruh Kesetaraan Jender dalam Mendorong Perempuan untuk Aktif dalam Serikat Pekerja. *Koran Perdjoeangan* XXIV (October): 11.

Purwanti, Aliyah, Ally Dalijo, El Nisya Mahendra, H. S. Geppy, Mega Vristian, Noena Fadzila, Ratna Khaerudina, and W. Srismitha. 2010. *Yam Cha: Kumpulan Karya Buruh Migran*. Hong Kong: Teater Angin Publisher.

Pye, Oliver, Ramlah Daud, Yuyun Harmono, and Tatat. 2012. Precarious Lives: Transnational Biographies of Migrant Oil Palm Workers. *Asia Pacific Viewpoint* 53 (3): 330–342.

Ragon, Michel. 2012 [1974]. *Histoire de la littérature prolétarienne de langue française: littérature ouvrière, littérature paysanne, littérature d'expression populaire*. Paris: Albin Michel.

Rahman, Zia, and Tom Langford. 2012. Why Labour Unions Have Failed Bangladesh's Garment Workers. In *Labour in the Global South: Challenges and Alternatives for Workers*, edited by Sarah Mosoetsa and Michelle Williams, 87–106. Geneva: International Labour Office.

Raihan, Ida. 2010. Lorong MRT. In *TKW Menulis*, edited by Bayu Insani and Ida Raihan, 177–183. Yogyakarta: leutika.

Ramaswamy, Vijaya. 1993. Women and Farm Work in Tamil Folk Songs. *Social Scientist* 21 (9–11): 113–129.

Rancière, Jacques. 1981. *La nuit des prolétaires. Archives du rêve ouvrier.* Paris: Fayard.

Reid, Anthony. 1972. On the Importance of Autobiography. *Indonesia* 13 (April): 1–3.

Repollo, Belen Esposo. 2015. Pusong Hapo (4-8-6). In *Get Lucky: An Anthology of Philippine and Singapore Writings*, edited by Manuelita Contreras-Cabrera, Migs Bravo-Dutt, and Eric Tinsay Valles, 82. Singapore: Ethos Books.

Reyes, Angelita. 1994. The Epistolary Voices of Indigenous Feminism in Mariama Bâ's *Une si longue lettre*. In *Moving Beyond Boundaries, Volume Two: Black Women's Diasporas*, edited by Carole Boyce Davies, 195–217. New York: New York University Press.

Robinson, Lillian. 2006 [1983]. Treason Our Text: Feminist Challenges to the Literary Canon. In *Background Readings for Teachers of American Literature*, edited by Venetria K. Patton, 245–259. Boston: Bedford/St. Martin's.

Robison, Richard. 1986. *Indonesia: The Rise of Capital.* Sydney: Allen and Unwin.

Rodgers, Susan (Ed.). 1995. *Telling Lives, Telling History: Autobiography and Historical Imagination in Modern Indonesia.* Berkeley: University of California Press.

Rostinah. 2002. Masalah Perburuhan Berubah menjadi Masalah Pidana. *Sepakat* 12 (1): 8–11.

Rotkirch, Anna. 2004. "Coming to Stand on Firm Ground": The Making of a Soviet Working Mother. In *On Living Through Soviet Russia*, edited by D. Bertaux, A. Rotkirch, and P. Thompson, 144–173. London and New York: Routledge.

Ruddick, Sarah. 1995 [1989]. *Maternal Thinking: Toward a Politics of Peace.* Boston: Beacon Press.

S. H. 1947. Tenaga Wanita Minta Perhatian. *Kereta Api* 37: 8.

S. Munar. 1948. Wanita Buruh. *Merdeka*, May 7.

Salsabilah. 2015. Surat Pendek untuk Nazik Almalaika. In *Buruh Menuliskan Perlawanannya*, edited by Bambang Dahana, Syarif Arifin, Abu Mufakhir, Dina Septi, Azhar Irfansyah and Alfian Al-Ayubby Pelu, 189–250. Bogor: Lembaga Informasi Perburuhan Sedane (LIPS) and Tanah Air Beta.

Samarakoon, Shanika, and Rasyad A. Parinduri. 2015. Does Education Empower Women? Evidence from Indonesia. *World Development* 66: 428–442.

Schaner, Simone, and Smita Das. 2016. Female Labor Force Participation in Asia: Indonesia Country Study. ADB Economic Working Paper No. 474. Manila: Asian Development Bank.

Scott, James. 1990. *Domination and the Arts of Resistance: Hidden Transcript*. New Haven: Yale University Press.

Semaoen. 1919. *Persdelict Semaoen*. Semarang: Sarekat Islam Semarang.

Sen, Krishna. 1998. Indonesian Women at Work: Reframing the Subject. In *Gender and Power in Affluent Asia*, edited by Krishna Sen and Maila Stivens, 35–62. London: Routledge.

_____. 2002. Gendered Citizens in the New Indonesian Democracy. *Review of Indonesian and Malaysian Affairs* 36 (1): 51–65.

Setiati. 1946. Indonesian Women Labour Union (Barisan Boeroeh Wanita Indonesia). *Voice of Free Indonesia* 27: 12–13.

Setiawan, Hersri. 2004. *Memoar Pulau Buru*. Magelang: IndonesiaTera.

Setyawati, Dinita. 2013. Assets or Commodities? Comparing Regulations of Placement and Protection of Migrant Workers in Indonesia and the Philippines. *ASEAS* 6 (2): 264–280.

Shaliha, Mell. 2014. *The Dream in Taipei City*. Surakarta: Indiva.

Shea, G. T. 1964. *Leftwing Literature in Japan: A Brief History of the Proletarian Literary Movement*. Tokyo: Hosei University Press.

Shiraishi, Takashi. 1990. Dangir's Testimony: Saminism Reconsidered. *Indonesia* 50: 95–120.

_____. 2011. The Making of a Jihadist: Itinerary and Language in Imam Samudra's *Aku Melawan Teroris*! In *Traveling Nation-Makers: Transnational Flows and Movements in the Making of Modern Southeast Asia*, edited by Caroline S. Hau and Kasian Tejapira, 281–303. Singapore and Kyoto: NUS Press and Kyoto University Press.

Siegel, James. 2001. Thoughts on the Violence of May 13 and 14, 1998, in Jakarta. In *Violence and the State in Suharto's Indonesia*, edited by Benedict Anderson, 90–123. Ithaca: Southeast Asia Program, Cornell University.

Silvey, Rachel. 2003. Spaces of Protest: Gendered Migration, Social Networks, and Labor Activism in West Java, Indonesia. *Political Geography* 22: 129–155.

_____. 2007. Unequal Borders: Indonesian Transnational Migrants at Immigration Control. *Geopolitics* 12 (2): 265–279.

Sim, Amy, and Vivienne Wee. 2009. Undocumented Indonesian Workers in Macau. *Critical Asian Studies* 41 (1): 165–188.

Situmorang, Manginar, Daniel Dolok Sibarani, and Juan Lingga. 2008. *Buruh Harian Lepas: Studi Kajian Hubungan Kerja, Upah dan Kesejahteraan di Perkebunan Sumatera Utara*. Medan: Kelompok Pelita Sejahtera.

Sjahrir. 1966 (1945). *Indonesische overpeinzingen*. Amsterdam: Bezige Bij.

Sjöholm, Fredrik. 2016. Foreign Direct Investment and Value Added in Indonesia. IFN Working Paper No. 1141. Stockholm: Research Institute of Industrial Economics.

Smith-Hefner, Nancy. 1989. Reading, Reciting and Knowing: Interpreting A Rural Javanese Text Tradition. In *Writing on the Tongue*, edited by A. Becker, 183–213. Ann Arbor: Center for South and Southeast Asian Studies, The University of Michigan.

Smyth, Ines, and Mies Grijns. 1997. Unjuk Rasa or Conscious Protest? Resistance Strategies of Indonesian Women Workers. *Bulletin of Concerned Asian Scholars* 29 (4): 13–22.

Snow, David. 2004. Framing Processes, Ideology, and Discursive Fields. In *The Blackwell Companion to Social Movements*, edited by David Snow, Sarah A. Soule and Hanspeter Kriesi, 380–412. Malden, MA: Blackwell Publishing.

SOBSI. 1957. Something About the Government Women Employees. *Indonesian Trade Union News* 7 (August): 4–5.

_____. 1961. *Peranan Buruh Wanita dalam Pembangunan: Dari Seminar Nasional Buruh Wanita, diselenggarakan oleh Dewan Nasional SOBSI di Djakarta, 11–14 Mei.* Djakarta: Jajasan Karja Bakti.

Soe, Hok Gie. 1983. *Catatan Seorang Demonstran.* Jakarta: LP3ES.

Soebagijo, I. N. 1982. *S.K. Trimurti: Wanita Pengabdi Bangsa.* Jakarta: Gunung Agung.

Soekarno. 1951. *Indonesia Menggugat.* Djakarta: S.K. Seno.

_____. 1975. *Indonesia Accuses!: Soekarno's Defence Oration in the Political Trial of 1930.* Edited, translated, annotated, and introduced by Roger K. Paget. Kuala Lumpur: Oxford University Press.

Soeprapti, I. N. 1946 (?) *Djedjak Dynamica Masjarakat.* Barisan Boeroeh Wanita.

_____. 1958. Kenangan dalam Detik-detik Proklamasi. In *Buku Peringatan 30 tahun Kesatuan Pergerakan Wanita Indonesia (22 Desember 1928–22 Desember 1958),* 224–226. Djakarta: Pertjetakan Negara, Kementerian Penerangan.

Soetjipto. 1947. Sengsara di Paberik: Lukisan Kaoem Boeroeh dalam Penindasan. *Loekisan Soeasana* 2 (1): 30–36.

Sohn, Kitae. 2015. Gender Discrimination in Earnings in Indonesia: A Fuller Picture. *Bulletin of Indonesian Economic Studies* 51 (1): 95–121.

Sorrita, Tarini. 2006a. *Penari Naga kecil: Kumpulan Cerpen.* Surabaya: JP Books.

_____. 2006b. Hamil. In *Nyanyian Imigran*, edited by Djodi Sambodo and Mega Vristian, 123–128. Malang: Dragon Family Publisher.

Spiller, Henry. 2010. *Erotic Triangles: Sundanese Dance and Masculinity in West Java.* Chicago: University of Chicago Press.

Spivak, Gayatri. 1988. Can the Subaltern Speak?. In *Marxism and the Interpretation of Culture*, edited by Cary Nelson and Lawrence Grossberg, 271–313. Urbana: University of Illinois Press.

Sri. 2012. Seruan kepada Kawanku, Buruh KBN Cakung dan KBN Marunda. *Suara Buruh* X (October): 10–11.

Steedman, Carolyn. 1986. *Landscape for a Good Woman: A Story of Two Lives.* London: Virago Press.

Stewart, Mary Lynn. 1989. *Women, Work, and the French State: Labour Protection and Social Patriarchy, 1879–1919.* Kingston: McGill-Queen's University Press.

Sudisman. 1967. Uraian Tanggungdjawab. *Djakarta*, 21 Djuli.

_____. 1975. *Analysis of Responsibility: Defence Speech of Sudisman, General Secretary of the Indonesian Communist Party at his trial before the Special*

Military Tribunal, Jakarta, 21 July 1967. Translated by Benedict Anderson. Melbourne: Works Co-operative.

Sudjinah. 2000. *In a Jakarta Prison: Life stories of Women Inmates*. Translated by Irfan Kortschak. Jakarta: Lontar Foundation.

_____. 2003. *Terempas Gelombang Pasang: Riwayat Wartawati dalam Penjara Orde Baru*. Jakarta Pustaka Utan Kayu.

Sukamdi, Setiadi, Agus Indiyanto, Abdul Haris, and Irwan Abdullah. 2001. Case Study 2: Indonesia. In *Female Labour Migration in South East Asia: Change and Continuity*, edited by Christina Wille and Basia Passl, 94–134. Bangkok: Asian Research Centre for Migration, Chulalongkorn University.

Sukanta, Putu Oka. 2004. *Di Atas Siang di Bawah Malam: Sketsa Perempuan & Renungan Seorang Eks Tapol*. Jakarta: Gagas Media.

_____. 2012. *Istana Jiwa: Langkah Perempuan di Celah Aniaya*. Jakarta: Jaringan Kerja Kebudayaan Rakyat and Lembaga Kreatifitas Kemanusiaan.

Sulami. 1999. *Perempuan, Kebenaran dan Penjara: Kisah Nyata Wanita dipenjara 20 Tahun karena Tuduhan Makar dan Subversi*. Jakarta: Cipta Lestari.

Sun, Wanning. 2014. "Northern Girls": Cultural Politics of Agency and South China's Migrant Literature. *Asian Studies Review* 38 (2): 168–185.

Surasto, Setiati. 1961. Buruh Wanita Harus mengadjak Seluruh Keluarga Buruh Ikutserta Dalam Merajakan Hari 1 Mei. In *Hidup! 1 Mei 1961*, 16–18. Jakarta: Biro P.P.K. D.N. SOBSI.

Suryakusuma, Julia 1996. The State and Sexuality in New Order Indonesia. In *Fantasizing the Feminine in Indonesia*, edited by L. J. Sears, 92–119. Durham: Duke University Press.

Suryomenggolo, Jafar. 2011. Defining "Indonesia" from the Margins: Working Class Autobiography as Part of the Nation's Collective Memory. *Indonesia and the Malay World* 39 (114): 221–243.

_____. 2012. Factory Employment, Female Worker's Activism, and Authoritarianism in Indonesia: Reading Ida Irianti's Pembelaan. *Critical Asian Studies* 44 (4): 597–626.

——— (Ed.). 2019. *At a Moment's Notice: Indonesian Maids Write on Their Lives Abroad*. Copenhagen: NIAS Press.

Suryomenggolo, Jafar, and Syarif Arifin (Eds.). 2012. *Kisah Moenadi: Otobiografi dan Tulisan-tulisannya*. Bogor: Lembaga Informasi Perburuhan Sedane.

Szumer, Zacharias. 2017. Sisters Doing It for Themselves: The Story Behind "Angka Jadi Suara." *Jakarta Post*, June 12.

Tagaroa, Rusdi, and Encop Sofia. n.d. *Buruh Migran Indonesia: Mencari Keadilan*. Jakarta: Lembaga Advokasi Buruh Migran Solidaritas Perempuan.

Tanesia, Ade. 2006. Maria Bo Niok, Domestic Helper-turned-Novelist. *Jakarta Post*, April 28.

Teew, A. 1994. *Indonesia Antara Kelisanan dan Keberaksaraan*. Jakarta: Pustaka Jaya.

Thukul, Wiji. 2000. *Aku Ingin Jadi Peluru: Kumpulan Puisi*. Magelang: IndonesiaTera.

_____. 2014. *Nyayian Akar Rumput: Kumpulan Lengkap Puisi Wiji Thukul*. Jakarta: Gramedia.

Tjandra, Surya. 2016. Labour Law and Development in Indonesia. PhD Thesis, University of Leiden.

———— (Ed.). 2009. *Hakim Ad Hoc Menggugat (Catatan Kritis Pengadilan Hubungan Industrial)*. Jakarta: Trade Union Rights Centre.

Tjandraningsih, Indrasari. 2000. Gendered Work and Labour Control: Women Factory Workers in Indonesia. *Asian Studies Review* 24 (2): 257–268.

————. 2003. Perempuan dan Keputusan untuk Melawan: Buruh Perempuan dan Perjuangan Hak. *Jurnal Analisis Sosial* 8 (2): 37–49.

Toer, Pramoedya Ananta. 1995. *Nyanyi Sunyi Seorang Bisu: Catatan-catatan dari Pulau Buru*. Jakarta: Lentera.

Trân, Angie Ngọc. 2013. *Ties that Bind: Cultural Identity, Class, and Law in Vietnam's Labor Resistance*. Ithaca: Cornell University, Southeast Asia Porgram Publications.

Traugott, Mark. 1993. *The French Worker: Autobiographies from the Early Industrial Era*. Berkeley: University of California Press.

Trimurti, S. K. 1946. Perdjuangan Buruh: Pra-advies pada Kongres Barisan Buruh Wanita di Kediri. *Kedaulatan Rakjat*, 24 Januari.

————. 1948. *A.B.C. Perdjuangan Buruh*. Jogjakarta: Pusat Pimpinan Partai Buruh.

————. 1980. *Hubungan Pergerakan Buruh Indonesia dengan Pergerakan Kemerdekaan Nasional*. Jakarta: Yayasan Idayu.

————. 1995. Permanente strijd. In *Verboden voor honden en inlanders: Indonesiër vertellen over hun leven in de koloniale tijd*, edited by H. C. Beynon, 49–61. Amsterdam: Mets.

Triutami, Astina. 2011. *Aku Bukan Budak*. Jakarta: Libri.

Tsing, Anna L. 1996. Alien Romance. In *Fantasizing the Feminine in Indonesia*, edited by L. J. Sears, 295–318. Durham: Duke University Press.

Ubon, Kompipote. 2002. Sexual Harassment in the Workplace: A Report from Field Research in Thailand, June 2002. The International Labor Rights Fund (ILRF) Rights for Working Women Campaign.

Uddin, Sharif. 2017. *Stranger to Myself: Diary of a Bangladeshi in Singapore*. Edited by Theophilus Kwek. Singapore: Landmark Books.

Umar, Risma, Salma Safitri, and Aliza Yuliana (Eds.). 2010. *Menguak Pelanggaran Hak Asasi Buruh Migran Indonesia. Catatan Penanganan Kasus Buruh Migran Perempuan-Pekerja Rumah Tangga (BMP-PRT), Solidaritas Perempuan tahun 2005–2009*. Jakarta: Solidaritas Perempuan.

Uno, Kathleen. 1993. One Day at a Time: Work and Domestic Activities of Urban Lower-Class Women in Early Twentieth-Century Japan. In *Japanese Women Working*, edited by Janet Hunter, 37–68. London and New York: Routledge.

Ventura, Rey. 2006 (1992). *Underground in Japan*. Quezon City: Ateneo de Manila University Press.

————. 2007. *Into the Country of Standing Man*. Quezon City: Ateneo de Manila University Press.

Vincent, David. 1981. *Bread, Knowledge and Freedom: A Study of Nineteenth-Century Working Class Autobiography*. London and New York: Methuen.

Vreede-de Stuers, Cora. 1959. *L'émancipation de la femme Indonésienne*. Paris: Mouton & Co.

Wahib, Ahmad. 1981. *Pergolakan Pemikiran Islam: Catatan Harian Ahmad Wahib.* Edited by Djohan Effendi and Ismed Natsir. Jakarta: LP3ES.

Watson, C. W. 2006. *Of Self and Injustice: Autobiography and Repression in Modern Indonesia.* Leiden: KITLV Press.

_____. 2009. Feminism and the Indonesian Nationalist Movement: A Reading of Soewarsih Djojopoespito's Novel. *Buiten het Gareel. Sari* 27: 125–142.

Wee, Vivienne, and Amy Sim. 2003. Transnational Labour Networks in Female Labour Migration: Mediating Between Southeast Asian Women Workers and International Labour Market. SEARC Working Paper Series No. 49, City University of Hong Kong.

Welvaartscommissie (H. E. Steinmetz, Ed.). 1914. *Onderzoek naar de mindere welvaart der Inlandsche bevolking op Java en Madoera.* IXb3: Verheeffing van de Inlandsche Vrouw, Deel VII. Batavia: Drukkerij Papyrus.

Werbner, Pnina. 2014. *The Making of an African Working Class: Politics, Law, and Cultural Protest in the Manual Workers' Union of Botswana.* London: Pluto Press.

White, Ben. 1993. Industrial Workers in West Java's Urban Fringe. In *Labour: Sharing in the Benefits of Growth?* edited by Chris Manning and Joan Hardjono, 127–138. Canberra: Department of Political and Social Change, Research School of Pacific Studies, Australian National University.

Widiawati, Helmy. 1995. Darmi: Buruh Pabrik Citra Rasa. In *Lika-liku kehidupan Buruh Perempuan,* edited by Masri Singarimbun and Sjafri Siarin, 10–42. Yogyakarta: Pustaka Pelajar dan Yayasan Annisa Swasti.

Widuri, Endang. 2008. Kesetaraan Gender. *Koran Perdjoeangan* XII (March): 11.

Widyawati, Rini. 2005. *Catatan Harian Seorang Pramuwisma.* Surabaya: JP Books.

Wieringa, Saskia. 2002. *Sexual Politics in Indonesia.* New York: Palgrave MacMillan.

_____. 2007. "If There is No Feeling..." : The Dilemma between Silence and Coming Out in A Working-Class Butch/Femme Community in Jakarta. In *Love and Globalization: Transformation of Intimacy in the Contemporary World,* edited by Mark B. Padilla, Jennifer S. Hirsch, Miguel Munoz-Laboy, Robert Sember and Richard G. Parker, 70–90. Nashville: Vanderbilt University Press.

Williams, Catharina Purwani. 2007. *Maiden Voyages: Eastern Indonesian Women on the Move.* Singapore and Leiden: ISEAS Publishing and KITLV Press.

Williams, Walter. 1990. *Javanese Lives: Women and Men in Modern Indonesian Society.* New Brunswick: Rutgers University Press.

Wilson. 2012. *Orang-orang yang Berlawan: Beragam Catatan dari Soekarno hingga Wiji Thukul.* s.l.: Opressiabook.

Wolf, Diane Lauren. 1990. *Factory Daughters: Gender, Household Dynamics, and Rural Industrialization in Java.* Berkeley: University of California Press.

Wolfe, Joel. 1993. *Working Women, Working Men: Sao Paulo and the Rise of Brazil's Industrial Working Class, 1900–1955.* Durham and London: Duke University Press.

Workers Rights Consortium (WRC). 2004. Worker Rights Consortium Assessment Re PT Panarub (Indonesia), Summary of Findings and Recommendations (7 September). www.workersrights.org/PT_Panarub_Updated_Summary_of_Findings_and_Recommendations.pdf.

Wright, Erik Olin. 1997. *Classes.* London: Verso.

Yeoh, B. S. A., and S. Huang. 2000. "Home" and "Away": Foreign Domestic Workers and Negotiations of Diasporic Identity in Singapore. *Women's Studies International Forum* 23 (4): 413–429.

Yi, Jodie, Chiao Lee, Stephanie Croft, and Tim McKinnel. 2018. *Misery at Sea: Human Suffering in Taiwan's Distant Water Fishing Fleet.* Taipei: Greenpeace East Asia.

Young, Iris M. 1994. Gender as Seriality: Thinking about Women as a Social Collective. *Signs: Journal of Women in Culture and Society* 19 (31): 713–738.

Zandy, Janet (Ed.). 1990. *Calling Home: Working-Class Women's Writings: An Anthology.* New Brunswick: Rutgers University Press.

Index

activists, 27, 50n25, 94, 100, 101,
104n7, 105nn12–13, 113, 151, 152,
166; female union, 12, 19n42, 31, 48,
86, 88, 92–94, 99–101, 103, 106n23,
106n29, 113, 137, 206; NGO, 13,
21n60, 57, 78, 90, 100, 116; union,
20n48, 20n52, 39, 56, 61, 81n41, 91,
106n31, 136
Aliansi Jurnalis Independen (AJI),
108n52
Asian financial crisis, 3, 17n6, 83, 148
authoritarian state, 3, 23, 83, 203;
political oppression by, 21n58, 24, 27,
78n12, 151, 152, 168, 204; working
class suppression by, 21n64, 28–31,
34–37, 39, 43, 47, 48, 52n43, 56,
59–60. *See also* New Order regime
autobiography, 6, 18n21, 49n13, 51n33,
52n41, 150, 171n28

babu, 171n29; *zeebaboe*, 146n1
Bandung, 29, 32, 149
Bangladesh, 106n31, 209n12
Bekasi, 55, 112, 123–26, 130–32, 136,
138n5
Botswana, 20n49, 21n60, 209n6

capitalism, 18n14, 144, 177, 195;
capitalist discipline, 208; capitalist

mode of production, 16, 28, 57, 207;
neoliberal, 3, 12, 14, 84–86, 88, 111,
123–24, 137, 208
China, 7, 209n4
class consciousness, 1, 25, 49n9, 52n43,
62, 90; collective consciousness, 36,
37, 91, 169. *See also* identity
Cold War, 7
colonialism, 2, 50n26; colonial court,
29, 32; colonial government, 2, 32,
34, 50n26, 51n28
Communist Party of Indonesia. *See*
Partai Komunis Indonesia (PKI)
corruption, 33, 55, 165
criminal court, 14, 24, 27, 31, 34, 38,
48, 49n5, 50n27, 202, 207

Dabindu, 7, 92, 106n24, 202, 209n1
dalang, 44, 58, 73, 76–77, 78n11, 81n41
democracy, 25n1, 30, 83, 105, 152, 170
diary, 147, 149, 150, 161, 169n7, 182,
198n23
divorce, 197n12

economic development, 1, 89, 201, 204,
206; after 1998, 91, 143, 171n35;
during New Order, 3, 11, 12, 21n64, 36
education, 36, 85; expenses, 18n29,
37; Freirean, 33, 50n25; primary,

229

About the Author

Jafar Suryomenggolo is associate member of the Centre Asie du Sud-Est (CASE), Paris, France, and Visiting research fellow at the Institute for Southeast Asian Studies, Jeonbuk National University (JISEAS), South Korea. His research focuses on working-class politics and political change in contemporary Southeast Asia.

His works include *Organising under the Revolution: Unions and the State in Java 1945–48* (2013), *At a Moment's Notice: Indonesian Maids Write on their Lives Abroad* (2019), *Environmental Resources Use and Challenges in Contemporary Southeast Asia* (co-edited with Mario Lopez, 2018), and *States and Societies in Motion* (co-edited with Khoo Boo Teik, 2020).

www.ingramcontent.com/pod-product-compliance
Lightning Source LLC
Chambersburg PA
CBHW022308280326
41932CB00010B/1022